In honor of Rick and Sally Osmer's tireless advocacy
for universal access to mental health services,
all proceeds from this book go to the National Alliance
on Mental Illness
(Mercer County, New Jersey chapter)

Consensus and Conflict

CONSENSUS AND CONFLICT

Practical Theology for Congregations
in the
Work of Richard R. Osmer

Edited by
KENDA CREASY DEAN
BLAIR D. BERTRAND
AMANDA HONTZ DRURY
ANDREW ROOT

Foreword by Friedrich Schweitzer

CASCADE *Books* • Eugene, Oregon

Cascade Books
An Imprint of Wipf and Stock Publishers
199 W. 8th Ave., Suite 3
Eugene, OR 97401

www.wipfandstock.com

PAPERBACK ISBN: 978-1-5326-5366-7
HARDCOVER ISBN: 978-1-5326-5367-4
EBOOK ISBN: 978-1-5326-5368-1

Cataloguing-in-Publication data:

Names: Dean, Kenda Creasy, editor. | Bertrand, Blair D., editor. | Drury, Amanda Hontz, editor. | Root, Andrew, editor.

Title: Consensus and conflict : practical theology for congregations in the work of Richard R. Osmer. / edited by Kenda Creasy Dean, Blair D. Bertrand, Amanda Hontz Drury, and Andrew Root.

Description: Eugene, OR: Cascade Books, 2019. | Includes bibliographical references and index.

Identifiers: ISBN 978-1-5326-5366-7 (paperback) | ISBN 978-1-5326-5367-4 (hardcover) | ISBN 978-1-5326-5368-1 (ebook)

Subjects: LCSH: Osmer, Richard Robert, 1950–. | Practical theology.

Classification: BT771.3 .C665 2019 (paperback) | BT771.3 (ebook)

Manufactured in the U.S.A.07/12/19

Contents

List of contributors

Blair D. Bertrand

Zomba Theological College, Zomba, Malawi and Theological Education by Extension in Malawi (TEEM).

Kenda Creasy Dean

Mary D. Synnott Professor of Youth, Church and Culture at Princeton Theological Seminary, Princeton, NJ.

Amanda Hontz Drury

Associate Professor of Practical Theology at Indiana Wesleyan University, Marion, IN.

Jessicah Krey Duckworth

Program Director in the Religion Division at Lilly Endowment Inc., Indianapolis, IN.

Drew A. Dyson

District Superintendent of the Raritan Valley District of the United Methodist Church of Greater New Jersey. He previously served as the James C. Logan Chair of Evangelism at Wesley Theological Seminary, Washington, DC.

Darrell L. Guder

Professor of Missional and Ecumenical Theology Emeritus at Princeton Theological Seminary, Princeton, NJ.

Thomas John Hastings

Executive Director of the Overseas Ministries Study Center (OMSC), editor of the *International Bulletin of Mission Research* (*IBMR*), and adjunct lecturer at Yale Divinity School, New Haven, CT.

Shin-Geun Jang

Professor of Christian Education, Presbyterian University and Theological Seminary, Seoul, South Korea.

Bo Karen Lee

Associate Professor of Spiritual Theology and Christian Formation at Princeton Theological Seminary, Princeton, NJ

Gordon S. Mikoski

Associate Professor of Christian Education, Director of the PhD Program, and editor of *Theology Today* at Princeton Theological Seminary, Princeton, NJ.

Richard R. Osmer

Ralph B. and Helen S. Ashenfelter Professor of Mission and Evangelism at Princeton Theological Seminary, Princeton, NJ.

Angela H. Reed

Associate Professor of Practical Theology and Director of Spiritual Formation at George W. Truett Theological Seminary, Waco, TX.

Andrew Root

Carrie Olson Baalson Professor of Youth and Family Ministry at Luther Seminary, St. Paul, MN.

Friedrich Schweitzer

Professor of Religious Education and Practical Theology at the University of Tübingen, Tübingen, Germany.

Nathan T. Stucky

Administrative Faculty and Director of the Farminary at Princeton Theological Seminary, Princeton, NJ.

Foreword

Richard Osmer and the New Practical Theology

Friedrich Schweitzer

To INTRODUCE—AND TO HIGHLY recommend—a book which is both fascinating to read and honoring a friend and distinguished colleague is a pleasure and an honor for me. The academic work and personal commitment of Richard Osmer truly deserve our appreciation and his many achievements certainly call for a *Festschrift* that celebrates them by taking clues from Osmer's work and by building upon his ideas and insights for the future. It is obvious to everyone who is familiar with Osmer and his work that in doing so, the focus must be on practical theology—the theological discipline to which he has contributed so much in his teaching and writing, his organizing and long-lasting leadership in many different capacities. Yet it is also obvious that, in this case, this topic must be approached in a special manner, with a constant eye on Osmer's characteristic ways of understanding—and of doing—practical theology himself. In other words, the book must be—and in fact, is—about Osmer's practical theology no less than about practical theology in general.

Not surprisingly, the various chapters in this fine volume often refer to Osmer's work of teaching and research at Princeton Theological Seminary. With their many facets and different perspectives they testify to the depth and breadth of his work as well as to his unique gift of inspiring, encouraging, and guiding other people—colleagues, junior faculty, as well as students at various levels. Princeton Theological Seminary has been the primary stage on which Osmer's many activities have been performed. Yet there is also another stage at a national and international level which has been no less characteristic of Osmer's continued commitment and far-reaching influence. Most of all, in 1991, he was one of the eight founders of the International Academy of Practical Theology (IAPT) which he then, as its first convener, brought to Princeton in 1993, thus giving bone and flesh to the emerging idea of a platform for international exchange and cooperation in practical theology. Without him, this Academy would not have come into existence, and without his leadership it would never have been what is has become.

In order to understand and to appreciate Osmer's special role in an international context, one has to be aware of the process through which the new practical theology emerged in the 1980s and how it continued to develop in the 1990s as well as into the new century until today. This is why I will offer a few observations concerning this particular dimension of Osmer's work while not repeating the more encompassing account of his work in general provided so aptly by others in the ensuing introductory chapter.

That practical theology could, or ever should, become a theological discipline of equal standing with the other theological disciplines was not viewed as an option throughout most of the history of theology, especially not in the United States. Although there were major American figures in this history whose work was quite influential nationally as well as internationally—in pastoral counseling, for example, or in the research on religious development in childhood and adolescence—it was not before the 1980s that practical theology could seriously be considered an "emerging field" in the United States.[1] Instead, practical theology appeared more like an addition to theology proper or as a useful but not research-oriented conveyor belt transporting the theology produced by the other disciplines into the various fields of church-related practice. Most of all, practical theologians like Osmer's friend Don Browning and Osmer's doctoral advisor James Fowler—together with a whole group of colleagues in other countries like Germany, the Netherlands, and South Africa—played a major role in this context.[2] From early on in his work which was then strongly focused on Christian education, Osmer placed his views and interpretations into a broader context, by drawing on biblical theology as well as on the theology of the sixteenth-century Reformers but also on practical theology. His groundbreaking book *A*

1. Browning, *Practical Theology,*

2. See for example, Schweitzer and van der Ven, *Practical Theology.* This book also contains the early papers from the International Academy of Practical Theology.

Teachable Spirit: Recovering the Teaching Office in the Church very clearly testifies to this.[3] It also forecasts Osmer's distinctive approach, which combines practical theology with a strong grounding in other theological disciplines that he considers indispensable interdisciplinary partners for practical theology. There is, to my knowledge, no other contemporary practical theologian who would base his or her work so clearly on in-depth biblical scholarship. Yet Osmer's practical theology has never been biblical in a one-sided sense or biblicist in any sense. Instead, he manages to bring biblical insights into continued conversation with other perspectives, for example, from the social sciences or from cultural and literary studies. This clearly is the first distinctive characteristic of his approach.

While Osmer first used practical theology as a context that could broaden his views on Christian education, he later developed it as a topic of its own, setting forth his own model of practical theology with its well-known four tasks: the "descriptive-empirical task," the "interpretive task," the "normative task," and the "pragmatic task."[4] This model builds upon the models developed in the 1980s, especially on Don Browning's *A Fundamental Practical Theology.*[5] Yet, it also takes these earlier understandings of practical theology beyond their original scope and, characteristically for Osmer's view, puts a much clearer emphasis on the need for a practical theology in the service of praxis, not in any naïve manner but in the sense of normative evaluations and orientations for praxis. It is probably fair to say that it is the normative and the pragmatic tasks which ultimately are decisive in Osmer's understanding. Yet, it is also obvious to him that the descriptive and interpretive tasks can never be side-stepped. It is the faithful attention to all four moments in the process of practical theology that marks Osmer's approach—a particular balance between the normative and the empirical in which I see a second distinctive characteristic.

It is easy to see that Osmer's interest in both praxis and practical theology is closely connected to his commitment to Christian congregations in which he sees an important embodiment of the Christian faith. Most of all, Osmer's *The Teaching Ministry of Congregations* makes this evident.[6] It also shows how Osmer's early interest in the congregational

3. Osmer, *A Teachable Spirit.*

4. Osmer, *Practical Theology.*

5. Browning, *A Fundamental Practical Theology.*

6. Osmer, *The Teaching Ministry of Congregations.*

task of teaching carries on in his later work but has been enriched and broadened in a number of important ways. First of all, there is a strong grounding in Pauline theology that now provides decisive directions for the understanding of what a Christian congregation needs to be and how the tasks of teaching are part of it. Second, there is the use of empirical approaches along the lines of congregational studies. Third, and not of least importance, there is a worldwide international-comparative perspective bringing experiences from South Korea, the United States, and South Africa into conversation with each other and with practical theology in general. In other words, the very concrete concentration on the congregation as a local form of Christianity goes hand in hand with Osmer's continued attention to globalization as the horizon in which practical theology has to make sense today and that it therefore has to address even where it refers to local congregations. In a world that has gone global, the local has ceased to be the opposite of the global—an insight which Osmer includes in his approach to congregational research. Practical theology must therefore be rooted in international cooperation and must make use of international comparison, for example, concerning congregations in different parts of the world. Internationalizing practical theology can thus be considered another distinctive characteristic of Osmer's approach.

International-comparative work of this kind can rarely be completed by one person alone. It is not surprising then that some of Osmer's contributions concerning international studies were carried out in cooperation with colleagues from other countries, leading to books in joint authorship. This is true, among others, for *Religious Education between Modernization and Globalization: New Perspectives on the United States and Germany* (published with Friedrich Schweitzer/Germany), as well as for his most recent publication, *The Future of Protestant Religious Education in an Age of Globalization* (with Hyun-Sook Kim/South Korea and again Friedrich Schweitzer).[7] In different ways, both of these books confirm the fruitfulness of Osmer's understanding of doing practical theology in new ways. This discipline cannot do justice to its tasks anymore if it is not deeply aware of the far-reaching challenges which globalization brings with it not only in terms of the economy but also of culture, religion and education.

7. Osmer and Schweitzer, *Religious Education between Modernization and Globalization*. Also Kim et al., *The Future of Protestant Religious Education*.

Another example of internationalizing research in practical theology is still under way, the major research project on confirmation work in the United States. This project evolved in dialogue with parallel research projects carried out in nine European countries.[8] On several occasions the projects in the United States and in Europe crossed hands in joint consultations in Finland and in Germany. It will be most exciting to see the results from these projects and to evaluate these results comparatively and in terms of their implications for practical theology.

So far, I have tried to identify a number of characteristics which mark Osmer's unique contribution to the advancement of practical theology. This emphasis remains important but it should not lead to the assumption that Osmer has been aiming for making one particular understanding of practical theology prevail, nationally or even internationally. While all scholars tend to favor their own approaches—why else would they maintain them?—Osmer's way of dealing with the varieties of practical theology has been distinctive. He tries to offer different categories or disciplinary maps that allow for a deeper understanding of the different approaches and that can bring them into conversation with each other.

Two articles from Osmer's rich bibliography deserve special mention in this context, both published—not by coincidence—in the *International Journal of Practical Theology*, for which Osmer served as one of the first acting editors for many years. The first of these articles is based on a lecture at one of the first meetings of the International Academy of Practical Theology. It attempts to provide a new kind of typology of different models of practical theology by showing how these models correspond to what Osmer calls different models of rationality: "rationality as argument," "rationality as rhetoric," "rationality as conversation," and "rationality as postfoundational science." This typology is meant to support international cooperation and dialogue in practical theology. "It is offered as a way of helping participants in the emerging international discussion of practical theology better understand their similarities and differences."[9] In other words, Osmer's intention is to develop a map of the field in order to make dialogue in practical theology possible.

The second article I want to take up here also comes from the context of the International Academy of Practical Theology. It was developed

8. Schweitzer et al., *Confirmation Work in Europe*. Also Schweitzer et al., *Youth, Religion and Confirmation Work in Europe*.

9. Osmer, "Rationality in Practical Theology," 40.

in response to an address by Bonnie Miller-McLemore, then president of the International Academy. Among others, Osmer describes his understanding of the use of a practical theology framework instead of only doing work in one of the specialized sub-disciplines of, for example, homiletics, pastoral care, or Christian education. According to his understanding, practical theology brings people into discourse with each other who otherwise might not be aware of what they share. Moreover, practical theology has become a major field of ecumenical encounter and cooperation. All this, Osmer concludes, is only possible if the pluralistic character of practical theology is acknowledged: "No practical theologian today can pretend to speak for the whole, that is, for *all* practical theologians." What then are they to do? "What they can do is to be forthright about the decisions informing their particular perspectives and locate them in relation to other, alternate perspectives."[10] For this reason Osmer continues by describing no less than six different "strands" in American practical theology alone: "Postmodern transforming practice strand," "American hermeneutical strand," "Dutch/South African empirical strand," "Christo-praxis strand," "American neo-Aristotelian practices strand," and "American Barthian strand."

These two examples can be seen as evidence of what I want to identify as another characteristic of Osmer's views on practical theology and even more of himself as a person. In a certain way, it can be said that he applies the four tasks of practical theology to this discipline itself—by not only doing practical theology in one particular way (his own) but by reflecting on what is going on in this field, how it can be better understood and interpreted, and most of all, how it can be improved.

I have had the privilege of being in continued conversation with Rick Osmer for more than twenty-five years. Our shared endeavors brought us together in the United States as well as in Germany but also in many other parts of the world, for example, Scandinavia, South Africa, and South Korea, where we co-lectured in a number of places. Our collegial relationship has turned into a long-lasting personal friendship, also including our families. This is why I want to end this foreword by expressing my deep gratitude—not only for the many impulses I have received from him and for his inspiring publications—but also for the many years that we have been in touch and have been able to share so much which is dear to us, personally, academically, and religiously.

10. Osmer, "Toward a New Story of Practical Theology," 67.

Bibliography

Browning, Don S. *A Fundamental Practical Theology: Descriptive and Strategic Proposals*. Minneapolis: Fortress, 1991.

———. *Practical Theology: The Emerging Field in Theology, Church, and World*. San Francisco: Harper & Row, 1983.

———. *A Fundamental Practical Theology: Descriptive and Strategic Proposals*. Minneapolis: Fortress, 1991.

Kim, Hyun-Sook, et al. *The Future of Protestant Religious Education in an Age of Globalization* New York: Waxmann, 2018.

Osmer, Richard R. *Practical Theology: An Introduction*. Grand Rapids: Eerdmans, 2008.

———. *A Teachable Spirit: Recovering the Teaching Office in the Church*. Louisville: Westminster John Knox, 1990.

———. "Rationality in Practical Theology: A Map of the Emerging Discussion." *International Journal of Practical Theology* 1 (1997) 11–40.

———. *The Teaching Ministry of Congregations*. Louisville: Westminster John Knox, 2005.

———. "Toward a New Story of Practical Theology." *International Journal of Practical Theology* 16 (2012) 66–78.

Osmer, Richard R., and Friedrich Schweitzer. *Religious Education between Modernization and Globalization: New Perspectives on the United States and Germany*. Grand Rapids: Eerdmans, 2003.

Schweitzer, Friedrich, and Johannes A. van der Ven, eds. *Practical Theology—International Perspectives*. Frankfurt: LIT, 1999.

Schweitzer, Friedrich, et al. *Confirmation Work in Europe: Empirical Results, Experiences and Challenges. A Comparative Study in Seven Countries*. Gütersloh: Gütersloher, 2010.

———. *Youth, Religion and Confirmation Work in Europe. The Second Study*. Gütersloh: Gütersloher, 2015.

Acknowledgements

"The dream begins, most of the time, with a teacher who believes in you."
—DAN RATHER

SOME BOOKS ARE MORE captured than written; this is one of them. It is a measure of Rick Osmer's influence—and of the affection his students and colleagues have for him—that so many people gladly gave of themselves to make this book possible. We would be remiss not to name those who gave more than most, whose unheralded generosity, long hours and late nights made possible capturing a glimpse of Rick's impact on the American renaissance of practical theology, and on an entire generation of American practical theologians.

Chief among these dedicated persons is Melissa Temple, whose incomparable cheer and relentless scrutiny turned multiple scruffy documents into publishable prose. Sally Osmer, too, was in the dugout, responding to last-minute requests to supply details and nicknames as we sought to offer a human portrait as well as an academic one. Distinguished practical theologian Friedrich Schweitzer—Rick's dear friend, avid supporter, and most honest critic from across the pond—shared many of the moments with Rick that are named in this book, especially the founding of the International Academy of Practical Theology. Friedrich's willingness to write this volume's foreword remains an unsurpassed gift to us, and to the reader as well.

We are exceedingly grateful for the support of Princeton Theological Seminary, especially to President Craig Barnes and Dean James Kay, who championed this project wholeheartedly—as well as to the members of the International Academy of Practical Theology. Matthew Wimer,

Rodney Clapp, and Stephanie Hough of Wipf and Stock and Cascade Books offered gentle editorial wisdom and grace, and the authors themselves—none of whom had time to meet our impossible deadlines, and all of whom did so gladly—deserve a page of gratitude all to themselves. Above all, thank you to Rick Osmer for being such an excellent sport about the whole thing, giving interviews (multiple times) to fill in biographical gaps, and for penning his own concluding thoughts about practical theology's future in light of the chapters in this book.

Some of the themes in this book are prominent in Rick's writing and teaching; others may surprise those who know him primarily from his publications. One that may surprise readers is Rick and Sally's passionate interest in mental health, and their deep dedication to serving those who struggle with mental illness. For that reason, the royalties received from this book go to the Mercer County, New Jersey chapter of the National Alliance on Mental Illness, where Rick and Sally volunteered for nearly two decades.

Illum oportet crescere, me autem minui.[1]

Kenda Creasy Dean
Princeton, New Jersey
May 24, 2018

---

1. "He must increase, but I must decrease" (John 3:30). This phrase, beside John the Baptist as he points to the cross in Matthias Grunewald's sixteenth century painting of the crucifixion, hung above Karl Barth's desk.

1

An Introduction

The Four Moments of Richard R. Osmer:

The Making of a Practical Theologian
Amidst Consensus and Conflict

BLAIR D. BERTRAND, KENDA CREASY DEAN,
AND AMANDA HONTZ DRURY

THIS INTRODUCTION FUNCTIONS AS a kind of map for the book you are about to read. Like all maps, introductions must balance adequate detail with appropriate scale. Too much detail overwhelms the reader, rendering the map useless. Scale relates specific places to the bigger picture. Go too big and the map becomes useless. Get too granular and you miss many relationships between salient details. None of us goes on a road trip with either a globe or the architectural renderings of our house.[1]

What guides us is the story we hope to become part of. Stories and maps are time-honored partners. Robert Louis Stevenson's *Treasure Island* was inspired by a map painted by his twelve-year-old stepson. Winnie-the-Pooh's Hundred Acre Wood was A. A. Milne's take on part of Ashford Forest in East Sussex. J. R. R. Tolkien (who mapped enemy trenches during World War I) doodled Middle Earth on one of his Oxford examination papers—and then spent years revising its coordinates,

---

1. Osmer uses an image very similar to this in *Practical Theology,* 80–81, 116.

1

gluing new versions on top of old ones. As he explained: "If you're go-ing to tell a complicated story, you must work to a map; otherwise you'll never make a map of it afterward."[2]

Richard R. Osmer's influence on the field of practical theology is just that: a complicated story, layered and mildly unpredictable, and this introduction serves as a kind of map to help you navigate the pages ahead. Osmer's influence on North American practical theology is seismic; his writing and teaching helped re-establish the field as a contemporary theological discipline with immediate relevance for Christian life, espe-cially for congregations. Osmer was central to forming the International Academy of Practical Theology in 1991 and is perhaps best known for conceiving the "consensus model" of practical theology—arguably the most accessible and widely used practical theological model in the world, thanks to the popularity of his book *Practical Theology: An Introduction* and to a generation of Osmerian protegees now teaching practical the-ology around the globe. Osmer not only helped reinvigorate an entire field of study that languished in Western theology after Schleiermacher, but his signature insistence that congregational practices like Christian education, youth ministry, spirituality, and evangelism are, in fact, deeply theological enterprises gave these fields new substance as well. By merg-ing practical theology with the contemporary "practices" of Christian life discussion, Osmer's approach to practical theology holds widespread ap-peal for scholars and reflective practitioners alike.

Yet when it comes to the *study* of practical theology, Osmer com-plicates things. He is more explorer than conqueror, more apt to follow bread crumbs than blueprints. His mark on the field of practical theology is the fruit of curiosity's winding path to wisdom rather than a systematic effort to prove or disprove hypotheses. Along the way, he posts trail signs for those who follow, indicating paths more than prescribing them. He is famous among his students for becoming captivated by a new intellectual conversation partner (or rediscovering an old one) every two or three years, sometimes from the sciences, sometimes from the arts, some-times from the theological disciplines (globalization, rhetorical theory, empirical research, children's fantasy literature, critical realism, spiritual direction, Lesslie Newbigin, and Karl Barth have all had their turns). He

2. Sibley and Howe, *The Maps of Tolkien's Middle Earth*, 5–7. For one of many ac-counts of the origins of *Treasure Island*, see Amrhein, "Robert Louis Stevenson." For a discussion of church planters as cartographers, see Kenda Creasy Dean and Mark DeVries's foreword in Baughman, *Flipping Church*.

takes a childlike delight in introducing this "friend" to his students as he explores every inch of what that conversation partner offers the practical theologian. Osmer's capacity for intellectual friendship is so vast that he never discards a dialogue partner; he merely adds another seat at the table for the next "friend" to practical theology that he takes under wing.

Like all cartographers, Osmer has dedicated his life to interpreting the terrain of practical theology rather than adjudicating it, poking air vents in disciplinary conversations rather than sealing up their leaky seams. This habit gives his approach to practical theology—like his approach to teaching, scholarship, and Christian life generally—an agility that allows him to tack back and forth between intellectual spheres. Most of the adulation and criticism Osmer received throughout his career stemmed from his refusal to park his theories in the political or intellectual parking spots others imagined for him.[3] Some of his books, especially those written for pastors, educators, or students, are direct, penetrating, clarifying. Others invite too many guests to the party: there is too much going on, too many pages, too many layers, too many characters, giving readers a glimpse of Osmer's own busy imagination as they join him for a joyful, lurching magic carpet ride that lands (it does inevitably land) on a new contribution to practical theology or congregational practice in the final pages. In fact, each of Osmer's books have gained a loyal following precisely because they reveal signposts to the faithful life that had become overgrown: the marks of the teaching ministry, the practices of congregations, the contours of spiritual direction or evangelism, the architecture of confirmation, and—most notably—the four moments of practical theological reflection.

This introduction, therefore, is intended to orient the reader to this volume and to the life of Richard R. Osmer. These two are related. The chapters ahead cover a number of important aspects of Osmer's career: 1) his early career, focused on Christian education, 2) the deepening of his mid-career interest in Christian spirituality, 3) his late-career shift towards mission and evangelism, and 4) his persistent interest in practical theology as a field and discipline. These four moments resonate with

---

3. Taken as a whole, conservatives wish he were more evangelical and liberals wish he were more progressive; scholars wish he would address the academy and practitioners wish he would be more accessible. Cf. Foster, "A Review of the Teaching Ministry"; Miller-McLemore, "Toward Greater Understanding of Practical Theology"; Smith, "Review of Richard Osmer." All of these are primarily appreciative reviews; but even fans have critiques.

the four moments of practical theology that Osmer identified and illuminated. But we advise you to approach this "map" to Osmer's life and career in the same way he approaches his own claims: provisionally, as a take, a "best account" rather than as a final one.[4] Maps, after all, tell stories better than they report facts: "Here be dragons," or "This way to treasure," or "At this point the water goes deeper." Osmer views practical theology not simply as a field of inquiry but as a story about the way God and humanity reach for one another—an account of the intersection between divine and human action. The through-line in all of Osmer's work is his insistence on making discourse about God central to every Christian practice, to the work of churches, and to the task of practical theological interpretation itself. Each author in this volume speculates on Osmer's influence in this regard, especially as his work comes to bear on the practices of congregations.

Origin Stories

Osmer recalls that while his parents did not "wear their faith on their sleeves," there was no doubt in his mind as a child that they understood their lives in terms of faith.[5] Faith meant living a moral life not in a legalistic sense, but by discerning "the right thing" from evidence and deliberation and then choosing it. Moral choice required knowing who and whose you were. Three years old when his younger brother Kenny passed away from leukemia, Osmer recalls seeing his parents navigate this devastating time while maintaining deep faith. Osmer remembers this tragically transformative experience as instilling confidence in faith's capacity to sustain people through the most difficult of circumstances. "I didn't understand faith," Osmer says, "but I could see it."[6]

It has been said that all research is autobiography, and Osmer's scholarship is no exception. A generation of "Harry Potter" fans in his classrooms led him to develop a course on "Moral Formation Through Children's Fantasy Literature"—the most popular course he ever taught—awakening in him a former passion. As a pre-teen needing to escape the pressures that he put on himself, Osmer had turned to science fiction

4. Charles Taylor explains his "best account principle" in Taylor, *Sources of the Self,* 58–59.

5. Osmer, Interview.

6. Ibid.

and fantasy literature as pressure valves. This literature challenged limits, declared new realities possible, and explored the moral composition of characters required to enter into a given "what if" scenario. Even dystopian science fiction inspired hope, imagining futures that shed new light on the present moment.

While an undergraduate at University of North Carolina-Chapel Hill, Rick began to imagine his own future in a new way when he met his roommate's twin sister, Sally. While traveling independently in Europe for separate summer educational opportunities, Rick and Sally agreed to meet in Italy. As Rick observes, it's quite difficult not to fall in love in Venice. A month after graduating from college, they were married.

Rick's post-graduation plan was to study world religions at Harvard. While in Boston, the Osmers supplemented their income by serving a small church together for two years. This proved to be pivotal period in Osmer's vocational discernment. Prior to his experience as a pastor, Osmer valued his church and his education, but failed to see how they overlapped. None of the maps he had previously considered for his life combined both his faith and his intellectual interests. As a young pastor, he realized that the study of world religions bore little resemblance to the lived experience of faith—nor would it prepare him to become a faith leader. Harvard had introduced Osmer to James Fowler and his "faith development" research, but he decided to transfer to Yale Divinity School to study Karl Barth under Hans Frei, David Kelsey, and George Lindbeck. Even so, Osmer would ultimately remember his seminary education as unhelpful when it came to practical theology or religious education. Harvard had no tenured faculty in practical theology during Osmer's time there; apart from being a student in James Fowler's first class on faith development, he received no encouragement in practical theology there. Yale's faculty included Randolph Crump Miller—a titan in the Religious Education Movement—but Osmer deemed him "a terrible teacher; nobody took his courses." (The irony of poor teaching in the Christian education area was not lost of Osmer.) Similarly, he was disappointed in the disconnect between his Yale courses on Barth and the practice of ministry: "I learned a lot of Barth, read a lot of Barth, but when I became a pastor I was clueless. I didn't know really how to make sense out of what practical theology is, and Barth is *really* difficult. And how do you connect what he says to what you're doing? So, I just put Barth on the shelf for a really long time."[7]

It was his year of Clinical Pastoral Education (CPE) that decisively shaped Osmer's vocation. Confronted with what one of his future mentors would call "the living human document,"[8] Osmer discovered an approach to education that took human experience seriously. Later, the "lab schools" offered by the Methodists at Lake Junaluska, loosely based on Dewey's famous lab schools in New York, provided a context for exploring experience-based education. At the lab school, Osmer discovered a way to encourage faith by connecting it to people's immediate experience, an approach that was particularly useful in the rural congregation he served. Alongside some volunteers, Osmer gingerly introduced a Sunday School program—and discovered his congregants' hunger, not just for the content of faith, but for a way of life infused and transformed by their walk with God.

This experience whetted Osmer's educational appetite. By then Fowler had joined the faculty of Emory University and Candler School of Theology in Atlanta. Osmer soon became Fowler's doctoral advisee, the first student admitted to Candler's "Theology and Personality" program (he ultimately became its first graduate as well). Beguiled by Fowler's understanding of how humans appropriate faith throughout the life cycle, Fowler's desire to push past Kantian categories towards lived experience reinforced Osmer's lab school discoveries about the importance of experience in religious formation. Fowler captured the dynamism of faith by conducting "faith interviews" (and by training his doctoral students to do the same) for a project called "Stages of Faith." Osmer became one of Fowler's most trusted research assistants, and eventually served as acting Assistant Director and Director of Educational Research at Candler's Center for Research on Faith and Moral Development.

Osmer had begun to form some critiques of Fowler's approach, concerned about reducing Christian faith to form and content. In Osmer's view, Christian faith is, above all, a relationship—and a particular relationship at that. The human/divine encounter had to be accounted for. Osmer grappled with this conundrum in his dissertation, investigating the teaching ministry through the Reformed lenses of Shelton Smith's and James Smart's neo-orthodox critique of the Religious Education

---

7. Ibid.

8. Cf. Gerkin, *The Living Human Document*, 97–117.

Movement. Fowler supported Osmer's theological drift away from Methodism towards Reformed theology—a lesson Osmer took to heart, and repeated with his own doctoral students: challenge, but always champion, your students.

With Fowler's support within the academy and Sally's support outside of it, Rick's career began to unfold. Faith and family became the couple's two foci, orienting every other detail of their lives. Even after they both left pastoral leadership, the Osmers remained dedicated to their church communities, celebrating their children's rites of passage and sometimes grieving timid pastoral leadership. Long before shifting his focus to evangelism, Osmer sensed its urgency. He was scandalized by what he viewed as mainline leaders' aversion to proclaiming the scandal of the gospel, "a stumbling block to Jews and foolishness to gentiles" (1 Cor 1:23). One colleague remembers a conversation following an Easter service, when Rick felt that a particular opportunity had been missed. "Of all days!" he exclaimed. "Today I came to church to encounter the Risen Christ, and instead I am leaving discouraged without meeting Jesus." Then he pointed to some visitors and asked his colleague rhetorically: "And them—what about them? How are they going to meet Jesus with sermons like that?"

The Osmers were committed to cultivating an "equal regard" marriage, to use his friend Don Browning's phrase, negotiating ways to nurture a family alongside two careers (Sally is an ordained United Methodist pastor and a respected leader in the non-profit sector). Osmer recalls how the birth of their first child led them to rearrange their schedules and reimagine their callings in order to be the kind of parents they wanted to be—a conversation that would be repeated often in the years to come. When they unexpectedly found themselves parenting a child with special needs, Osmer once again refocused his professional commitments, limiting travel and speaking to focus on teaching and writing, which afforded him more time at home. The most recent "reimagining" of Osmer's calling accompanied the birth of his two grandchildren, who largely set the stage for Rick and Sally's decision to retire. Of all the mantles Rick has worn throughout his career, the one that gives him the most delight is "Grandpapapapa."

Practical Theologian in Context

In his consensus model of practical theology, Osmer identified four "moments" in the process of practical theological reflection which he labeled as the *descriptive-empirical*, the *interpretive*, the *normative*, and the *pragmatic* moments. As Osmer put it, "What is going on? Why is this going on? What ought to be going on? How might we respond? Answering each of these questions is the focus of one of the core tasks of practical theological interpretation."[9]

The chapters ahead give an eclectic and broad glimpse of these four moments but missing from most of them is how Osmer's career has been shaped by the changing religious culture in which his work has been situated. Osmer's career serves as a kind of barometer for these shifts as they have played out in institutions, in the practice of Christian formation, and in the global significance of practical theology itself. Osmer's ministerial career spanned forty-one years. He received his M.Div. from Yale Divinity School in 1977 and retired from Princeton Theological Seminary in 2018. He also served on the faculty of Candler School of Theology (1983–1986; PhD 1985) and Union Theological Seminary at Richmond (1986–1990), but his time at Princeton Theological Seminary (1990–2018) most clearly established him as a practical theologian. Osmer himself has given an account of his time at Princeton Seminary, reflecting on the experience of being part of a long line of Princeton practical theologians.[10] Any retrospective of Osmer's career must account for the institutions that have helped shape him, and that he has helped shape, most of all Princeton Seminary.

In a broader sense, the shape of Christian witness and formation in the United States has undergone tectonic shifts during Osmer's career, especially the mainline denominations with which Osmer has been primarily associated. In 1977 it was still possible to see Christian education as the primary vehicle for enculturating North Americans into the social institution of the church. Today, mainline churches offer little in the way of a recognizable culture into which to socialize young people—and convincing critiques of enculturation models, from both theological and socio-cultural perspectives, call into question many of the educational practices twentieth-century churches took for granted. Instead, many would argue that the appropriate starting point for Christian formation

9. Osmer, *Practical Theology*, 4.

10. Mikoski and Osmer, *With Piety and Learning*, 31–133.

in the early twenty-first century is evangelism, broadly conceived in Osmerian terms as reawakening North Americans, in and beyond existing congregations, to the active presence of God at work in their midst. Osmer's evolving teaching and research interests reflect this shift; in 2013, he voluntarily relinquished his named chair in Christian education in order to become Princeton Seminary's Ashenfelter Professor of Mission and Evangelism.

A map that faithfully traces Osmer's career also must account for the international horizon present in his work. A founding member of the International Academy of Practical Theology, Osmer hosted the Academy's founding meeting at Princeton Theological Seminary in 1991. He co-edited an early book tracing the effects of globalization on youth ministry and religious education. His work continues to resonate in parts of the global church, especially in South Africa and Korea. Still, Osmer's focus on congregations as the base unit of Christian practice and as the primary locus of his research makes his signature in the field distinctly American. His global work gives his US focus welcome humility, substantially mitigating the risk of parochialism or of making American church practices normative.

Before going further, we should address a common misconception about Osmer's consensus model of practical theology, the so-called "four moments" that you will hear echoing throughout this volume. Although these moments in the process of practical theological reflection, as outlined by Osmer, are often interpreted as spiraling around each other in sequence, Osmer maintains that each moment is present in all the others—and that all four moments (not just the normative moment) are "theological" in nature. Influenced by his friendship with Princeton Seminary colleagues Darrell Guder, George Hunsinger, and Bruce McCormack, Osmer returned to reading Karl Barth late in his career. He became drawn to the idea of dialectical inclusion as a way to understand how systematic, biblical, and practical theology relate to one another—and, by extension, to describe how each moment in practical theology relates to all the others. Each moment has a specific focus but necessarily includes the entirety of the other to make sense. Dialectical inclusion not only describes Osmer's thinking about practical theology; there is a kind of dialectical inclusion at work in Osmer's life as well. To understand one moment in Osmer's vocation, it is necessary to include all the others, which are held together in dialectical tension. To be specific, let us briefly outline the four "moments" of Richard R. Osmer's work that serve as the outline for this volume.

The Educator

For thirty-one of his forty-one years of ministry, Osmer's job description had the word "education" in his title. Twice he served congregations as the minister of education. In the academy, he served as Instructor in Christian Education at Candler School of Theology while completing his doctorate (1983–1984), Assistant Professor of Christian Education at Candler (1984–1986) and at Union Theological Seminary (1986–1990), and the Thomas W. Synnott Professor of Christian Education at Princeton Theological Seminary (1990–2012). His first five books all addressed the church's teaching ministry—*A Teachable Spirit: Recovering the Teaching Office in the Church* (1990), *Teaching for Faith: A Guide for Leaders of Adult Groups* (1992), *Confirmation: Presbyterian Practices in Ecumenical Perspective* (1995), *Religious Education between Modernization and Globalization* (2003, co-authored with Friedrich Schweitzer), and *The Teaching Ministry of the Congregations* (2005). In short, most of Osmer's professional life centered around practicing, teaching, and writing about various aspects of Christian education.

Even so, Osmer often found himself at odds with dominant understandings of American religious education in the late twentieth century. He lost little sleep over the dissonance. He considered these "older models" to be "generic" at best, and "shell games" at worst, smuggling in normative theological commitments under the guise of philosophy, modern education, and the social sciences. He countered that theology should determine what counts as "ministry" and "teaching" in congregations, eschewing the phrase "religious education" in favor of "the teaching ministry."[11] He was far more interested in how faith comes alive in the life of the believer than in educational philosophy or technique. Defending the Presbyterian Church (USA)'s new catechism as an instrument for personal exploration rather than a mechanism to ensure that children are "properly indoctrinated," Osmer criticizes the twentieth-century Religious Education Movement's tendency to caricature catechetical instruction, and the movement's explicit prioritization of process over content. Calling the Religious Education Movement "a failure," he states

11. Osmer, *The Teaching Ministry of Congregations*, xviii.

flatly: "Too much is at stake for the church to accept uncritically a continuation of trends that have undercut its teaching ministry throughout this century."[12]

Osmer's solution is to adopt a broader understanding of discipleship formation than religious educators—not to mention most congregations—practice or even recognize. Writing in 2005, he said: "We cannot think exclusively in terms of formal education offered in class-like settings. Rather, we must also think in terms of relationships and formational practices that shape people as they participate in a way of life."[13] Despite his passionate investment in congregations, the complexities of faithful discipleship capture his imagination more than the dynamics of incorporating people into existing church cultures. Even those aspects of his work that focus largely on enculturation (his role as chair of the PCUSA's catechism committee and his lifelong interest in confirmation come to mind) were, for Osmer, less about cultivating new generations of church members than about shaping a way of life, embodied in congregations, that would reflect Christ in the world. When asked in 1998 whether the PCUSA's new catechisms would be considered authoritative, the *Los Angeles Times* quoted Osmer's reply: "Only if they enable the contemporary church to confess Jesus Christ today."[14]

The chapters of this section reflect some of Osmer's many interests as an educator. In Chapter 2, Amanda Hontz Drury investigates a largely unexamined aspect of Osmer's teaching interests—his conviction that children's fantasy literature shapes moral imagination. Drury believes that this literature opens human imagination in ways that allow us to approach Christ as "little children." Kenda Creasy Dean argues in Chapter 3 that Osmer's interest in young people's theological formation, and his long insistence that youth are necessary to the church's theological and ecclesial identity, anticipated the so-called "theological turn" in North American youth ministry thirty years later. Jessicah Krey Duckworth explores catechesis as formation into a way of life, and suggests that focusing on the formation of newcomers to faith—new members, children, the newly baptized—can have the effect of forming the rest of the community as well.

12. Osmer, "Restructuring Confirmation," 66, 68–69.

13. Osmer, *The Teaching Ministry*, 27.

14. "New Presbyterian Catechism Proposed," *Los Angeles Times.*

The Spiritual Director

It surprises some people familiar with Osmer's theological work and intellectual bent that he is trained as an Ignatian spiritual director. Former students are more likely to name the spiritual driver of the education faculty at Princeton Seminary as the late James Loder, who coupled theoretical brilliance with charismatic prayer practices and the occasional exorcism. More recently (and less exotically) students might name Kenda Creasy Dean's warm Methodist pastoral sensibilities, Gordon S. Mikoski's sacramental inclinations, or Bo Karen Lee's rootedness in historical and ascetical traditions as the spiritual rudders of the Education and Formation "subarea." Invariably, Osmer is remembered as the towering intellectual force.

Yet Osmer spent much of his career at Princeton Seminary quietly carving out a Reformed approach to spirituality for both himself and others. True to his upbringing, Osmer's spirituality was enacted more than professed, but it pervaded his personal life and his teaching. Students recall his habit of praying before class, devoting class time to unpacking their spiritual autobiographies alongside paper assignments, or taking part in spiritual retreats with Osmer and a colleague or two at the beginning or end of a semester.

Osmer was fascinated by the possibility of a spirituality that was genuinely Reformed in both theology and practice. This ruled out many popular understandings (or misunderstandings) of spirituality as an individualistic, emotional, or intellectually vacuous pursuit. Sometimes Osmer's spiritual interests showed themselves in course material for classes like "Spiritual Awakenings," co-taught with historian Kenneth Appold. For Osmer, German pietism became an opportunity to talk about small group ministries; the Great Awakening was an occasion to explore Jonathan Edwards' treatises on discernment and religious affections; the origins of Pentecostalism presented students with opportunities to make sense of personal charismatic experiences. Osmer insisted on contextualizing the personal, spiritual dimension of learning within the academic rigors of history and the discipline of practical theology.

One dimension of Osmer's understanding of Reformed spirituality is a discerning openness to the "other," a practice that marked his research as well as his devotional life. "It is important for practical theology . . . always to operate with several perspectives simultaneously and to appropriate them in an intentionally eclectic fashion," Osmer wrote in his inaugural lecture.[15] While perpetually engaging with the social sciences, especially psychology and sociology, Osmer insisted that any empirical dialogue partner with practical theology must approach the human subject as a person and not an object. Profoundly influenced in his doctoral program by Charles V. Gerkin, whose approach to pastoral care understood the subject as a "living human document," Osmer chose to engage social scientists whose work left room for a theological anthropology. Osmer's interest in the research of sociologist Christian Smith, for instance, emerged especially from Smith's meta-theoretical work *What Is A Person?* and from Smith's defense of critical realism and personalism.

Osmer understood even qualitative empirical research to be an act of spiritual openness and presence—ultimately, an act of willing vulnerability to the human other and the divine other. In research, wrote Osmer, the practical theologian must be simultaneously open and present to the human "other," and to the "Other" who is God, listening intently to both.[16] His posture acknowledged the possibility of God's prior action in a given situation—a hallmark of Reformed spirituality, whether the task at hand is cultivating mission (i.e., God is the one with a mission in which you and I may participate) or the spiritual life of the laity.

Ultimately, Osmer's interest in spirituality took shape in the book *Spiritual Companioning: A Guide to Protestant Theology and Practice* (2015) penned with his former student Angela H. Reed, and his teacher in spiritual direction, Marcus Smucker. In chapter 5 of the present book, Reed examines how Osmer's understanding of practical theology aids and contributes to understanding of spiritual companioning as a form of leadership in contemporary Protestant congregations. In Chapter 6, Nathan Stucky wonders how teachers and learners can know a God of reconciliation when the very form of their education embodies the divisions Christ came to heal. He explores new possibilities for ministry and theological education, influenced by Osmer's insistence that practices carry epistemological weight, taking shape at Princeton Seminary's "Farminary," where theological formation and small-scale redemptive

15. Osmer, "Practical Theology as Argument," 71.

16. Osmer's explanation of the empirical/descriptive moment in *Practical Theology: An Introduction* describes a "spirituality of presence" as something typified by a priest attending simultaneously a situation's complex dynamics, and to the presence of God at work in the world. A priest, argues Osmer (and by extension, a practical theologian), must be open to both this world and to the world to come. The empirical becomes a spiritual act through openness and presence. See Osmer, *Practical Theology*, 35–36.

agriculture happen side by side. Bo Karen Lee follows suit by exploring the necessary relationship between spirituality and mission in Chapter 7, and describes how co-teaching with Osmer allowed her own awareness of this connection to blossom.

The Evangelist

In many ways, Osmer's approach to spirituality as openness and presence led directly to his interest in evangelism. While acknowledging the importance of conversion, Osmer prefers to view evangelism as "awakening," an image that acknowledges God's prior presence in the world, and in an individual's life, before the evangelist arrives. The evangelist's role, for Osmer, is to catalyze the recognition of God's presence. For Osmer, this is never merely a "church growth" strategy or a defensive posture aimed at pinning people to their pews. He approaches evangelism as he approaches his empirical research—from a position of genuine curiosity about and delight in the "other," acknowledging that God is already at work.

Several factors led to Osmer's unexpected 2013 shift from a named chair in Christian education to becoming Princeton's Ralph B. and Helen S. Ashenfelter Professor of Mission and Evangelism. One obvious factor was the shifting ecclesial landscape. American congregations had changed dramatically since Osmer's early days as a pastor. Over time, Osmer became convinced that the church could no longer assume an ecology of formative institutions—families, churches, schools, communities—that worked together to nudge people towards faith. While secularization in the United States differs from its counterparts in other parts of the world, it is no less a factor in eroding traditional mechanisms of Christian formation. The task of the Christian educator, Osmer came to believe, was no longer to find more effective ways to nurture nascent faith. It was to bear witness to the *possibility* of faith, and to live as though God is a plausible option for twenty-first century people who are increasingly, and quite happily, religiously unaffiliated.

Osmer adopted two broad responses to this changing context. The first was to re-evaluate past efforts and methods of handing on the faith. Re-evaluating the church's educational practices meant examining how practices that had been shaped under Christendom could continue to be relevant in a post-Christendom world. The most notable re-evaluation was a reassessment of churches' confirmation practices. The mainline churches with which Osmer worked most closely, including the Presbyterian Church (USA), had a history of confirmation, a subject that Osmer had researched and written about in his 1995 *Confirmation: Presbyterian Practices in Ecumenical Perspective*. Around 2013 the question became, "Is there something in this practice that can respond to the current context?" Osmer marshalled scholars from five denominations to find out, and under the leadership of Osmer and Katherine Douglass, the massive three-year, mixed method, five-denomination *Confirmation Project* was born.

Osmer's second response was to focus on a neglected and increasingly urgent practice in mainline Protestantism: evangelism. In the United States, evangelism had fallen prey to Christendom's assumption that being born into a "Christian" country made one a Christian, making evangelism either irrelevant, or a tool for growing your church. The myth of American Christendom, perpetuated by mainline denominations throughout the twentieth century, tended to equate faithfulness with middle class decency, which meant that whatever passed for evangelism amounted to little more than reclaiming backsliding Christians or convincing lukewarm churchgoers to join a more fervent faith group. Neither represented a true awakening to God.

Osmer had long been convinced that Christian formation and mission went hand in hand; the church makes disciples, not for bolstering its rosters, but for the sake of participating in God's mission in the world. Osmer's view of mission as incarnational witness fit easily with his view of evangelism—and Osmer was aghast that, in the ecclesial context of the early twenty-first century, a flagship mainline seminary with over forty-five faculty had no one teaching it. The retirement of Osmer's colleague Darrell L. Guder, the theologian who made "missional church" a household word, accentuated the problem. Osmer proposed shifting from education to evangelism to address this deficit—forcing yet another re-examination of what Christian education actually means in a context where not only the quality of faith, but the *possibility* of faith, is in question.

Section Three focuses on Osmer's interest in mission and evangelism from three distinct theological and cultural perspectives. In Chapter 8, Darrell L. Guder traces the mutual relationship between practical theology and missional theology, especially as they relate to Guder's articulation of missional theology. In Chapter 9, Thomas John Hastings, a long-time mission co-worker in Japan and now Executive Director of the Overseas Mission Study Center, offers a practical theological analysis of missional theology influenced by his experience in Asia. Hastings demonstrates how Osmer's work in areas as wide ranging as practical theology methodology to the development of a new catechism has surprising cross cultural relevance. Finally, in Chapter 10, Drew A. Dyson proposes a missional practical theology for American churches working with emerging adults, and demonstrates with case studies how Osmer's reformulation of evangelism can reframe ministry within a mainline context.

The Practical Theologian

If there has been one identity that has persisted throughout Osmer's life, it is that of practical theologian. Osmer always found that his identity as educator, spiritual director, and evangelist fit best within the broader, more inclusive identity of a practical theologian. In the Epilogue to *Practical Theology: An Introduction*, Osmer sketches out a brief history of theological education, and argues that because the context that gave rise to theological education has changed, theological education must now change as well. In contrast to the theological encyclopedia, Schleiermacher's response to the scientism and secularization encroaching on churches in the late eighteenth century, Osmer advocates a dialogical model of theological education, a cross-disciplinary engagement with human sciences that stops short of adopting science's abstract, universalizing principles and epistemological methods. Practical theology, for Osmer, moves from "a sharp distinction between disinterested, pure scholarship and applied science to the recognition that scholarship is grounded in and oriented toward practice, reflecting constellations of value, interest, and power."[17]

This vision of practical theology led Osmer to abandon guilds oriented around particular sub-fields, like education, in favor of organizations committed to invested, praxis-oriented research. In the North American context, Osmer was an active participant in the Association of Practical Theology (serving as the President in 1991–1992), and his work with the International Academy of Practical Theology led to the founding of the Academy's journal, *The International Journal of Practical Theology*, in 1991.[18] As interest in practical theology grew, its animating principles,

17. Osmer, *Practical Theology*, 237.

18. Cf. Osmer, "Practical Theology: A Current International Perspective," 1–7.

scope and content became more contested—leading to both appreciation and scrutiny of Osmer's work by members of the organization he helped found, as well as by scholars he helped educate and encourage.[19]

Yet important as these guild conversations have been, the hot lava core of Osmer's work remains the North American congregation. Just as shifts in the cultural and intellectual context necessitate new theoretical understandings of practical theology at a theoretical level, so shifting congregational realities require new forms Christian ministry and practice. The four essays in this section posit Osmer's significance for the field of practical theology as a whole, but also have implications for congregational leaders. In Chapter 11, Blair D. Bertrand notes the importance of Osmer's alignment with Karl Barth as his main theological conversation partner, accentuating theological norms in practical theology. It is generally acknowledged that Osmer has always had a focus on theology but Bertrand argues that this is true of other practical theologians, including congregational leaders, as well. In Chapter 12, Andrew Root addresses a long-standing division in the academy between those who, like Johannes van der Ven, advocate for a practical theology driven by the empirical and those who, like Osmer, lean towards the theological. Root makes the case for the theological and its importance for congregations. Shin-Guen Jang, in Chapter 13, explains why the perichoretic content of faith can and should determine the form and manner of the teaching ministry, and by extension, practical theology itself. Finally, in Chapter 14, Osmer's colleague and co-author Gordon Mikoski situates Osmer's work within the long tradition of practical theology at Princeton Theological Seminary, a tradition of practical theology that has long found its origins in the shaping of congregations.

Consensus and Conflict

Let us close with a word about the title of this book. On one level, the phrase *Consensus and Conflict* acknowledges an irony. Known for his "consensus" model of practical theology, Richard Osmer's career nonetheless unfolded against a backdrop of unprecedented ecclesial change

19. Cf. Miller-McLemore, "Toward Greater Understanding of Practical Theology," and Hastings, *Practical Theology and the One Body of Christ*. These colleagues in no way seek to invalidate Osmer's project, and in fact draw from it substantially. Osmer's review of Hastings's book, despite Hastings's critique, calls it "brilliantly and persuasively argued."

and conflict as the descriptions, interpretations, norms, and strategies of faith communities became increasingly contested. When Osmer graduated from Yale Divinity School in the placid spring of 1977 (the biggest conflict in the US that year was Darth Vader's vendetta against the Force), he could not have suspected the shifting tectonic plates of culture groaning underfoot, or imagined how those shifts would forever change the church he was newly ordained to serve. The "consensus" model of practical theology was born in a moment in history when the church, as Osmer knew it, was experiencing anything but consensus.

On the other hand, this period of ecclesial ferment is what allowed the "four moments of Richard R. Osmer"—educator, spiritual director, evangelist, practical theologian—to emerge. Osmer's signature "tacking back and forth" between disciplines, conversation partners, and ecclesial interests allowed him to hold loosely a church in transition. He is more interested in the church's significance and potential for a changing world than in the increasingly polarized skirmishes that have preoccupied mainline congregations throughout his career. For example, while personally sensitive to issues of gender, class, and race, none of these form the spine of Osmer's research—a frequently noted shortcoming of his work. While engaging multiple disciplines in his work, he avoids various correlational methods that have dominated practical theological interpretation, methods that give two fields of study or practices equal footing as they pose questions to one another.[20] Instead, he refers to his preferred theological method as "transversal cross-disciplinarity"[21]—a method that explores intersections and divergences between two fields with common interests, without attempting to establish their parity.

At the end of the day, in addition to expanding the scope of practical theology's interests, we believe Osmer will be remembered for bolstering the field in three ways. First, he will be remembered for distilling the field's methodological architecture into the "four moments" that constitute the consensus model of practical theology. Second, his own breadth of interests demonstrate the flexibility of the consensus model,

20. Joseph E. Bush critiques Osmer's normative task for making practical theology more about meaning-making than emancipatory praxis—although he later quotes Osmer as saying precisely the opposite, as noted in the following paragraph. Bush, *Practical Theology in Church and Society*, 149.

21. For a summary of transversal rationality, see van Huysteen, "Postfoundationalism and Interdisciplinarity." Osmer's appropriation of transversal disciplinarity for practical theological method is described in Osmer, *The Teaching Ministry*, 303–17.

as well as its usefulness for understanding multiple practices of Christian life and leadership. Finally, Osmer's insistence on a "normative" moment in practical theological reflection offers an important counterweight to the field's increasing reliance on social science and empirical research. Osmer openly champions the church's need to be in conversation with disciplines beyond theology; much of his work has been devoted to modelling interdisciplinary conversations. Osmer steadfastly maintains that theology makes a distinctive and necessary contribution to interdisciplinary work.

In the end, it is not enough that practical theology is ideologically current, methodologically sound, or even practically accessible. For Osmer, identity, methodology, and accessibility in practical theology matter only to the extent that they help the church concern itself with the things that concern God. Thus, Osmer can claim, along with liberationist practical theologians that "the real crisis confronting theology is not one of meaning, but one of human suffering."[22] Osmer's primary educational concern has always been how to make practical theology fruitful for congregations' work that forms people to participate in God's redemption and transformation of the world. The true test of practical theology's validity—and the true test of a career as a practical theologian—is its potential to reveal divine grace in the midst of the lived life of human communities. As Osmer puts it: Does practical theology "contribute to social transformation that alleviates suffering?"[23] In short, does practical theology *matter*? Does it make a difference to people who cling to one another in small rural churches in North Carolina, to the daily struggles of communities served by his students, to the urgent concerns of his own son and daughter and grandchildren? The authors in this volume share a conviction: namely, that in Osmer's case, the answer is unequivocally yes. It matters, Rick. It matters.

22. See Matthew Lamb, *Solidarity with Victims*, in Osmer, *Practical Theology*, 167.

23. Ibid.

Bibliography

Amrhein, John. "Robert Louis Stevenson," Treasure Island, The Untold Story. http://www.treasureislandtheuntoldstory.com/robert-louis-stevenson.htm.

Baughman, Michael. *Flipping Church: How Successful Church Planters are Turning Conventional Wisdom Upside Down*. Nashville: Discipleship Resources, 2016.

Bush, Joseph E. *Practical Theology in Church and Society*. Eugene, OR: Cascade, 2016.

Foster, Charles. "A Review of the Teaching Ministry of Congregations." *Journal of Religious Education* 101 (2006) 430–43.

Gerkin, Charles V. *The Living Human Document: Revisioning Pastoral Counseling in a Hermeneutical Mode*. Nashville: Abingdon, 1984.

Hastings, Thomas John. *Practical Theology and the One Body of Christ: Toward a Missional-Ecumenical Model*. Grand Rapids: Eerdmans, 2007.

Mikoski, Gordon S., and Richard R. Osmer. *With Piety and Learning: The History of Practical Theology at Princeton Theological Seminary*. Berlin: LIT Verlag, 2011.

Miller-McLemore, Bonnie J. "Toward Greater Understanding of Practical Theology." *International Journal of Practical Theology* 16 (2012) 104–23.

"New Presbyterian Catechism Proposed." *Los Angeles Times*, March 28, 1998. http://articles.latimes.com/1998/mar/28/local/me-33510.

Osmer, Richard R. Interview by Amanda Drury, May 18, 2018, telephone interview.

———. *Practical Theology, An Introduction*. Grand Rapids: Eerdmans, 2008.

———. "Practical Theology as Argument, Rhetoric, and Conversation." *Princeton Seminary Bulletin* 18 (1997) 46–73.

———. "Practical Theology: A Current International Perspective." HTS Teologiese/Theological Studies 67 (2011) 17. https://hts.org.za/index.php/HTS/article/view/1058.

———. "Restructuring Confirmation." *Theology Today* 49 (1992) 46–67.

———. *The Teaching Ministry of Congregations*. Louisville: Westminster John Knox, 2005.

Reed, Angela, et al. *Spiritual Companioning: A Guide to Protestant Theology and Practice*. Grand Rapids: Baker, 2015.

Sibley, Brian, and John Howe. *The Maps of Tolkien's Middle Earth*. New York: Houghton Mifflin, 1994.

Smith, Kevin. "Review of Richard Osmer: *Practical Theology, An Introduction*." *Conspectus: The Journal of the South African Theological Seminary* 10 (2010) 99–113. https://www.sats.edu.za/userfiles/Conspectus,%20vol.%2010.pdf.

Taylor, Charles. *Sources of the Self: The Making of Modern Identity*. Cambridge, MA: Harvard University Press, 1989.

van Huysteen, J. Wentzel. "Postfoundationalism and Interdisciplinarity: A Response to Jerome Stone," *Journal of Religion and Science* 35 (2000) 427–39.

SECTION ONE

THE EDUCATOR: FORMING THE FAITHFUL

2

Frodo's Magnificat

Shaping the Imagination through Children's Fantasy Literature

AMANDA HONTZ DRURY

I'VE SPENT YEARS READING fantasy literature alongside Rick Osmer, first as a master's student taking his "Fantasy Literature and Moral Formation" course, then as a doctoral student precepting that same course. Now, our reading alongside of one another consists of occasional emails: "Have you read . . . ?" "Have you seen the latest . . ." Within this past year, however, Rick shifted from sending me titles to sending me his own work—the children's fantasy literature he spoke aloud to his children while they were growing up. Now, as he shares the stories with his grandchildren, he is putting these stories to paper. Children's fantasy literature with a bent towards moral formation is not new. What is striking about Rick's stories, however, is the ways in which his characters embody Christian practices. Strength, wisdom, and courage are not always found in the genie's bottle or the magic wand. The reader sees transformation of the character taking place through the cultivation of mindful Christian practices. Rick's stories are, if you will, practical theological fairy tales.

Frodo's Magnificat: Children's Fantasy Literature and the Kingdom of God

Fantasy is not mere childish escapism. There is a political aspect to it—we won't try to change this world unless we are able to imagine another reality. One could say all change starts with fantasy.—Carol Funcke

My favorite Bible story about children is when Jesus overturns the tables at the temple.[1] Perhaps it is not often referred to as a story about children, but in Matthew's Gospel, the story of Jesus turning out the money changers ends with the young. It's easy to miss this ending with all the donkeys, palm branches, and cheering crowds. It's easy to get caught up in the transformation of Jesus from parade marshal to rogue protester as he starts yelling and turning over tables. For some reason, however, Jesus the agitator captivates children:

"But when the chief priests and the scribes saw the amazing things that he did, and heard the children crying out in the temple, 'Hosanna to the Son of David,' they became angry."[2] Somewhere between the triumphal entry and the table throwing, Jesus loses friends. We went from crowds of people cheering to just children. It sounds like Jesus scared away everyone but the kids. Where the adults were confused, the children were curious. Where the adults showed consternation, the children showed courage.

This shouldn't surprise us. The kingdom of God, we read over and over again, belongs to children (this is why the phrase, "children are the future of the church" is so maddening—as if the kingdom of God belongs to children, and when they grow up they will inherit the local church as well). Somehow, children are able to see aspects of the kingdom of God that the rest of us cannot. And apparently, this is a good thing: "I praise you, Father, Lord of heaven and earth," Jesus declares, "because you have hidden these things from the wise and the intelligent and have revealed them to infants."[3]

"Truly I tell you," we read in Matthew's Gospel, "unless you change and become like children, you will never enter the kingdom of heaven."[4] Much has been written on what it means to "become like children" with

---

1. Matt 21:12–17.
2. Matt 21:15.
3. Matt 11:25.
4. Matt 18:3.

people differing on what exactly this means.[5] Rather than jumping into these conversations, however, I propose we sneak in a side door and attempt to eavesdrop on a world children often find themselves in: the world of children's fantasy literature.

Sneaking in the side door of children's fantasy literature gives us the chance to see the kingdom of God by using our moral imaginations. Using stories in this way makes sense. The "good life" of the kingdom, James K.A. Smith asserts, "captures our hearts and imaginations not by providing a set of rules or ideas, but by painting a picture of what it looks like for us to flourish and live well." "This is why," he continues, "such pictures are communicated most powerfully in stories, legends, myths, plays, novels and film rather than dissertations, messages, and monographs." This attraction to the good life plays out at a "precognitive level . . . it is not primarily our minds that are captivated but rather our imaginations that are captured, and when our imagination is hooked, we're hooked . . . Attracted by it and moved toward it, we begin to live into this vision of the good life and start to look like citizens who inhabit the world that we picture as the good life."[6] Children's fantasy literature tills the soil for the kingdom of God—it allows the kingdom of God to germinate through 1) calming the watchful dragons of myopic realism, 2) opening our ears to the testimony of children, and 3) awakening within us a moral imagination to envision a new world.

Become Like Children: Sneaking Past the Watchful Dragons

Is there something we lose concerning the kingdom of God as we grow old? Is seeing God's kingdom more difficult as we age? "Become like a child" we read over and over again. I wonder when the lips of those cheering children were silenced? At what point in their growing up would they have lost that courageous curiosity?

Not long ago the University of North Dakota released a study on how people might tap into their "inner child." Psychologists Darya Zabelina and Michael Robinson recruited seventy-six undergraduate students and split them into two groups.[7] Both groups were told that school was

---

5. See Balthasar, *Unless You Become Like This Child*; Bunge, *The Child in the Bible*; Harwood et al., *Infants and Children in the Church*.

6. Smith, *Desiring the Kingdom*, 53.

7. Zabelina and Robinson, "Child's Play."

cancelled and were then instructed to write for five to ten minutes on what they might do with their extra time. One of the groups received an additional instruction: "You are seven years old." The control group wrote of sleep, work, and other obligations. The "seven-year-olds," however, came up with more whimsical answers often tied to creativity, spontaneity, and play. The possibilities imagined by the "seven-year-olds" seemed boundless. One of the findings of the study was that simply by *pretending* to be a child awakened long-dormant parts of our imagination. In order to have a more childlike mindset, *try*.

While we are capable of *trying* to act like children, reading children's fantasy literature moves us to a more unself-conscious state. When we read, our imaginations are stoked in such a way that we catch a glimpse of the delight of a child who sees things her older counterpart cannot. It connects us to that which we've lost as we've aged; it sneaks us past the guardians our adult sense of realism has stationed at the entrance to our imagination.

If we do have what C. S. Lewis calls "watchful dragons" that stop anything too fantastical or childlike, then perhaps, as Lewis says, fairy tales will enamor us and sneak right past the winged beast.[8] Lewis explains:

> I thought I saw how stories of this kind could steal past a certain inhibition which paralyzed much of my own religion in childhood. Why did one find it so hard to feel as one was told one ought to feel about God or about the sufferings of Christ? I thought the chief reason was that one was told one ought to. An obligation to feel can freeze feelings. And reverence itself did harm. The whole subject was associated with lowered voices; almost as if it were something medical. But supposing that by casting all these things into an imaginary world, stripping them of their stained-glass and Sunday school associations, one could make them for the first time appear in their real potency? Could one not thus steal past those watchful dragons? I thought one could.[9]

When fantasy literature sneaks past the "watchful dragon," it nudges the sleeping imagination along the way. I propose we turn to children's fantasy literature to help cultivate within us a childlike lens through which we might broaden our understanding of the kingdom of God. If pastors

---

8. It is worth noting there are differences between fantasy literature and fairy tales, however, fairy tales are a subsection of the larger fantasy genre.

9. Lewis, *On Stories*, 70.

are challenged to preach with the Bible in one hand and the newspaper in another, then perhaps fantasy literature should rest in one's back pocket.

Certainly, *trying* to be like a child is an option, but perhaps there is something beyond volition. Yes, we can try harder, but there is also a sense that children's fantasy literature allows us to simply *be*—to be caught up in the currents of make-believe and imagination.

Receiving the Testimony of Children

All dreams are not false; some dreams are truer than the plainest facts. Fact at best is but a garment of truth, which has ten thousand changes of raiment woven on the same loom. Let the dreamer only do the truth of his dream and one day he will realize all that was worth realizing it.—George MacDonald

Oddly enough, almost immediately after Jesus calls his followers to "become like children," he seems to change his story. "Whoever welcomes one such child in my name welcomes me," he declares.[10] Which is it? Do we become like children or are we instead those who welcome children? Matthew gives us a fascinating yet ambiguous shift of personhood. We do not just become children, we also welcome children.

If we want to become more child-like it helps to start by taking seriously the things that children say. The story of Princess Irene in George McDonald's *The Princess and the Goblin* traces the tension between the children who see and experience remarkable things and the adults who refuse to believe them. "'When I tell you the truth, Lootie,' said the princess, who somehow did not feel at all angry, 'you say to me 'Don't tell stories': it seems I must tell stories before you will believe me.'"[11]

Much of children's fantasy literature revolves around the trope of children speaking truth and the adults not believing them.[12] Harry

---

10. Matt 18:5.

11. MacDonald, *The Princess and the Goblin*, 166.

12. "It's a longstanding 'rule' of child and adolescent literature that in order to free the juvenile protagonists to act independently, the parents/adults must first be removed from the picture: The Boxcar Children are orphans, the Hardy Boys are off camping on their own, the kids in *The Mixed up Files* move in to the museum, the Peanuts adults are out of the frames and speak in gibberish . . . and so on. So, in addition to the shared childhood experience that adults don't take us seriously, there is also a writer's desire to allow for child heroism via obtuse grown-ups." Randy Dewing, email to the author, January 29, 2018.

Potter insists on the return of Voldemort. Meg from *A Wrinkle in Time* maintains her father's survival despite incredulity from Mr. Jenkins. *The Lion, The Witch and The Wardrobe* holds within it an unusual reversal in which the elderly professor instructs Lucy's siblings that they really should believe their little sister's testimony. Lewis then proceeds to remove children from the adults like the professor in order for them to serve as their own heroes in their stories. This removal implies Lewis's willingness for children to serve as "trustworthy narrators of their own experiences."[13] Thank goodness for children who insist on sharing their experienced reality, even if it means waking us up three times in a single night when they hear the voice of God.

What is more, testifying is a communal practice. It is not a testimony unless there are hearers to receive the message. When we listen to and take seriously the testimony of children, we are not only showing children that we believe them to be capable vessels of the Holy Spirit, we are also reminding ourselves that the message of God is not the sole property of those who've conquered puberty. When children know their testimonies are taken seriously, we are assisting them in articulating and solidifying their identities in Christ Jesus as well as our own in the process.

So often God seems to delight in using the weak instead of the strong. This is quite fitting with our fairy tales as ultimately, the genre of children's fantasy literature—and fantasy literature in general—is one of subversion. We also see these subversive elements woven throughout the biblical narrative. Before Hobbits defeated dark lords, we had boys slaying giants. A baby in a basket escaped death though the loving act of a mother long before another baby was shielded by his mother's love and ultimately became known as "the boy who lived." Repeatedly, we see the gospel proclaimed to the poor, the lame, the widowed, and the weak—it is a story of subversion. And God seems quite well pleased to subvert what is "proper" in favor of entrusting his words to women and children.

We don't read children's fantasy literature to become better listeners. As illustrated above, the problem isn't *hearing* what children say, it's imagining their words to be true. One could argue that as we grow, we lose our capacity to imagine. This was certainly the case with Susan who grows up and abandons her belief in Narnia. She becomes a Narnian apostate, claiming that all the stories her siblings tell are the product of overripe imaginations.

---

13. Ibid.

J. K. Rowling took issue with Lewis's treatment of Susan in Lev Grossman's *Time* article from July 17, 2005: "There comes a point where Susan, who was the older girl, is lost to Narnia because she becomes interested in lipstick. She's become irreligious basically because she found sex. I have a big problem with that."[14] Rowling is referring to a conversation from *The Last Battle*:

"'My sister Susan,' answered Peter shortly and gravely, 'is no longer a friend of Narnia.'

'Oh Susan!' said Jill. 'She's interested in nothing nowadays except nylons and lipstick and invitations.'"[15]

If Rowling is correct that Lewis is using Susan to speak out against sex or a particular form of feminism then I too would "have a big problem with that." Looking at this passage in context, however, Lewis's critique seems to have less to do with the lipstick and more to do with the problem of abandoning childhood faith in order to become more "sophisticated" as evidenced by Lady Polly's response to Jill:

"'Grown up, indeed,' said Lady Polly. 'I wish she *would* grow up. She wasted all her school time wanting to be the age she is now and she'll waste all the rest of her life trying to stay that age. Her whole idea is to race on to the next silliest time of one's life as quick as she can and then stop there as long as she can.'"[16] Lewis's critique seems to be less about a woman's sexuality and more about one's shunning of childish things and the subsequent refusal to believe. In Susan's defense, it is quite difficult to hold on to one's childhood imagination as one grows up—so much so that, in order to take seriously the testimony of children, we must have robust imaginations.

Awakening Imaginations:
What We Knew Before We Knew Too Much

Reality is merely an illusion, albeit a very persistent one.—Albert Einstein

Sometimes we see what is most true with our imaginations. Fantasy is not an escape from reality; rather, C. S. Lewis writes, "we do not retreat

14. Grossman, "J. K. Rowling Hogwarts and All,"

15. Lewis, *The Last Battle*, 169. That is not to say that there are not explicit or implicit sexist undertones in Lewis's stories, simply that there could be an alternative interpretation in this particular case.

16. Ibid.

from reality: we rediscover it. As long as the story lingers in our minds, the real things are more themselves . . . [D]ipping [things] in myth we see them more clearly."[17] Children see reality in a way that adults cannot (or would not), and we read fantasy literature in an attempt to see as children see.

We need this childlike lens because the older we get the less creative we are. It seems that as we age we lose something that once came naturally to us. We know this is the case with language.[18] The older we get, the fewer sounds we can make. While we might acquire new words and understandings of the vernacular, we also lose linguistic abilities to participate in other languages. There are somewhere around 869 identified phonemes—or units of sound that distinguish one word from another. Infants aged six to eight months can discriminate the full range. "After that," John Dowling writes, infants "use just a subset—those that they hear and thus distinguish. Conversely, young children can imitate virtually any sound an adult makes, but this ability is also lost with age. By one-and-a-half years, babies start to make sounds characteristic of the languages to which they are exposed, and their ability to make sounds characteristic of other languages slowly disappears."[19] As the infant grows, she slowly loses her ability to reproduce the sounds she once gurgled easily. She unlearns sounds in order to speak the words of those around her. As the child grows accustomed to her native tongue, her linguistic abilities are pruned until they are within the boundaries of the surrounding vernacular. Learning to speak means unlearning certain sounds.

Just as we lose the ability to make sounds, so too we lose the ability to think creatively. In 1968 George Land and Beth Jarman of NASA came up with a test to determine "divergent thinking" among rocket scientists and engineers. Land and Jarman applied the test to children as a way to measure their creativity. They were startled to see that 98 percent of the children tested scored at a "genius level." Amazed by these findings, the duo followed the children, conducting tests as they aged. What they saw was a decline in the children's ability to think creatively as they aged.

17. Lewis, *On Stories*, 138.

18. We go from Susan, the child queen of Narnia, to Susan who has grown and is "no longer a friend of Narnia," her lived experiences in Narnia reduced to a pretend game she used to play.

19. Dowling, *The Great Brain Debate*, 64.

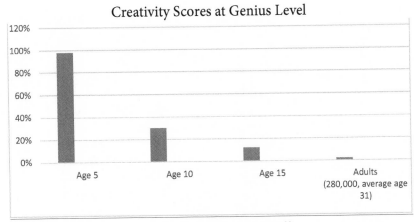

George Land's Creativity Test (1968)[20]

Amazingly, these results have been replicated over and over again. Both the NASA study and the "School is Cancelled" study listed above assert that while adults tend to lose creativity as they age, that creative spark has not necessarily gone out. Our creativity is not dead; it becomes dormant and simply needs to be awakened. The creative spark is present, as evidenced by the dreams of our subconscious that are often fraught with a creativity unparalleled in our waking hours.[21]

What does an awakened imagination have to do with the kingdom of God? We will have a difficult time imagining a new world in heaven if we are unable to imagine a new world on earth. Fantasy literature opens us up to that which is other. It pushes against the boundaries of what we see as real and leaves us wondering if perhaps there is more. This is not necessarily an intentional question we ask, like "Is there life outside of earth?" Rather, it is something we are swept up into. We do not consider fantasy literature; it consumes us. In other words, when we read children's fantasy literature, we move from *trying* to be like children to being caught up in a childlike state.

With a moral imagination, we cannot help but wonder just how different we are from a character like Tolkien's Gollum. The creature steals, fights, and perhaps worse, betrays, and yet throughout the books, we follow Bilbo's lead and are often filled with pity for the creature. Gollum represents the figure we all could become should circumstances play out differently. We are all, as it seems, a simple quarrel away from the path of

20. Land, "The Failure of Success."
21. Nir and Tononi, "Dreaming and the Brain."

Gollum. Tolkien stokes our compassion throughout the story, giving us glimpses into almost alternate views of Smeagol. Gollum sees Fordo and Sam asleep and we read:

> A strange expression passed over his lean hungry face. The gleam faded from his eyes, and they went dim and grey, old and tired. A spasm of pain seemed to twist him, and he turned away, peering back up towards the pass, shaking his head, as if engaged in some interior debate. Then he came back, and slowly putting out a trembling hand, very cautiously he touched Frodo's knee—but almost the touch was a caress. For a fleeting moment, could one of the sleepers have seen him, they would have thought that they beheld an old weary hobbit, shrunken by the years that had carried him far beyond his time, beyond friends and kin, and the fields and streams of youth, an old starved pitiable thing.[22]

When the Gollums appear, we reach a fork in the road and must choose between compassion or disdain. These authors encourage us to maintain strong convictions—yet always with compassion. Characters like these prompt us to approach the kingdom of God with open hands, palms up. We take what we think we know and hold it lightly with the knowledge that God often uses the "foolish things of the world to shame the wise."[23]

This is the same imagination that calls us to hold out hope for the good in others. It may look like Snape is muttering incantations to cause you to fall off your broom, but it's also possible those mutterings are counter-curses keeping you in the air. Fantasy literature opens up the door for us to see the good where everyone else might see the evil. It opens us up to the thought of salvation coming from an unexpected source.

Often at the end of children's fantasy literature there is revealed an unexplored depth of imagination. And so stories end with "They lived happily ever after," implying there is more to the narrative and it only gets better from here. Frodo boards the ship for the Grey Havens "where the leaves fall not."[24] And the Narnians take their final journey: "All their life in this world and all their adventures in Narnia had only been the cover and the title page: now at last they were beginning Chapter One of the Great Story which no one on earth has read: which goes on for ever: in

---

22. Tolkien, *The Two Towers*, 366.

23. 1 Cor 1:27.

24. Tolkien, *The Return of the King*, 252.

which every chapter is better than the one before."[25] Children's fantasy literature paves the way for an unfathomable kingdom that has no end. "Further up and further in."[26]

Conclusion

My favorite Bible story about adults is from Mark 10:13–16, where Jesus blesses the children:

> One day some parents brought their children to Jesus so he could touch and bless them. But the disciples scolded the parents for bothering him. When Jesus saw what was happening, he was angry with his disciples. He said to them, "Let the children come to me. Don't stop them! For the Kingdom of God belongs to those who are like these children. I tell you the truth, anyone who doesn't receive the Kingdom of God like a child will never enter it." Then he took the children in his arms and placed his hands on their heads and blessed them.

This is not a children's story. This is a story for adults. Children don't need to hear this story—they already know they are welcome on Jesus' lap (that is why they are in the story in the first place). This story is for the rest of us caught in the myopic reality of adulthood. It is those of us who are closest to Jesus who need to hear this story.

25. Lewis, *The Last Battle*, 228.
26. Ibid., 206.

Bibliography

Balthasar, Hans Urs von. *Unless You Become Like This Child*. San Francisco: Ignatius, 2015.

Bunge, Marcia J. *The Child in the Bible*. Grand Rapids: Eerdmans, 2008.

Dowling, John. *The Great Brain Debate: Nurture or Nature*. Princeton, NJ: Princeton University Press, 2007.

Grossman, Lev. "J. K. Rowling Hogwarts and All." *Time*, July 17, 2005. http://content. time.com/time/magazine/article/0,9171,1083935,00.html.

Harwood, Adam, Kevin E. Lawson, Jason Foster, David Liberto, David P. Scaer, and Gregg Strawbridge. *Infants and Children in the Church: Five Views on Theology and Ministry*. Nashville: B&H Academic, 2017.

Land, George. "The Failure of Success." TedXTuscon (February 16, 2011). https:// www.youtube.com/watch?v=ZfKMq-rYtnc (accessed February 8, 2019). Study originally reported in George Land and Beth Jarman, *Breakpoint and Beyond: Mastering the Future Today*. Leadership 2000, 1998.

Lewis, C. S. *On Stories: And Other Essays on Literature*. San Diego: Harvest, 2002.

———. *The Last Battle*. New York: Harper Collins, 2002.

Nir, Yuval and Giulio Tononi. "Dreaming and the Brain: From Phenomenology to Neurophysiology," *Trends in Cognitive Sciences* 14 (2010) 88–100. https://www. ncbi.nlm.nih.gov/pmc/articles/PMC2814941/.

MacDonald, George. *The Princess and the Goblin*. Philadelphia: J.B. Lippincott & Co, 1872. net-Library, e-book, pdf.

Smith, James A. K. *Desiring the Kingdom: Worship, Worldview, and Cultural Formation*. Grand Rapids: Baker Academic, 2011.

Tolkien, J. R. R. *The Return of the King*. New York : Del Rey, 1986.

———. *The Two Towers*. Wilmington: Mariner, 2012.

Zabelina, D. L. and M. D. Robinson. "Child's Play: Facilitating the Originality of Creative Output by a Priming Manipulation." *Psychology of Aesthetics, Creativity, and the Arts* 4 (2010) 57–65.

3

Accidental Prophet

Richard R. Osmer and the "Theological Turn" in Youth Ministry

KENDA CREASY DEAN

THE FIRST ARTICLE I ever read written by Richard R. Osmer was fished out from under an unruly stack on my seminary advisor's desk. "Here," she said, emphatically thrusting a slim journal into my hands. She had marked the page, knowing that I—the only seminarian that either of us knew who actually *wanted* to do youth ministry—would devour it. "You're going to want to read this," she said. And then, ominously, indicating the byline: "Keep your eye on that young man. He's going places."

It was 1989, the year of Tiananmen Square, the fall of the Berlin Wall, and Madonna's "Like a Prayer" video. George Herbert Walker Bush was the United States' forty-first President. The Exxon Valdez bled almost eleven million gallons of crude into the Alaskan sea; Stephen Hawking published *A Brief History of Time*. Michael Keaton was *Batman*. Taylor Swift was born. And congregations were beginning to come to grips with the fact that young people, who had been spilling out of North American churches steadily since the 1960s, were not coming back—or, more disorienting to us still, were never really "churched" in the first place.

By 1989, the youth ministry resource industry was in full swing, a testament to the widespread belief that the adolescent exodus from North American churches was linked to lackluster resources and poorly trained leadership. The generally held assumption was that improving the quality of these variables would stem the outgoing tide. Two scrappy American youth ministry resource companies—Youth Specialties and Group Publishing—had come of age, and their user-friendly youth curriculum, flashy program resources, and energetic training conferences underscored the narrative that most churches told themselves: if we can just make youth programs more appealing and attract more professionally prepared leaders, teenagers will stay. By design, most of the available youth ministry literature leaned toward personal reflections on "what works" with teenagers, and could be read in an hour.

Still, research from fields like education, developmental psychology and sociology had begun to make inroads in youth ministry. In 1991, the Carnegie Council on Adolescent Development identified two goals shared by Protestant, Catholic, and Jewish religious youth work in the United States: to impress upon young people a religious identity, and to usher them safely into adulthood.[1] For churches, the most common route to both was to address young people's developmental, sociological, and cultural "needs" in church so youth would not look elsewhere to fulfill them. In other words, religious communities set out to provide young people with optimal conditions for physical, psychological, and spiritual health, and to make the rough places plain as adolescents grew in wisdom and stature and favor with God.[2] It was a job most pastors happily outsourced to volunteer or professional youth workers.

Fresh from seminary, newly ordained, and as gung ho as they come, I was one of them.

Little did I know that three years later I would be sitting in Rick Osmer's office as his first doctoral advisee, exasperated by churches' easy dismissal of young people—but also exhausted from "meeting adolescents' needs," and frustrated by churches' inability to imagine youth ministers as more than service providers. Theology was seldom discussed by youth ministers beyond hackneyed catch-phrases (helping youth "meet Jesus," "get saved," or "grow into mature Christian adults," depending

1. See Dean, "Youth Ministry," n.p.

2. For example, Mark Senter has written: "Youth ministry has always been a transaction between young people themselves or caring adults and young people they perceive to be in need." See Senter, "History of Youth Ministry Education," 83. I disagree with the sweeping nature of this statement—much that happens in youth ministry is neither transactional nor necessarily a reaction to young people being "in need"—but Senter's description is an accurate observation of a common *perception* about youth ministry, especially in evangelical circles. Osmer uses the language of "needs" in adolescents primarily developmentally.

on your theological tradition).[3] Most of us were far too busy meeting teenagers' needs to reflect deeply on what any of this actually meant, or on whether youth ministry could (or should) accomplish these things. Meeting adolescent needs was important work, after all. Yet what made youth ministry *ministry* remained elusive. Meanwhile, despite ample scriptural warrant for God's "preferential option for young people,"[4] mainline churches' leadership systems retained a clear bias for age and experience, and typically overlooked the potential theological contributions of young people and those who served them.

Seeds of a Theological Turn for Youth Ministry[5]

In the late 1980s Robert Lynn from the Lilly Endowment's religion division convened mainline Protestant Christian educators—including Union Theological Seminary (Richmond)'s new professor of Christian education, Richard R. Osmer—to discuss the "state of youth ministry." These gatherings marked the beginning of Lilly's generation-long emphasis on congregations and young people. Osmer's prescient piece in 1989, "Challenges to Youth Ministry in Mainline Congregations," was the culmination of those conversations. Osmer framed the issue squarely: the problem wasn't youth—it was the *church*.

> It is time to take a new look at the mainline churches' ministry with youth . . . An important part of the dissatisfaction of today's youth with the church stems from an absence of a spiritually challenging and world-shaping vision that meets their hunger for a chance to participate in a worthy adventure . . . Ultimately, the spiritual needs of youth transcend the legitimate requirements of wholesome companionship, entertaining events, and even worthwhile service projects. What they ask from the church is no so much something to *do* as something to *be*.[6]

3. There were rare but notable exceptions to this pattern; cf. Little, *Youth, World and Church*; Ng, *Youth in the Community of Disciples*.

4. Little, "Introduction."

5. The first book to describe this turn was Root and Dean, *The Theological Turn in Youth Ministry*. The book's dedication to Richard R. Osmer and Roland Martinson acknowledges their seminal roles in approaching youth ministry theologically.

6. Osmer, "Challenges to Youth Ministry," 5, 6, 7.

With that, the gauntlet was thrown, igniting an explicit ecclesiologi-cal thrust in youth ministry.[7]

Thirty years later, the dispiriting truth is that every challenge Osmer named in his 1989 manifesto remains true for youth ministry today. This is despite a generation of leaders who have substantially professional-ized youth ministry training, launched an active academic "subfield" in Western theological education, and made resources and education in youth ministry readily available. Surely churches' lack of influence on contemporary young people, despite these substantial changes, requires explanation. Yet my main purpose in this essay is to argue that Osmer's essay was more prophetic than its author realized. In offering a fresh lens for the ways churches think about young people, Osmer anticipated a shift—still too nascent in 1989 to fully make out—that thirty years later would be called "the theological turn" in youth ministry.

In the years to follow, Osmer sometimes sowed the seeds of a "theo-logical turn" explicitly, but more often he simply assumed them in his teaching and writing. (To my knowledge, he never assigned this article to his students; it remains a hidden part of the Osmer corpus, appearing only once in print.) Yet these seeds grew into a forest of publications from Osmer's students and their progeny—including many of the authors of this volume—not to mention a generation of pastors and Christian thought leaders who insisted that young people, and therefore any min-istry that involves them, are theological subjects worthy of a theological mission . . . and that if the church offers them anything less, we are frauds.

The More Things Change

In his essay, Osmer identified eight characteristics of mainline congre-gations' youth ministries that, in his view, castrated churches' ability to hand on Christian faith to new generations, with devastating effects on adolescent faith (*see Figure 1*). Several refrains recur throughout the article. Without a "spiritually challenging, world-shaping vision," avers Osmer, young people experience church as "spiritually innocuous"—and therefore unworthy of their time, attention, or commitment. Without creatively renegotiating Christian practices for new generations (a role Osmer explicitly champions for youth ministry), even youth who value

---

7. I see this as augmenting rather than replacing the evangelical thrust that charac-terized twentieth-century youth ministry's evangelical roots.

their childhood church experience fail to see its relevance for their futures. When churches avoid the most pressing issues of society (a charge the young Osmer levies with some force), they fail to address matters that daily concern adolescents, leaving youth to conclude that theology has nothing to do with them.

It is striking how little has changed in thirty years. Despite a more professionalized workforce, heightened clergy awareness about young people, and a limited but noticeable theological conversation around youth ministry, churches have failed to foster robust faith in young people, restore them to the fold, or guarantee a central place for youth ministry in North American congregations. In short, the challenges facing youth ministry in 2019 look very much like those enumerated by Osmer a generation earlier. Still absent from most churches is a spiritually challenging and world-shaping vision that meets adolescents' hunger to participate in a worthy adventure. Still persistent in most congregations is a reluctance to confront the comfortable standards of American culture. Still dwindling is adolescent church participation—in fact, we now have data showing that religious faith among young people is significantly *more* precarious today than in 1989. So what can we learn from Osmer's views on youth ministry besides its stubborn resistance to change? What about his understanding of adolescent faith helped inspire a "theological turn" that took almost thirty years to unfold?

The Shackles of Low Expectations

Underlying Osmer's observations about North American youth ministry is his determination to confront churches with their failure to nurture the potential theological and ecclesial contributions of young people. Osmer believed that failing to prioritize youth ministry placed *the church itself* in jeopardy, not because youth are "the future of the church" or an antidote to membership losses, but because young people's absence creates a *theological* crisis for congregations.

Seven Challenges to Mainline Congregations in Forming Young Faith

Richard R. Osmer (1989)

1. Lacking a spiritually challenging, world–shaping vision that can stand up to the dominant culture's vision of "comfort"

2. Limiting adolescent's contributions to specialized programs for teens, segregating and marginalizing young people from the congregation

3. Focusing almost exclusively on teenagers' psychological development, ignoring the critical importance of social influences and expectations on young people

4. Leaving youth to draw their identities and affirmations from youth culture instead of offering a counter–cultural identity drawn from Christian tradition

5. Failing to offer an antidote to pervasive narcissism by giving teens significant opportunities to participate in justice ministries

6. Failing to help families leverage their decisive influence on religious identity

7. Overlooking the congregation's importance—especially in the form of trusted adult leaders and peers—in modeling for youth a Christian vision and way of life

Figure 1

With few exceptions, most advocates of youth ministry in 1989 focused on the risks teenagers faced in a culture that offered them more attractive options than Christian communities. Put another way, adolescents' developmental "needs" were being met more adequately *outside* churches than in them. This disjuncture created a chasm between adolescents and congregations that, it was commonly believed, placed youth in spiritual jeopardy and dangerously weakened the membership rosters of the institutional church. Without youth as "the church's future," American mainline congregations—whose steep declines in membership and influence had become undeniable—seemed doomed to a speedy demise.

Osmer turns this "problem" of youth ministry on its head. He challenges two implicit assumptions in this narrative: first, the assumption that youth ministry should be strengthened to ensure institutional survival, and second, the assumption that adolescents are wrong to seek meaning and purpose apart from congregations. Osmer wonders if this analysis is backward. What if institutional survival was not all it cracked up to be? What if congregations did not offer ecclesial teaching *worthy* of adolescents' allegiance? What if young people searching for a "worthy dream," to paraphrase Stanley Hauerwas, simply couldn't find one in church?

To make his case, Osmer does not point to the cultural and demographic trends that might plausibly contribute to adolescents' increasing absence from North American religious life.[8] Nor does he blame young people themselves for abandoning churches in favor of other interests. Instead, Osmer interprets young people's *de facto* exodus from mainline Christianity as a stinging rebuke on churches' refusal to offer youth a compelling counter-narrative to those peddled by the broader culture—and often embodied by congregations. "The mainline churches' failure to present their own task in more starkly radical terms is an indication of their abdication to the comfortable standards of American culture," Osmer charges.[9] The challenge for churches with young people, says Osmer, is to offer a vision not unlike the one that won teens like Mary, Agnes, Joan of Arc, Teresa of Lisieux, and the Uganda martyrs—a vision that invites "an irrevocable (and therefore fully adult) commitment to God's work in the world."[10]

> In their zeal, these [young saints] consented to being thrust immediately into the midst of the ferment that inevitably results when the Spirit of truth confronts the spirit of the age; they asked for and were granted the privilege of moving to the front lines in the battle with sin and evil, where they would be most vulnerable to the action of grace and, in some cases, to martyrdom.[11]

8. Sociologist Robert Wuthnow, for example, posits demographic and social factors as contributing to young people's declining presence in churches, including delayed marriage, fewer children born later in life, uncertain economic stability, more higher education, declining civic participation, loose social connections, and the proliferation of options thanks to the internet and globalization. See Wuthnow, *After the Baby Boomers*.

9. Osmer, "Challenges to Youth Ministry," 7.

10. Ibid., 6.

11. Ibid.

Osmer contrasts contemporary congregations' approach to youth ministry with the call to radical self-giving and even martyrdom that punctuates the biographies of history's young saints, whom history portrays not as victims, but as agents of considerable power. "At no point did these youthful saints see themselves as the 'church of tomorrow,'" observes Osmer wryly. Meanwhile, contemporary youth ministry focuses on "devising strategies for keeping young people in the church because it is a place they will be 'safe' from the terrors of the street or the seductions of the shopping mall."[12] Then he lands his most devastating punch:

> Our hopes for [our youth] are modest and reasonable. For the most part, they mirror the expectations we have for ourselves. We ask no more than that they grow up to be 'good' people . . . To this end, we program activities which are certainly wholesome, sometimes edifying, and almost always 'fun.' . . . Of course, some youth do remain in the church, and most of these do turn out to be 'good' people. But many . . . leave the church because it asks nothing significant of them. They leave the church because it is spiritually innocuous.[13]

In short, as long as churches present Christian discipleship as "manageable and unthreatening, youth will fail to find sufficient scope there for their very considerable zeal." We should not be surprised, Osmer concludes, if youth look elsewhere.[14]

Twenty-five years later, Osmer's analysis of the situation was corroborated by sociologist Christian Smith in the longitudinal National Study of Youth and Religion (NSYR), the largest study of adolescent religiosity ever conducted in the United States. The NSYR concluded that American's default religion—practiced by young people because they learn it from their parents and their churches—is "moralistic therapeutic deism," a do-good, feel-good, consumerist religious outlook that reduces God to a divine butler or cosmic therapist.[15] Smith and his colleagues believe that moralistic therapeutic deism had "colonized" American churches, having supplanted experiences of the Trinity, holiness, justification, forgiveness, Eucharist, heaven, hell, and so on with the language of happiness, niceness, and earned heavenly reward. "It is not so much that Christian-

12. Ibid.

13. Ibid., 7.

14. Ibid.

15. For a discussion of God-images of teenagers who are moralistic therapeutic deists, see Smith with Denton, *Soul Searching*, 165.

ity is being secularized," writes Smith. "Rather . . . [it] is actively being colonized and displaced by a quite different religious faith."[16] In other words, young people don't practice moralistic therapeutic deism because they have misunderstood what churches teach them. Rather, they practice it because this *is* what churches teach them.

Much has been made of these findings' significance for religious life in North America. A religion whose highest ambition is to meet young people's needs—to keep them safe ("sober virgins," in the words of one youth pastor I know) [17] and connected to a church community that supports them—instrumentalizes faith, draining it of theological grit (which does not stop it from being a useful therapeutic or civic exercise). Smith's research was quickly followed by the Pew Research Center's discovery of a dramatic drop in religious affiliation among young adults.[18] Suddenly a new possibility emerged: if churches had inadvertently colluded with American culture to promote something like moralistic therapeutic deism, would increased church involvement counter pallid faith in adolescents, or contribute to it?

The Theological Significance of Youth Ministry

If moralistic therapeutic deism flattens and homogenizes faith into a generic, interpersonal version of American civil religion, the story of Jesus invites young people into something starkly different.[19] Osmer posits the church as "the only institution with an investment in forming a counter-culture awareness in its members."[20] For Osmer, youth ministry is critical for raising the most urgent questions facing the church and world, which at bottom are always theological. Youth ministry inevitably "brings into focus some of the most significant theological issues presently before the church," says Osmer. "Virtually every issue of central importance to the mainline churches' future comes to expression in [ministry with young people]."[21]

16. Ibid, 171.

17. See Rood, *Bold Parenting.* "Sober Virgins" is the topic of chapter 4.

18. Pew Research Center, "Nones on the Rise," par 1–6. See also Lipka and Mc-Clendon, "Why People with No Religion," par 3.

19. Smith with Denton, *Soul Searching,* 168.

20. Osmer, "Challenges to Youth Ministry," 10.

21. Ibid., 3.

For this reason, mainline churches' ambivalence toward youth ministry reveals for Osmer "a broader theological uncertainty" in the church as a whole.[22] In spite of research suggesting that most American adolescents want more time with adults—not less—churches tend to give youth their own "space," their own minister, their own meeting times and programs (whether this is intended to benefit young people or adults is unclear).[23] Such a "one–eared Mickey Mouse" model of youth ministry, as it is sometimes called (*see Figure 2*), isolates young people from the rest of the church, and marginalizes them from "the real centers of power, responsibility, and commitment in congregational life."[24] When youth are incorporated into the life of the church, on the other hand, they remind us of our theological mission, and force us to confront the disconnect between the story of Jesus and the "comfortable standards of secular culture," thereby maintaining the church's truth-telling power. This prevents congregations from falling into what social theorist Ulrich Beck calls a "zombie" category: a social concept that is dead, but kept alive by those invested in continuing the fiction of traditional institutions.[25]

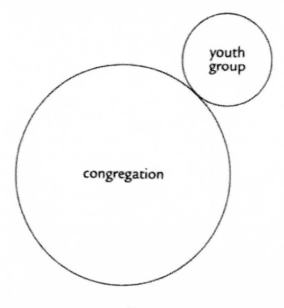

Figure 2

22. Ibid., 3.

23. Nichols and Good, *America's Teenagers*, 246–48.

24. Cummings-Bond, "The One-Eared Mickey Mouse," 76–78.

25. See Beck and Beck-Gernsheim, *Individualization*, 203.

Five Theological Gifts of Youth Ministry

Osmer does not explicitly outline youth ministry's theological potential, but he is adamant that young people and youth ministry make contributions that safeguard the church against spiritual impotence. He aims his remarks at congregations, pointing out how youth ministry theologically anchors the broader church.[26]

Prophetic Witness

The most obvious way youth ministry helps the church remain "the church" is by raising difficult theological issues that congregations would often rather avoid. Because youth ministry dives headlong into adolescents' lived concerns, there is no skirting issues of race, gender, justice, economics, and institutional mission. All of these are complex, cultural extensions of adolescent questions around identity, belonging, and purpose—questions that point to larger conversations about who we are in relationship to God. Despite its reputation for "fun and games," youth ministry raises some of the most perturbing questions of human existence. Young people who explore these questions with their faith communities experience faith as a practice field for bearing one another's burdens while naming and navigating the sins of institutions and societies as a whole.

Missional Vision

Osmer accuses mainline churches of becoming so infatuated with meeting the "needs" of adolescents, as those needs are outlined by developmental psychology, that they become captured by consumerism, reducing youth ministry to one more salve available to apply to the aches and pains of adolescence. Osmer eschews this reductionist interpretation of the church, and of youth ministry specifically. Anticipating his much later emphasis on missional theology, Osmer insists that ministry must not be prescribed by a theory of human development, nor should adolescence be romanticized on the one hand, or viewed as a series of

26. Early in his career, Osmer plainly questioned the "theological integrity" of parachurch and independent Christian organizations, a position he later softened, particularly in relationship to Young Life.

unavoidable lifecycle crises on the other. Osmer's concern is not simply intellectual misappropriation (though he has strong words for churches that oversimplify social science in order to "apply" it to ministry), but the fact that the developmental paradigm "represents a theologically bank-rupt way of using the social sciences in Christian ministry."[27]

> The language of "needs," psychologically understood, is used to undergird a view of the church and its ministry as competing in the spiritual supermarket to offer the most satisfying product to religious consumers. The most successful churches do the best job of meeting people's needs. Youth ministry alone is not guilty of this mentality, for it is widely pervasive in mainline Chris-tianity. Clearly, however, it does come to expression in [youth ministry].[28]

Osmer's experience as a pastor in western North Carolina gave him an enduring appreciation for the importance of context in ministering to a person. He saw practical, not just theoretical, costs to organizing youth ministry around assuaging developmental "crises." Besides diminishing the role of the Holy Spirit in adolescent formation, to assume "crisis" is just part of adolescence has the effect of minimizing many teenagers' very real pain—pain that congregations could help diminish. Osmer argues that "many characteristics of contemporary youth are not inevitable life cycle crises, but the result of very specific patterns of culture and concrete institutional arrangements."[29] Where those patterns and institutional arrangements create harm, churches must challenge them on young people's behalf, and offer youth life-giving alternatives.

Theological Agency

Like countless other researchers, Osmer underscores the crucial role of families in shaping youth's religious identities. Osmer notes that adoles-cents still identify with their parents' God-images,[30] but he champions young people's movement toward "owned" faith (i.e., faith as a durable aspect of identity, usually in adulthood). He acknowledges a role for

---

27. Osmer, "Challenges to Youth Ministry," 4.
28. Ibid.
29. Ibid, 9.
30. Ibid, 13.

doubt and "searching" as part of this process.[31] By helping young people construct a scaffolding for faith, argues Osmer, youth begin to see themselves not as the "church of tomorrow" but as agents of ministry, effective immediately, called by God as "partners" in mission with roles to play in their home churches that extend beyond teen programs.[32] Similarly, by offering young people a pool of trusted adults and peers, youth ministry plays an important role in launching those partnerships, giving young people models of mature faith who become exemplars for teenagers' own emerging faith identities. Congregations that help youth "test drive" these new roles and new God-images help them exercise agency as theologians as they construct a faith that is genuinely their own.

Constructive Practical Theologians

Osmer critiques mainline churches' failure to recognize youth ministry as an imaginative space for instructing youth in the texts and traditions of Christianity. He is forthright about the importance of teaching Christianity's historic practices, not for the sake of perpetuating old traditions, but for "helping [youth] develop a deeper and more personal relationship with God."[33] Since Osmer is convinced that the "pressing issues" facing youth and youth ministry—and therefore the church—are theological in nature, he deems it essential, if youth ministry is to be *ministry*, for congregations to equip young people with robust theological tool kits. These tool kits include practices like prayer and testimony, language for Jesus, and significant adult role models who show young people what cobbling a life together with these tools can look like.

At the same time, Osmer recognizes that such instruction places historic Christian practices in the hands of newcomers to the tradition, which inevitably means new adaptations and uses for those practices. Osmer affirms this innovation as part of young people's calling, and thus lays the groundwork for understanding youth ministry as a kind of ecclesial

31. The influence of John Westerhoff's book *Will Our Children Have Faith?* on North American Christian educators in the 1980s is evident here, as Osmer uses Westerhoff's paradigm to describe the trajectory toward mature faith, moving from "experienced/received" faith through "searching" faith during adolescence to "owned" or mature faith as an adult. See chapter four of Weserhoff, *Will Our Children Have Faith?*

32. Osmer, "Challenges to Youth Ministry," 18.

33. Ibid, 15.

laboratory—the "research and development" arm of the church, so to speak. In this R&D space, fresh approaches to theology and practice are welcomed and tested as young people reshape their communities to reflect a God who cares deeply about them, and who invites their creativity.

Barometers of the Human Condition

Many adults enter youth ministry because it's one of the few places in the church that allows you to rearrange the furniture, metaphorically (and often literally). Congregations are prone to giving young people they love far more room—and more rope—for ecclesial experimentation than, say, pastors who want to switch things up. What is really going on in this laboratory, however, is not simply random ideation: young people are testing to see if the Christianity they have been handed holds water. They wonder: Is God up to the task of helping me figure out what it means to be human—what it means to be *me*—as I grapple with questions of identity, belonging, and purpose for the first time? Is the gospel of Jesus Christ relevant to the world I experience, and does it make a difference? Is there room for me in this faith community, and what role do I play here? Answering these questions inevitably results in theological and ecclesial renovation as young people form their assumptions about faith, the church, and the world—assumptions they will very likely carry with them into adulthood.

This brings us full circle in terms of the theological importance of youth ministry for Osmer. The most significant experiences in any person's life are the moments in which we discover what it feels like to be utterly human. These moments of vulnerability, in small and awkward ways, are shards of glass that reflect God's light into the world. As churches struggle for significance with adolescents, we need look no further than the love story that is the good news of the gospel: this God, in whose image young people are made, thought they were worth dying for, and did. Like every story of true love, the life with God that the church promises is fraught with risk and unknowing; it is a route to death, and a route to life. That is what makes it a worthy dream.

Osmer knows that young people's search for a worthy dream serves as a proxy for the church's own search for God in a secular age. At our best, churches also ask the questions of adolescence: Who are we, and why are we here? To whom do we belong, and how do we become grafted into that tribe? How do we make sense of this world, and what are we called to contribute? These questions point toward something approximating the divine, because we answer them differently depending on our degree of confidence in *that which is beyond us*. We too need a worthy dream, a story to be part of a story with infinite significance, purpose, and grace. Young people will not settle for less. Neither should we.

More Than Meeting Needs

Osmer's challenges to the mainline churches about youth ministry remind us that what makes ministry matter to young people is not what the church *does*, but what the church *is*: an embodiment of a story of life-rattling significance, a body that not only makes room for young people but embraces them as essential limbs. Unless we start from a "worthy dream" of Christ-centered hope, churches will continue to "serve" young people with programs that "meet their needs." We will retain our modest hopes and reasonable expectations for adolescents and the church. We will remain "spiritually innocuous."

The last thirty years have demonstrated that this is unlikely to change when we lack the will or clarity to unwind God's story from its entanglement in the values of North American culture. Osmer forecasts the theological turn in youth ministry by reminding us, in so many words, that the church needs young people—not to bulk up our membership, or to carry on our institutions—but to give the church a "crown to grow into," as Howard Thurman called it. Osmer believed this is a higher calling than the one churches have settled for. As Osmer admitted, a renewed interest in youth ministry "is not going to save the mainline churches . . . What it *can* do is serve as an avenue into these broad and complex issues" that challenge the identity and purpose of the church itself. May it be so.

Bibliography

Beck, Ulrich, and Elisabeth Beck-Gernsheim. *Individualization: Institutionalized Individualism and Its Social and Political Consequences.* Translated by Patrick Camiller. London: Sage, 2002.

Cummings-Bond, Stuart. "The One-Eared Mickey Mouse Model of Youth Ministry." *Youthworker* (1989), 76–78.

Dean, Kenda Creasy. "Youth Ministry in Protestant, Catholic, and Jewish Religious Youth Organizations." White paper. New York: Carnegie Council on Adolescent Development, 1991.

Lipka, Michael, and David McClendon. "Why People with No Religion Are Projected to Decline as a Share of the World's Population." *Pew Research Center*, April 7, 2017, accessed January 28, 2018. http://www.pewresearch.org/fact-tank/2017/04/07/why-people-with-no-religion-are-projected-to-decline-as-a-share-of-the-worlds-population/.

Little, Sara. "Introduction." *Affirmation* 2 (1989), i–xvi.

———. *Youth, World and Church.* Richmond: Westminster John Knox Press, 1968.

Ng, David. *Youth in the Community of Disciples.* Valley Forge, PA: Judson, 1984.

Nichols, Sharon, and Thomas Good. *America's Teenagers: Myths and Realities: Media Images, Schooling, and the Social Costs of Careless Indifference.* London: Lawrence Erlbaum Associates, 2004.

"Nones on the Rise." *Pew Research Center*, October 9, 2012, accessed May 15, 2018. http://www.pewforum.org/2012/10/09/nones-on-the-rise/,

Osmer, Richard R. "Challenges to Youth Ministry in Mainline Congregations." *Affirmation* 2 (1989) 1–26.

Rood, Lars. *Bold Parenting: Raising Kids to Be More than Just Rule-Keepers.* Loveland, CO: Group/Simply Youth Ministry, 2013.

Root, Andrew, and Kenda Creasy Dean. *The Theological Turn in Youth Ministry.* Downers Grove, IL: InterVarsity, 2011.

Senter, Mark. "History of Youth Ministry Education." *Journal of Youth and Theology* 12 (2014) 83.

Smith, Christian, with Melinda Denton. *Soul Searching: The Religious and Spiritual Lives of American Teenagers.* New York: Oxford University Press, 2005.

Westerhoff, John. *Will Our Children Have Faith?* 3rd ed. New York: Morehouse, 2012.

Wuthnow, Robert. *After the Baby Boomers: How Twenty- and Thirty-Somethings Are Shaping the Future of American Religion.* Princeton, NJ: Princeton University Press, 2007.

4

Learning a Way of Life

The Catechetical Gift of Newcomers

Jessicah Krey Duckworth

Nearly every night at their bedtimes, my husband and I recite the Lord's Prayer with each of our children. Give or take the occasional nights missed, we've recited the Lord's Prayer as a family about 13,000 times in fourteen years. Our children have heard the Lord's Prayer whispered in their ears long before they could speak. More times than I can recall, they've interrupted the prayer to ask a reflective question about the world or to remind us about their field trip the next day. We have made up melodies to sing the prayer, prayed the Lord's Prayer in "pirate"—"arrr-men"—or said the whole prayer in a monotone voice to see who bursts out laughing first. Now that they stay up later, I'm often deeply absorbed in my own evening work when the voice from the second-floor sounds, "Hey Mom." Like the church bell tolling to remind the workers in the field to stop and pray, I rise from my chair and ascend the stairs to join them in their evening prayers.

Praying is a practice that is learned. Our children were not born praying to God, even though they were certainly surrounded by prayer as they were being born. They learned the posture and words of Christian prayer through their experience with it at mealtime and bedtime and during other celebrations within the institution of our family, in our home. On the flip side, their personalities and interests have shaped what, when, and how my husband and I teach our children to pray. Both of us carried expectations about which traditions from our own upbringings we wanted to pass on to our children and thoughts about what we wanted to do differently. In time, together we created the established practice of prayer that our family engages in today, making adaptations for different stages of life and responding to our children's observations, their curiosities and their own ideas for how to carry out our prayer practice. And each day, in, with and under this practice, and in spite of our frequent attempts to thwart routine because we are human after all, Jesus' promised presence, where two or three are gathered, shows up.

When our family's collective voices join our congregation in the Lord's Prayer during Sunday morning worship, it is often the eighth time our children have prayed Jesus' prayer in a week. Thanks to regular participation in Christian worship, our family has a broad repertoire of prayer practices to draw upon, including litanies and liturgies, psalms, hymns and songs, intersessions and communion prayers. The psalms of thanksgiving and lament we recite in worship provide language for the vast range of human experience and emotion, from celebrating life's joys to grieving life's tragedies. Experiencing the profound witness of other Christians praying or asking for prayer through intercessory prayer, my children live their lives trusting that God hears the prayers of the faithful even when—or rather, especially when—the opposite appears to be the case. Even though God may not intercede in the way that our prayers demand, God ushers in life in the midst of suffering and despair. In prayer with others we encounter Jesus where Jesus promises to be—in, with, and under the means of grace.

Forming a Way of Life

Learning how to pray is only a part of becoming a disciple of Jesus Christ. Praying is one practice.[1] Within the life of a congregation, the practice of prayer is situated among a constellation of Christian practices that include Scripture reading, baptism, holy communion, mutual care and consolation, rites of passage, Bible study for all ages, mission and service, to name a few. Experienced together, over time, these practices make up the congregation's comprehensive way of life[2] or, said in another way, the

1. "Practices are the discrete, socially shared forms of action that embody . . . praxis." Osmer, *Teaching Ministry of Congregations*, 95.
2. "Praxis is the comprehensive way of life of a congregation." Ibid.

ethos that reflects and interprets Jesus' vision for a way of life.[3] As practical theologians, pastors and congregational leaders are called to cultivate this life-shaping ethos by establishing, coordinating, and sustaining communal practices, informed by Scripture and Christian tradition, so that families and fellow Christians encounter the promises of God. This attention to a congregation's identity and ethos, carefully considered in light of contemporary contexts, is what practical theologian Richard R. Osmer calls formation.[4]

Through formation in Christian practices, individual Christians learn how to practice discipleship through participation in the community's way of life. Beyond formation, there are also moments when pastors and congregational leaders invite Christians to reflect on specific teachings from Scripture and the tradition. This, Osmer calls education.[5] Congregations do both. For instance, congregational leaders create opportunities for Christians to pray the Lord's Prayer while also creating space to teach the Lord's Prayer. To teach the Lord's Prayer is to invite the questions such as, "Who is the Lord?" and "Why did the Lord have a prayer?" To respond to these questions, Christians will likely turn to Scripture itself.

The practice of prayer provides a window on how a way of life is formed that embodies the vision of Jesus. In Luke's Gospel, the disciples implored Jesus. "Lord, teach us to pray, as John taught his disciples."[6] And Jesus did. Jesus gave his disciples a prayer practice—words to say over time with confidence. And directly after teaching his prayer, Jesus shared a story about a man who shows up at midnight asking his Galilean friend for three loaves of bread—not for himself, but to provide hospitality for a traveler who has just arrived. In spite of the friend's indifference, he helps anyway because tradition requires, and his neighbor persists. Jesus wraps up his story with a teaching, "Ask, and it will be given you; search, and you will find; knock, and the door will be opened for you."[7] And, "how much more will the heavenly Father give the Holy Spirit to those who ask him!"[8] Through the story, Jesus encourages a particular

---

3. Osmer and Schweitzer, *Religious Education between Modernization and Globalization*, xviii, 54.

4. Osmer, *Teaching Ministry of Congregations*, 27.

5. Ibid.

6. Luke 11:1.

7. Luke 11:9.

8. Luke 11:13.

way of life shaped by the practice of prayer and grounded in the promise that God hears and responds to the prayers of God's children. Through a practice and a parable, Jesus gives his disciples a way that this distinctive way of life can be passed on.

Pastoral leaders are often overwhelmed at the magnitude of formation. How is one to teach the stories and practices of Christian tradition while tending to the daily spiritual needs, not to mention practical urgencies, of an entire flock? Rather than bear the responsibility to be the sole catechists for a church while also attending to the praxis of the congregation, this essay suggests that pastoral leaders may trust the resources for this kind of formation to already exist in what might seem like the least likely vessel: in the flock itself, in congregational members, and more foolishly yet, in the young people and newcomers within congregations.

Catechesis as Response

Traditionally, this way of teaching—enacting a story through practices that can be handed on from one generation to another, much as Jesus taught his own disciples—is called *catechesis*. Originally, catechesis referred to oral religious instruction or handing on the community's tradition. In Greek, *catechesis* means "to sound" or "to echo" in the ear. Rather than dull, doctrinaire learning, however, catechesis involves the rich tapestry of the stories, wisdom, and encouragement to live a particular way of life that are shared through a teacher's voice and that echo in the learners' ears. Moreover, *catechesis*, as Luke's Gospel story suggests, is deeply responsive to the learner's experience. When the disciples ask Jesus to teach them as John taught his disciples, they already possess an interpretive lens for prayer. The disciples are rooted in a prayer tradition and ask their question from within the frame of John the Baptizer's way of life. While Luke's Gospel does not say exactly how or what John taught his disciples to pray, what is clear is that the prayer Jesus taught likely trusted the formation provided by John's teaching, and very likely the other common practices of prayer in the first century as well. Biblical scholars confirm that Jesus' prayer stands in continuity with the tradition of Jewish prayer.[9] Nonetheless, the prayer is also a new text and becomes a new tradition birthed in dialogue with, and in response to, Jesus' disciples and their questions.

9. Miller, *They Cried to the Lord*, 328.

Scripture provides various examples of people faithfully pressing Jesus with questions rooted in their own experiences and interpretations of Scripture, tradition, and commitments to a particular way of life. Jesus trusts the life experience of his interlocutors as a resource. He takes their frameworks for a way of life seriously and his responses often contribute to the emergence of a new teaching or practice altogether. A classic example is in Mark's story of Jesus' visit to Tyre, when a parent bows down before Jesus to ask him to drive out the demon in her daughter. Jesus tells the woman, who was not from Israel but from Greece, "Let the children be fed first, for it is not fair to take the children's food and throw it to the dogs." She replies, "Sir, even the dogs under the table eat the children's crumbs."[10] Reacting to her testimony, Jesus sends her home to her daughter who now has been healed. The woman professes what she knows to be true in her faith experience—that Jesus can heal and that his promise extends beyond Israel. Her interpretation unexpectedly sounds as gospel in Jesus' ears and in Mark's story becomes Jesus' own tradition—his own way of life. In turn, this Gospel story sheds light on how Christians interpret Scripture and tradition.

Beholding God's Presence, Proclaiming God's Promise

Ultimately though, the purpose of encounters with Jesus is not Jesus' reaction or even the new interpretation of tradition that extends Jesus' ministry. Rather, the purpose is to proclaim and make evident the presence of God and the promise of God's steadfast love and peace. The parent from Tyre is not seeking to argue a point in the abstract. She is seeking healing for her beloved child. Her plea is a matter of life and death. Jesus, confronted with the suffering of a mother's heart, responds with life, with healing and hope. "For saying that, you may go—the demon has left your daughter," he says (Mark 7:29). Through Jesus' act of healing, the woman from Tyre and her daughter now have the means to live into the reality of what God has envisioned for their lives—this is the kingdom of God come near, God's life-filled intention for all of creation. Here *catechesis* is dynamic, rooted in lived experience yet also pointing away from itself towards something greater—the power and promise of God. For twenty-first century church leaders seeking change and innovation on behalf of their congregation, this is an important point. Catechesis, and

10. Mark 7:27–28.

the emergence of new traditions or practices that might flow from it, are not ends in and of themselves, but rather are means for beholding divine action.

A dynamic catechesis seeks to interpret the heart of the gospel in light of concrete situations and experiences within the contemporary community of faith in order to facilitate encounter with Jesus Christ. This is evident in the letters passed between Paul and the early churches as each community seeks to figure out what faithfulness to Jesus Christ looks like. In his letter to the churches in Galatia, Paul must confront the fact that some in Galatia are turning to a different gospel. Similarly, Paul's letters to the church in Corinth respond directly to the arguments arising within the community of faith about how to be a Christian community. Paul does not reify God's promise of the past to God's promise in the present or even to God's promised future in the Sprit. His catechesis, rooted in his own Damascus Road experience, consistently points towards the promise of God that makes all things *new*.

In his book on the teaching ministry of congregations, Osmer writes:

> Paul's interpretive freedom stems from his overwhelming sense that God did something radically new and different in Jesus Christ . . . Paul also interprets Scripture and tradition with a certain degree of freedom because he believes the Holy Spirit is doing something new and different among his congregations. Walking in the Spirit is not merely a matter of continuing the traditions of the past, but of attending to the signs of new creation in their very midst.[11]

Paul invites and expects Christians to engage in dialogue with the tradition as it is lived out in their life together through their real-life experiences. Leaning on Paul, Osmer invites contemporary congregations to stand in this interpretive dynamic framework as they engage in catechesis.[12] He defines catechesis as "an interpretative activity undertaken by congregations and their individual members who see themselves as participants in the Theo-drama of the triune God and are seeking to better understand their roles in this drama by deepening their understanding

---

11. Osmer, *Teaching Ministry of Congregations*, 29.

12. Osmer identifies three central tasks of Paul's teaching ministry, only one of which is catechesis. Exhortation and discernment are the other two tasks. While I appreciate these distinctions of the teaching ministry, I use *catechesis* broadly to encompass the whole process of learning to be a disciple of Jesus Christ.

of Scripture and Christian tradition."[13] The Theo-drama is God's present activity in the world today in which Christians are called to participate.

Trusting that experience can interpret the Christian tradition does not seem very wise. Indeed, Osmer encourages congregations as they interpret the present activity of the Holy Spirit to test critically experiences of the Spirit in light of Scripture and tradition. However, as theologian Mary Solberg contends, "Theology is not about God; it is about how it is with us—in the presence of God-in-relation-to-us in the person of Jesus Christ. This is not out-of-this-world theology, this is theology for real life as we live it, in the first, sixteenth, and twenty-first centuries."[14] Theology for real life, Solberg insists, means that pastors and congregational leaders create the conditions that help Christians trust life experience as the core material of theological exploration.

Taking up Martin Luther's theology of the cross, Solberg describes the kind of knowing that is shaped by the theology of the cross. "An epistemology of the cross describes the movement from lived experience to compelling knowledge, a movement that involves seeing what is the case; comprehending one's implication in it and coming to accept accountability to act on what is known."[15] Seeing "what is the case" is that moment when a Christian, caught unawares by an encounter responds, "I had no idea . . ."[16] Sometimes, disillusionment is so powerful that Christians can't help but proclaim unbelief out loud. At other times when paradigms to understand the world are disrupted, especially for adults, words of unbelief do not come as easily. Expressing disillusionment seems easier for children. Their curiosity leads them to see "what is the case" through their imagination and play. Too many adults learn to ignore and inhibit their curiosity and wonder. Pastors and congregational leaders are called to create spaces where disillusionment can be confessed so that real life as we live it can be the core material of theological interpretation.

Catechesis happens where meaning erupts from honest encounter between lived experience and the Christian tradition and the gospel can unexpectedly sound in the least likely of places. At the foot of the cross, "God's foolishness is wiser than human wisdom, and God's weakness is

13. Osmer, *Teaching Ministry of Congregations*, 237.

14. Solberg, "All that Matters," 148.

15. Solberg, *Compelling Knowledge*, 19.

16. Solberg, "All that Matters," 151.

stronger than human strength."[17] Learning to be a disciple, in community, at the foot of the cross, where real life is trustworthy as an interpretive framework for the Gospel, *is* a cruciform catechesis.

A Catechetical Moment in Context: Teaching the Lord's Prayer

Set within a cruciform catechesis, where the gospel is proclaimed by unlikely sources, within the community of faith, the Lord's Prayer as a practice of prayer in the home and in congregations has shaped the imaginations of Christians across the ages, and even the imaginations of our own children. At five years old, our son pressed us with real life questions rooted in his curiosity and wonder. "Why doesn't the Lord's Prayer say God very often? When we pray we should include God by saying God does this, God does that, God is like this, you know. The Lord's Prayer doesn't say that," he said. In his prayers that night we changed the pronouns to God's name. "Hallowed be God's name. God's kingdom come, God's will be done." This change satisfied his curiosity for the night.

When he was six, he told us his favorite part of the Lord's Prayer was, "Give us this day our daily bread." He immediately followed with a question, "Why doesn't the Lord's Prayer include wine? Shouldn't it be, 'give us this day our daily bread and wine'?" The connection he made between daily bread and the bread and wine of Holy Communion was not an accident. He had recently participated in first communion classes at our congregation and weekly throughout his life he had seen communion shared. Yet, underneath my son's questions was the importance of an argument about the norms of faithful practice. In both cases he used the word "should." At five and six he already had interpretive and normative frames, and was curiously asking questions about the received prayer practice of the Lord's Prayer as it interplayed with other prayers at home and the prayers and actions in worship that surrounded Holy Communion. In turn, he opened up the imaginations of those adults around him toward new possibilities of God's acting in the world.

Catechesis is not something experienced by individuals alone. Our son asked these faithful questions within the community of our congregation and of the home. As Osmer points out, "In a very real sense, the praxis of a congregation provides its members with their first interpretation of

17. 1 Cor 1:25.

Scripture and tradition. It is here that they build up habits, perceptions, and expectations about a life of discipleship for better and for worse."[18] Through communal practices, congregations help Christians—like my son—make connections between the tradition, daily living, and the active presence of God. It is pastors and congregational leaders who find themselves tending these connections.

Becoming a Catechetical Community

For much of the twentieth century, mainline Protestant congregational leaders could count on a broad ecology of institutions to inform their ministry decisions with biblical and theological scholarship and resources that supported the congregation's formation and education practices. This ecology included the scholarly inquiry and theological education of seminaries, colleges, and universities and robust educational resources produced by national and regional denominational leaders. By the beginning of the twenty-first century, this ecology had weakened and the burden of creating or selecting resources to support congregational ministry fell more squarely on the shoulders of congregational leaders, especially pastors.[19] Anticipating the weakening of the ecology as early as 1990, Osmer wrote *A Teachable Spirit* arguing for the rehabilitation of the institutional offices, agencies, and structures that determine the church's normative beliefs and practices. Faculties, congregational leaders, and denominational leaders should have a shared responsibility to ensure that the biblical and theological tradition of the church are taught to each new generation in the faith. Calling for a strong teaching office of the church, Osmer concludes *A Teachable Spirit* by placing honest hope in pastors "to lead congregations to an understanding of themselves as centers of teaching and practical theological reflection."[20] As practical theologians, informed by the tradition and carefully considering their ministry context, Osmer calls upon pastors to be catechists.

In his later work, which focuses on the teaching ministry of congregations, Osmer describes four patterns of interpretation and teaching in catechesis. Congregational leaders are called to 1) interpret texts of Scripture and tradition; 2) interpret the present activity of the Spirit; 3)

---

18. Osmer, *Teaching Ministry of Congregations*, 244.

19. Osmer, *A Teachable Spirit*, 178–81.

20. Ibid., 253.

interpret congregational praxis; and 4) interpret continuing creation.[21] Osmer's hope is that as practical theologians, informed by the tradition and carefully considering the praxis of the congregation, pastors and congregational leaders might carry out the role of catechist on behalf of the church.

While many congregational leaders take this role seriously, far too many pastors shoulder the burden of interpretation on their own. If this is how many pastors understand their part in the Theo-drama within the weakened ecology of the teaching office, it is no wonder that they are exhausted. Moreover, pastors are increasingly called to catechesis beyond the congregation, helping homes, schools, sports fields, workplaces, and the public square become formative spaces as well.[22]

The Catechetical Power of Newcomers

Here is a modest proposal. What if pastoral leaders directed what energy they have towards newcomers in the faith, creating welcome processes that foster relationships between newcomers and established members of the congregation, so that newcomers and established members may become the body of Christ—Christ's presence—for one another?[23] This action affirms that the real lives of people is the greatest resource the church has for catechesis—as foolish as it might sound.

Whether a newborn or a new employee, a new in-law or a new member, a newcomer's presence reminds the established members of a community that their praxis and meaning making are not clearly evident. And this is by design—a cruciform design. Like younger members of a family, newcomers within a congregation ask questions about the norms of faithful practice because these practices do not yet fit within their interpretive landscape. The real lives of newcomers bring questions, and their questions invite response from established members. In turn, new meaning often erupts. And perhaps, new practices and traditions themselves are born. "Lord, teach us to pray, as John taught his disciples"

21. Osmer, *Teaching Ministry of Congregations*, 240.

22. See Osmer and Schweitzer, *Religious Education between Modernization and Globalization*, part III. In this section Osmer and Schweitzer engage four locations for religious education: paideia and society, congregation, religious dimension of individual, and the family.

23. For more on newcomer welcome processes in congregations see Duckworth, *Wide Welcome*.

(Luke 11:1). "Sir, even the dogs under the table eat the children's crumbs" (Mark 7:27–28). "Why doesn't the Lord's Prayer include wine? Shouldn't it be, give us this day our daily bread and wine?" Newcomers—in families and in congregations—bring real life into the Christian community's praxis, and this real life awakens new possibilities of gospel promise in the ears of established members and newcomers alike.

Late last year, our home congregation welcomed a new family visiting from a Baptist congregation. The parents take home catechesis seriously. We know this because it is their children who respond first to a question about a Bible story during children's time in worship. Recently this yet still-new family attended our congregation's intergenerational faith formation experience called Messy Church.[24] Five-year-old Hazel and her older sister Tessa visited the drama station, for which I was the facilitator. That night, children and adults acted out a skit based on John's version of Jesus feeding the five thousand with a boy's lunch. At one point in the skit, Jesus (played by older sister Tessa, who can read) says, "Let us pray" to bless the fish and bread. Hazel (playing one of the disciples) immediately bowed her head, closed her eyes and began to recite the Lord's Prayer aloud. She prayed the whole prayer intently, ending with a big "Amen." The adults listened with glances and gaping jaws in wonder and awe. At the end of Hazel's prayer, Tessa said indignantly, "Can I say *my actual* prayer now?" I nodded reassuringly, and she read the skit's rather generic meal prayer. Hazel's response to Jesus inviting prayer was as it should have been. Jesus obviously expected his disciples to pray *his* prayer. The established member's eyes all met each other recognizing the holy moment that occurred. The kids kept going with the skit.

As newcomers, young and old, enter into the congregation's praxis, they tend to disrupt the established members' established practices and meaning. The Spirit's disruptive work ushering in newcomers is dizzying. No congregational leader can keep up with the varieties of ways that the Spirit is activating opportunities for formation and education when newcomers and established members encounter one another: "Now there are varieties of gifts, but the same Spirit; and there are varieties of services, but the same Lord; and there are varieties of activities, but it is the same God who activates all of them in everyone. To each is given the manifestation of the Spirit for the common good" (1 Cor 12:4–5). And that is

24. Messy Church, as an idea, began at St. Wilfrid's church in Cowplain, England, to reach children with God's story. See http://www.stwilfridscowplain.co.uk/. The idea is now a movement—https://www.messychurch.org.uk/.

the point. Sharing the responsibility of catechesis with the people of God illuminates the activation of the Spirit's gifts. Facilitating the relationship between newcomers and established members as they engage in the praxis of the congregation concentrates leaders' effort and relieves their burden, as God catalyzes the increase in gifts, services, and activities.

God shows up in many and various ways in the world and within the lives of the people and the creation God loves. This much is certain. Yet, Scripture—the norm of faith—points faithful people to look for God in the places God promises to show up: as people read and engage Scripture; as two or three people are gathered in the name of Jesus to pray; as real life in all its pain and joy is confessed; as means of grace are stewarded and distributed by the church to people yearning for mercy and life abundant; as newcomers encounter established members, standing in received truth while also creating new possibilities. In these trusted and unlikely places, God's power realizes God's promise, not over against our real lives but through them, for the sake of the world.

Within our real life at home, our children continue to disrupt the comfortable gospel my husband and I are used to—each and every day—with their curiosity and wonder. As practical theologians, and parents, we are called to create spaces in our home where real life encounters the gospel. So, I rise from my chair and ascend the stairs to pray for the 13,001st time so that we might be foolish together, these newcomers to faith and I, as we figure out how to follow Jesus through the power of the Spirit in this world God loves.

Bibliography

Duckworth, Jessicah Krey. *Wide Welcome: How the Unsettling Presence of Newcomers Can Save the Church*. Minneapolis: Fortress, 2013.

Miller, Patrick D. *They Cried to the Lord: The Form and Theology of Biblical Prayer*. Minneapolis: Fortress, 1994.

Osmer, Richard R. *A Teachable Spirit: Recovering the Teaching Office in the Church*. Louisville, KY: Westminster John Knox, 1990.

———. *The Teaching Ministry of Congregations*. Louisville: Westminster John Knox, 2005.

Osmer, Richard R., and Friedrich Schweitzer. *Religious Education between Modernization and Globalization: New Perspectives on the United States and Germany*. Grand Rapids: Eerdmans, 2003.

Solberg, Mary M. "All That Matters: What an Epistemology of the Cross Is Good For." In *Cross Examinations: Readings on the Meaning of the Cross Today*, edited by Marit Trelstad, 139–53. Minneapolis: Augsburg Fortress, 2006.

———. *Compelling Knowledge: A Feminist Proposal for an Epistemology of the Cross*. Albany, NY: State University of New York Press, 1997.

SECTION TWO

The Spiritual Director: Testing the Spirit

5

Practical Theology and Spiritual Companioning

Angela H. Reed

Not long after I arrived at Princeton Theological Seminary to begin doctoral studies, Richard R. Osmer invited me to read a few sections of his working manuscript, *Practical Theology: An Introduction*. He encouraged me, a fledgling PhD student, to comment on his discussion of the spirituality of congregational leaders. I felt both honored and overwhelmed at the invitation from this theological visionary and wise practitioner who seemed to think I might have something to offer about the intersection between congregational spiritual formation, a topic I had a passion for, and practical theology, a field of study I was just coming to know. With generous hospitality, he welcomed my few, hesitating insights.

I soon discovered that Osmer has a spirit of humble curiosity that drives him to be a lifelong student. He sought recommendations for spiritual direction training programs and ultimately studied with Dr. Marcus Smucker, who had been my professor and instructor in the practice. The three of us met together to explore questions about spirituality, theology, and congregational life. These conversations culminated in a book entitled *Spiritual Companioning: A Guide to Protestant Theology and Practice*.[1] As we engaged in the work, I began to notice that the communal process of reflecting and writing seemed to take on qualities of the

---

1. Reed et al., *Spiritual Companioning*.

companioning relationships we were describing. The relational process that evolved as we wrote somehow mirrored the content. Like many who have come before and after me, I was intellectually and spiritually companioned and guided by Dr. Richard Osmer in a manner that has profoundly shaped my work as a teacher, scholar, and minister.

The Intersection of Practical Theology and Spiritual Companioning

One of Osmer's most important contributions to practical theology is a commitment to exploring cross-disciplinary questions for the benefit of the church. The Western Christian tendency to separate the scholastic from the monastic and pastoral work from mysticism continues to shape our thinking and practice. Even areas of study such as Christian spirituality and practical theology, which bend traditional disciplinary lines, can suffer from the "silo effect" when they do not interact easily or frequently. Students of spiritual practices such as spiritual direction and companioning are likely to read historical spiritual masters such as Teresa of Avila but ignore theories that raise important questions about spiritual formation in relation to a congregation's theology and practice. In a similar way, training in practical theology may emphasize theological reflection on congregational activities while giving little attention to historical Christian spirituality and spiritual practices that shape formational community and encounters with God. Each area of study is driven by its own resources, methods, and questions.

Whether or not we readily acknowledge it, the fields of practical theology and Christian spirituality and their respective tasks and practices necessarily interact in congregational ministry. In *Practical Theology: An Introduction*, Osmer notes that leadership in Christian community is "inherently a spiritual matter" which requires openness to the guidance of the Holy Spirit and transformation toward the image of Christ.[2] All of the tasks of practical theology require divine engagement and discernment. It is also true that historic Christian practices like spiritual companioning and direction necessarily involve practical theological reflection because companioning arises out of theological and ethical convictions. Osmer's work in practical theology and spiritual direction offers a road map that enables church leaders to be intentional about defining and shaping

2. Osmer, *Practical Theology*, 27.

the art and skill of spiritual companioning in light of essential practical theological concerns.[3]

In this chapter, we explore the value of Osmer's practical theological tasks for one dimension of Christian spirituality, the ministry of spiritual companioning. As we have already seen in this volume, Osmer identifies four core tasks: descriptive-empirical, interpretive, normative, and pragmatic. Each one has a role in a hermeneutical spiral of practical theological interpretation enabling congregational leaders to return repeatedly to the various tasks in a pattern of ongoing growth and deepening understanding.[4] These tasks provide insight into the development of spiritual companioning ministries in congregational life.

What is Spiritual Companioning?

In order to consider these intersections, we must give brief attention to what we mean by relationships of spiritual companioning. This seems especially important given the wide variety of "spiritual practices" within and beyond the church in our time. Forms of spiritual companioning arise from a long and rich history in the Christian tradition. These practices are especially evident among various groups across the spectrum of Christian traditions, including Jesus and his followers, the New Testament Church, the desert mothers and fathers of the fourth and fifth centuries, various historical monastic orders, early Anabaptist communities, and Methodist bands and classes. Contemporary relationships of spiritual companioning have particularly strong roots in the practice of spiritual direction, a one-with-one relationship between a trained spiritual director and a directee seeking to grow in the spiritual life.[5] A growing number

3. A major impetus for *Spiritual Companioning* was the goal of bringing wisdom from these two fields of study together in order to encourage and strengthen congregations and their leaders. While it was not explicitly discussed in the book, we drew upon components of Osmer's four tasks of practical theology to describe and shape practices of spiritual companioning in the church. This becomes evident in the following headings found in most chapters: "Understanding the Cultural Context," "Listening to Scripture," "Mining the Protestant Tradition," "Practicing Spiritual Companioning," and "Exploring the Stories of Congregations." See Reed et al., *Spiritual Companioning*.

4. Osmer, *Practical Theology*, 11.

5. Janet Ruffing explores six typological historical models of spiritual direction beginning with the desert fathers and mothers, in Ruffing, *Uncovering Stories of Faith*, 2–17.

of programs in theological schools and independent institutes provide educational instruction and preparation in this one-with-one practice.

Spiritual companioning can be described as "a way of accompanying others in intentional relationships of prayerful reflection and conversation that help them notice God's presence and calling in their personal lives, local communities, and the world."[6] Companioning relationships provide support and accountability for responding to the invitations of God. The term "companioning" is used "in *verb form* because these kinds of relationships are much more than casual connections—they require an intentional, *active* commitment to a way of being with others and with God."[7] Intentional relationships of spiritual companioning in congregations can be shaped according to the needs of the community, taking various forms including one-with-one spiritual direction, peer spiritual friendships, small groups, family and congregational connections, and other types of relationship.

Spiritual companioning or direction is one among many ancient Christian practices being retooled for contemporary life to support the formation of faith. As faith communities seek to recover ancient forms of practices such as spiritual companioning or direction, the goal is not to identify one definitive approach to the practice that all must engage in, but rather to adapt the practice for specific contexts as congregations articulate ways in which the practice may support faith formation.[8] Bringing the tasks of practical theology to bear on the use of the practice allows congregational leaders to do this with integrity in light of the community's theological commitments and the needs and calling of the congregation. One way to enter into practical theological reflection on spiritual companioning is to consider a case study in light of Osmer's four tasks—the narrative of Jason Wells, a seminarian in his mid-twenties exploring spiritual companioning at Cedar Springs Community Church.[9]

---

6. Reed et al., *Spiritual Companioning*, xx.

7. Ibid.

8. Richter, "Religious Practices in Practical Theology," 235–36.

9. For the purposes of anonymity, names and details have been changed in the case study.

Jason's Story of Spiritual Companioning

Jason had just completed his first semester in seminary when he received a call that his father had passed away unexpectedly. The news was staggering for Jason, and he struggled to come to terms with the reality of the family's loss and the immediate need to provide solace and support to his mother and brother. Jason began to make frequent trips to his home town several hours away, and he became increasingly overwhelmed by the demands of school and work alongside family commitments. Jason was also deeply disappointed that he had not been close to his father in recent years, and he felt significant guilt over it. This disappointment was compounded by his desire to understand God's presence and guidance in the midst of the loss. Just when he most longed for divine comfort, God seemed truly absent. Jason chose to participate in worship in spite of the inner emptiness and did appreciate the congregation's reflections on loss particularly in the season of Lent.

Just before his father's death, Jason had begun participating in a new spiritual direction group at Cedar Springs Community Church led by Kristen Terry, a trained spiritual director. During Jason's times of sharing, he reflected on his journey through grief. After a few months, Jason was final able to admit that he could not pray about his father. In all honesty, he could barely pray at all. It was difficult to acknowledge this broken dimension of his life with God, and Jason wondered what the inability to pray might say about his future in ministry. The group listened carefully to Jason's story over time and prayed on his behalf when he could not pray for himself.

Other concerns arose as Jason moved through the grief, including difficulties in his family relationships. Jason's brother, Paul, urged their mother to sell land and other assets. Jason disagreed with this idea, and tension arose between the brothers. As Jason told these parts of his story, group members were occasionally tempted to offer practical suggestions. With Kristen's gentle guidance, they were able to remain focused on the key purpose of the group process: attending to the presence and activity of God in everyday life. Jason found the group to be a spiritual community of healing and hope during an especially difficult season in his life. He could not imagine getting through that time without them. Jason remained with the group for two years after his father's death, and then went on to graduate from seminary and serve in pastoral ministry.

The Descriptive–Empirical Task: A Call to Listen

As we consider Jason's experience of group spiritual direction, it is evident that the descriptive-empirical task is a foundation for spiritual companioning. The core question of this task is, "What is going on?" Osmer suggests that a spirituality of presence involving priestly listening is an essential dimension of practical theology.[10] This may be the task in which the work of practical theology and spiritual companioning interacts most clearly. In both cases, the emphasis is upon taking a posture of attending to the presence of another in a way that is prayerful, focused, and engaged, offering empathy and warmth. This kind of listening is truly rare and demanding. Neither spiritual companioning nor the tasks of practical theology can be accomplished without it.[11] The listening process involves attending to narrative, allowing the participants to tell the stories of their everyday lives. The process requires listening and responding to assist the storyteller in clarifying a representation of their life experiences as they attempt to interpret them through spiritual, social, cultural, psychological, and other frameworks.

As pastors and spiritual companions listen and long for the healing and guidance of God in another's life, they may be tempted by a sense of urgency to bring quick resolution. This was certainly a temptation in Jason's group. In emergency situations, quick responses are necessary. More often, attempting to "fix" what is wrong in people's lives by offering simplistic solutions or hasty advice blocks the ability to offer a genuine spirituality of presence. If Jason's group had focused on solving relational problems between the brothers, they would have been distracted from the true intent of spiritual companioning.

In order to attend adequately to the interpretive and normative tasks, spiritual companions must wait patiently and watch for the broader scope of the narrative to unfold. Prayerful listening is required to move past the reflexive desire to "help" and enter more deeply into encounter and engagement with God and with another while listening for the presence and activity of God. In the words of priest and spiritual director, Margaret Guenther, "This ministry of presence is a living out of intercessory prayer, as the holy listener waits and watches. Sometimes the listening takes place in the warmth of the stable, sometimes in the pure white light on the high mountain apart, sometimes in desolation at the foot of

---

10. Osmer, *Practical Theology*, 34.

11. Lunn, "Paying Attention," 219.

the cross, and sometimes with fear and great joy in the encounter with the risen Christ."[12]

There are many ways in which the field of practical theology contributes to a deepening understanding of waiting and watching in the descriptive-empirical moment. To begin, the practical theologian has a broad range of elements to explore in the greater "web of life."[13] Spiritual direction gives primary attention to the religious dimensions of human experience. Companioning may take on a form of "research" by attending to the larger life stories of others, acknowledging that the relationship with God is shaped by family life, societal pressures, congregational engagement, physical health and well-being, and many other influences. Practical theology recognizes that spiritual frameworks interface with social constructs such as race and gender.

Few resources in spiritual companioning literature recognize or address these concerns as an element of holy listening. The experience of prayer and relationship with God may be influenced by a call to justice in a sermon, by interactions with co-workers that bring gender issues to the fore, or by shame over mounting debt and financial instability. Understanding the descriptive-empirical task of practical theology opens up the possibility of exploring unexpected elements rooted in societal systems that influence life experiences and impact spiritual formation. In the case of Jason's group, it is essential for them to recognize the complex web of life in which he is engaged. His spiritual journey is impacted by relationships with his living family members and his deceased father, his preparation for ministry in seminary, and his sense of call. Creating space for the larger web of life enables participants to wait and watch, recognizing that God engages human beings in every dimension of life.

Within the congregation, a focus on spiritual companioning for individuals or small groups alone may be limiting when leaders consider the broader "web of life" that connects the entire community's system. This may involve creating a culture of spiritual companioning by exploring together what it means to provide language and tools for spiritual guidance through various ministries. Growth may begin with congregational leaders who view their ministries through the lens of spiritual guidance in order to support the entire congregation as it seeks to discover the presence of God. Congregational leaders grow in this role as they

---

12. Guenther, *Holy Listening*, 145.

13. Osmer, *Practical Theology*, 15–17.

carry the community in prayer and watch for signs of God's presence and guidance.[14] At Cedar Springs, several ministers and lay people are training in spiritual direction programs in order to shape various ministries including worship, pastoral care, administration, and mission according to the vision of spiritual companioning.

The Interpretive Task: A Call to Use Our Tools with Care

Jason's spiritual companions also benefit from attending to the core question of the interpretive task: "Why is this going on?" Osmer argues that a spirituality of sagely wisdom is necessary for the interpretive task, and it requires that congregational leaders continue to love God with their minds beyond the walls of seminaries and theological schools.[15] The interpretive task contributes to deepening clarity about the evolution of an individual's images of God, experiences of prayer, and life within the church. The task involves offering space for companions to be conscious of the ways in which they are influenced by various psychological and sociological theories alongside other arts and sciences. This requires a faith that is willing to engage with the world, recognizing that we will never be fully removed from the culture we inhabit, and we can learn from the intellectual resources of culture to interpret what we hear and observe as practical theologians and spiritual companions. An essential element of sagely wisdom is the ability to discern which theories are persuasive for a given episode, situation, or context. We must also be aware of the audiences we draw upon to help us determine the theories we choose to employ.[16]

The gifts of the interpretive task for spiritual companioning are numerous. Some practitioners of spiritual direction have already made good use of the resources of psychology and sociology to inform spiritual

14. Rice, *The Pastor as Spiritual Guide*, 62.

15. Osmer, *Practical Theology*, 81–82.

16. For example, Osmer chose life course theory, a concept of human development rooted in sociological research, to identify essential issues and questions for spiritual companioning throughout the journey of life. Osmer argues that life course theory serves spiritual companions better than life cycle theory because human growth and development does not necessarily follow consistent patterns and predictable crises. Osmer goes on to explore the importance of storytelling in spiritual guidance as it applies to life course theory through the witness of God's interaction with the people of Israel in scripture. In this way, the interpretive moment is shaped by normative commitments. See Reed et al., *Spiritual Companioning*, 125–50.

companioning relationships. Psychologist and spiritual director David Benner advocates for *psychospiritual* preparation among spiritual directors.[17] It is impossible for human beings to separate spiritual and psychological aspects of functioning. What we learn from the interpretive task of practical theology is to judge wisely when we select and employ psychological and other theoretical tools for the sacred calling of walking alongside people on the spiritual journey. We must own the interpretive resources we engage and understand their foundations and frameworks in light of our theological and ethical commitments.

The benefit of a breadth of knowledge in psychology and related disciplines is certainly evident in Jason's case. His experience of God, particularly his struggles in prayer, are probably intertwined with the grief and guilt he feels about his relationship with his father. A spiritual companion who interprets Jason's relationship with God in light of his loss will recognize that processes like this cannot be rushed or controlled by others. Jason may experience a variety of thoughts and emotions as he contemplates the loss, and wise spiritual companions will serve Jason well by creating hospitable spaces for any "negative" emotions such as anger with God. The interpretive task also raises questions about other resources Jason may benefit from at this time, including psychological or pastoral counseling.

The Normative Task: A Call to Claim Our Roots

One of the most important elements of Jason's spiritual work in the companioning group is theological. Who is the God that Jason struggles to pray to and what is God's role in Jason's life? The normative task addresses theological commitments by asking the core question: "What ought to be going on?" Osmer posits that the normative task includes theological interpretation, ethical reflection, and good practice. Practical theology is a form of theology, not social science "lite." Methods, concepts, and sources of theological discourse are necessary to create constructive theological perspectives. The work of practical theology, then, is to bring these perspectives us into conversation with other fields, including the

---

17. Benner, *Sacred Companions*, 155–56. Some spiritual direction theorists have given less attention to psychological theories, focusing primarily on other resources including the historical writings of Christian spiritual masters such as St. Ignatius in order to understand the inner workings of the human soul.

classical theological disciplines.[18] As we do this, however, we must recognize that there are multiple trajectories to interdisciplinary conversation. There are numerous perspectives on the relationship between theology and experience in spiritual direction. I believe that practices of spiritual companioning are well suited to the confessional trajectory that gives priority to theology in interdisciplinary dialogue. In this approach, theological roots ground us. Human experience is highly valued but is not equal to theological understandings of divine revelation.[19]

The normative moment is central to the entire process of practical theological reflection and to the ministry of spiritual companioning. This task addresses the essential reality that every person seeking spiritual guidance has theological commitments that may not be clearly articulated or even recognized. For example, a directee might say, "I believe God loves me, *but* . . ." Moments like this may require exploration of both theology and human experiences in everyday life to see how they may or may not coincide. This is certainly true for Jason. His spiritual companions encouraged him to consider his image of God, recognizing that what Jason believes about God and about prayer may not match what he perceives about daily life experiences. A belief that God is always present and benevolent can be sustaining in periods when God seems more absent than present. Jason's group can help him explore any disconnect between what he believes and what he experiences in relationship with God. He may not be able to trust what he *feels* about God at this time, depending instead upon what he *believes* to be true.

The normative task helps us recognize that spiritual guidance or direction relationships alone are not enough for a life of faith. In my perspective, they do not provide adequate biblical and theological resources or the critical theological language needed for discernment.[20] Spiritual guidance practices belong together with a wider group of formational practices including worship, fellowship, Christian formation and education, witness and service, and a personal devotional life. In our cultural context, it is possible to seek out a spiritual guide to meet one's own spiritual needs and avoid the church altogether. Spiritual formation is personal and communal, and it ought to attend both to interiority and outward

18. Osmer, *Practical Theology*, 163.

19. Osmer, "Empirical Practical Theology," 89–90.

20. The particular normative commitments that are placed in conversation with spiritual companioning practices will vary depending upon faith traditions and specific communal and individual theological perspectives and practices.

action. Spiritual companioning rooted in the practices of healthy congregational life may contribute to spiritual growth and development. In Jason's case, participating in public worship during Lent creates space for theological reflection on suffering and loss in a way that cannot be fully accomplished through spiritual companioning practices alone.

Another important contribution of the normative task is the belief that spiritual companioning itself has the potential to be one normative practice generating new understandings of God and the Christian life.[21] This plays out regularly when a directee offers a confession and hears a word of forgiveness and acceptance or is named aloud in prayer and encouraged to receive God's loving compassion. Time and again spiritual companioning reshapes and redefines theology by creating spaces for struggling with concepts of divine and human action and learning to use the tools and skills of discernment. Spiritual guides must also be doing their own theological reflection in order to companion others with integrity. These commitments influence approaches to attentive listening and the manner in which questions are posed. While our theologies may not seem central to priestly listening, we are deeply rooted in our convictions as we engage with those we companion.

The Pragmatic Task: A Call to Action

As Jason and his group members grow in the life of faith, they will frequently ask the core question of the pragmatic task: "How might we respond?" This task provides us with the opportunity to shape and reshape plans for practice and then to embrace action. The invitation is missional, prophetic, and it may involve confession and a call for change and growth. The work of spiritual companioning necessarily results in action. It is not a process of contemplation alone. Jason found that his group regularly invited him to consider how he might act in the world in light of his relationship with God.

Jason recalls one particular experience that involved a specific response. After he shared about tensions with his brother, Kristen invited the group to pause, and she encouraged Jason to enter into a practice of imaginative prayer. He pictured himself sitting with Jesus in his family home. His brother, Paul, entered the room. Kristen encouraged Jason to talk with Jesus about Paul, exploring what Jesus saw when he looked

---

21. Osmer, *Practical Theology*, 152–53.

at Paul. After a period of silence, Kristen asked Jason about the experience of prayer. Jason noted that Paul seemed to be under considerable strain, fearing for the future in the midst of his own loss and grief. It was a profound experience for Jason to attempt to look at Paul through the eyes of Jesus with the compassion of Christ. Some weeks later, Jason returned to the group and reported that he had reached out to Paul, and the brothers had taken a hopeful step toward repairing their relationship. The group rejoiced with Jason and promised to continue praying for ongoing restoration.

The pragmatic task of practical theology can be painfully prophetic at times, and it requires the commitment of servant leaders who are willing to call for change. A spirituality of servant leadership coincides beautifully with the roles of spiritual companions who avoid telling another what to do in the spiritual life and instead come alongside as the individuals they serve set the agenda and seek God for themselves.[22] But companions must also raise difficult questions at times, holding others accountable for right living and acting. If Jason had not chosen to show love toward his brother, group members may have felt a call to gently raise the issue. The work of the pragmatic task reminds us that growth and change must be the result of prayer and reflection, something that is not always assumed in contemporary spiritual direction practice. If we hold a theology of redemptive action and solidarity in suffering, we will choose to live out the consequences of the encounter with God in the world. Spiritual companioning relationships create space for reflection on the pragmatic steps we might take as we discern a way forward.

Concluding Thoughts

Even as ancient Christian practices like spiritual companioning resurface and draw the attention of contemporary church communities, we need practical theologians to raise important theological questions in order to develop our practices faithfully. The vision and wisdom of Dr. Richard Osmer will continue to guide these essential conversations and form practical theologians and spiritual companions for many years to come.

---

22. Osmer, *Practical Theology*, 196–97.

Bibliography

Benner, David. *Sacred Companions: The Gift of Spiritual Friendship and Direction.* Downer's Grove, IL: Intervarsity, 2002.

Guenther, Margaret. *Holy Listening: The Art of Spiritual Direction.* Cambridge: Cowley, 1992.

Lunn, Julie. "Paying Attention: The Task of Attending in Spiritual Direction and Practical Theology." *Practical Theology* 2 (2009) 219–29.

Osmer, Richard R. "Empirical Practical Theology." In *Opening the Field of Practical Theology: An Introduction,* edited by Kathleen Cahalan and Gordon Mikoski, 77–94. Lanham, MD: Rowman & Littlefield, 2014.

———. *Practical Theology: An Introduction.* Grand Rapids: Eerdmans, 2008.

Reed, Angela H., Richard R. Osmer, and Marcus G. Smucker. *Spiritual Companioning: A Guide to Protestant Theology and Practice.* Grand Rapids: Baker, 2015.

Rice, Howard. *The Pastor as Spiritual Guide.* Nashville: Upper Room, 1998.

Richter, Don. "Religious Practices in Practical Theology." In *Opening the Field of Practical Theology: An Introduction,* edited by Kathleen Cahalan and Gordon Mikoski, 233–52. Lanham, MD: Rowman & Littlefield, 2014.

Ruffing, Janet. *Uncovering Stories of Faith: Spiritual Direction and Narrative.* Mahwah, NJ: Paulist, 1989.

6

Re-Grounding Theological Education

NATHAN T. STUCKY

EVERY FALL, A NEW crop of eager seminary students arrives at Princeton Theological Seminary (PTS). Upon arrival, the new cohort yields to the same fate as generations of students who preceded them: new student orientation. They undergo this orientation to their seminary education in the same space where they will soon take requisite survey courses that are designed to lay a proper foundation for theological education: Intro to Old Testament, Systematic Theology, Church History. They sit in auditorium-style seating, rows of chairs slightly arced, all facing a lectern that sits front and center.

More happens in this space than most realize. Here, the journey of formal theological education begins. The space acts on the learning and the learning community. It encourages certain ways of being and learning. It limits others. Furthermore, the impact of this space goes beyond shaping the learning community. This is, after all, a seminary. The space impacts theologies. It shapes how those in the space understand the life and being of God. Assumptions about theology and theological education necessarily bend depending on the learning environment and how the learning environment is utilized.

Students and faculty sit in lecture halls, seminar rooms, and libraries, studying the God who made the heavens and earth, who wrapped divinity in matter through incarnation, and who invited disciples to remember the incarnate One through bread and wine, grain and grape. But there's a problem: this learning takes place in a space removed from the very content of the curriculum. This learning happens in lecture halls where interior walls divide one course of study from another and where walls of literal stone often divide learners from the soil, trees, and the ground that surround them.

Of course, formal theological education—either in academy of congregation—has never been reduced completely to a lecture hall (consider dining and fellowship halls, lawns and dorms). Yet the irony remains: Students study Creator, creation, and incarnation while divided from creation, each other, and the very land and people who bear grain and grape in the first place. How can we as teachers and learners in theological education possibly know *this* God while such a division persists? How did this division come about? What might it look like to heal this division? What new possibilities for ministry and theological education might emerge on this journey to healing?

This chapter wrestles with these questions. In it, I want to explore the history of Christian faith in the West to begin understanding the origins of this division; I want to explore the division as uniquely theological—that is, deeply reflecting and impacting our convictions about the life and being of God; and I want to look at recent examples of theological education at Princeton Theological Seminary. Hopefully, these examples point forward to a theologically robust and less divided future. Ultimately, I will suggest that faithful formation of communities according to the deepest theological convictions of the Judeo-Christian tradition requires an intimate and intentional relationship with creation. Anything less risks obscuring rather than unveiling the very image of the triune God.

How Did We Get Here? Willie James Jennings and *The Christian Imagination*

In his book *The Christian Imagination*, Willie James Jennings works primarily to articulate the origins of race. He digs into centuries of history in order to articulate the very beginnings of colonialism. Yet before digging into the depths of this history, Jennings starts his book in the garden of his childhood home. Jennings's mother knew this garden intimately. It was a source of life for her and her family, yet the story Jennings tells is not one of intimate knowing, but rather of bewildering anonymity.

On a summer day when Jennings was twelve, two men from a local Reformed Church visited Jennings and his mother in this garden. They

came on a missionary journey to share about their church and its ministries. Yet even though the men came from a congregation that sat just two
hundred yards from the backyard garden where they stood, they arrived
as strangers, completely oblivious to the vibrant Christian faith already
flourishing in the Jennings home. Spatial proximity failed to predict any
accompanying neighborly intimacy. Not only did the men not know the
Jennings family, they also failed to inquire about them. They came to talk,
not listen, to give, not receive. The strangeness of the encounter lingers
with Jennings to this day. He asks, "Why did they not know us?"[1] Jennings' pursuit of answers to this question leads him ultimately to his deep
exploration of the genesis of colonialism and the advent of racial logic.

Though the full scope of Jennings's work is intricate and multi-
layered beyond what I can cover here, a central part of his argument
connects with the aforementioned division in contemporary theological education. Jennings argues that the colonial moment—the moment
when racial logic and destruction spread like cancer throughout the
world—that moment depended on and grew out of a division between
human identity and land in the mind of the colonizer. He writes, "Colonialism established ways of life that drove an abiding wedge between the
land and peoples."[2]

Jennings recognizes vast political and economic forces at work as
colonialism emerges. Empires seek expansion—more land and more
resources—yet the full force of Jennings's argument lies beyond and be-
neath politics and economics. Jennings doesn't merely describe the wedge
between land and identity that propels colonialism and racial logic. He
gets behind the division to the theology that drives it.

Jennings sees supersessionism as the major theological error here,
and he traces its beginnings back as least as far as the fifteenth century.
Within this view the church replaces Israel as God's chosen people. Supersessionism then combines with doctrines of papal authority and apostolic succession to bloat the church's sense of itself. Church and empire
conflate, believing Christ has handed all authority over, and ownership
of creation, to the church for the purpose of the salvation of the world
and the expansion of the empire.[3] Thus, there is no such thing as seizing
another people's land because Christ has already given all lands to the

1. Jennings, *The Christian Imagination*, 1–4.

2. Ibid., 292.

3. Ibid., 28.

colonizer; the colonizer becomes the (white) norm of Christ-likeness; and all lands and peoples are subject to the dominion and judgment of the colonizer. Resistance provokes forced submission . . . in the name of Christ. This, of course, is heresy, and it all coincides with the division between identity and land, space, and place.

More accurately, the division between identity and land, space and place *is* the theological error. The colonizers fail to recognize God as a "landed" or "placed" God. They forget the geography, culture, ethnicity, and landscape inherent to the identity of the Jewish Jesus, the Galilean. They lose sight of the intimate interconnections among God, people, and land inherent to the faith of the One they profess to represent. They forget that revelation of God's identity and experience of God's presence have always been tied to particular lands and places—Adam and Eve in the garden, Abraham and Sarah at the oaks of Mamre, Jacob at Bethel, Jesus at Nazareth.

This theological misperception—the loss of the intimate link between land and God's identity—yields a twofold anthropological misperception. On one hand, as colonizers lose sight of an intimate connection between land and identity within the life of God, they also lose sight of it within themselves. Their own identity is divided from the land. On the other hand—and of utmost importance for Jennings's broader argument—the colonizers fail to see themselves as a people adopted by someone else's God. They fail to see that the gospel has already been transposed from the land, language, and culture of its first audience into their own land, language, and culture.[4] They fail to see that the God of Israel has come to them.

This is the error of supersessionism. Church supersedes Israel, oblivious to the fact that the identity of the God they profess to serve utterly depends on Israel. In some sense the very name *Israel* signals the loss. To say Israel is to express an identity irreducible to either land or people. And when this theological error enmeshes with insatiable colonial hunger, the consequences are devastating. As Jennings notes, we have barely begun wrestling with the consequences of this error. We struggle to even perceive the error because we are buried so deeply inside of it.[5]

4. Jennings, "The Colonization of Land."

5. In discussing the displacement at work in colonialism, Jennings notes that both colonizer and colonized are displaced. The critical difference, of course, is that the colonizer willingly leaves his home. This reality leads Jennings to acknowledge the depth of the challenge. "With this leaving [Europeans willingly leaving their homes]

In thinking about the emergence of colonialism, the destruction of lands and peoples that follows in its wake, and the theological error that Jennings describes, a simple question about the incarnation helps clarify the error at work here. The question is, how did Christ enter the world? Some would say the world longed for a conquering emperor—a display of force that would set the world aright. Instead, the all-powerful Creator of the universe comes as an infant child to an unwed teen mother with livestock and lowly shepherds keeping watch. The Lord of the universe comes to a particular land, a particular time, and a particular place, and before engaging any public ministry spends decades learning. Jesus learns the language, the culture and customs, the land and geography, the food and the festivals, and only after these decades of simply being native to his place does he begin a public ministry.

For the purposes of this chapter, we may say that through the incarnation, Christ enters a new land. Contrast Christ's entry into a new land with that of the colonizers. The contrast is stunning. Rather than immersing themselves in the lands, cultures, and languages of indigenes, colonizers impose themselves and their fractured, landless identities, leaving the bodies of native people and native lands scourged. Jennings casts this tragedy of colonialism in the terms of failed hospitality.

> Other peoples and their ways of life had to adapt, become fluid, even morph into the colonial order of things, and such a situation drew Christianity and its theologians inside habits of mind and life that internalized and normalized that order of things . . . Indeed, it is as though Christianity, wherever it went in the modern colonies, inverted its sense of hospitality. It claimed to be the host, the owner of the spaces it entered, and demanded native peoples enter its cultural logics, its ways of being in the world, and its conceptualities.[6]

Again, consider Christ. Christ arrives in the world as utterly dependent guest. Even in the years of Jesus' public ministry, we find Jesus again and again a guest at someone else's table. Yes, Jesus does ultimately extend an invitation to his table, but there again we encounter not a division between the life and work of this God and the created, material world, but rather a most intimate union: teacher, disciples, table, bread and wine

---

. . . one approaches the depths of this theological mistake. It will not be easy to articulate the material reality of displacement because it is the articulation of a loss from within the loss itself." Jennings, *The Christian Imagination*, 37.

6. Ibid., 8.

inextricably bound together at a meal celebrating God's deliverance of the Israelites from captivity on a journey to a promised land. The Savior enters intimately into the life and mess of the world in order that the world may know its life in Christ. The contrast with the colonial agenda again stands out starkly. Instead of domination or forced subjugation, the image here is of mutual indwelling rooted deeply in the earth—identities indelibly linked to land, neighbor, Christ, and all the particularities of place.

The comparison of Christ and colonizer should lead those of us in contemporary theological education to ask difficult questions. The mission of both Christ and colonizer is educational. Both seek to shape others into their images, but their methods and their accompanying relationships to land and space could not be more different. We must ask, then, whether contemporary theological education is repeating the errors of colonialist education in its ignorance of land and commodification of land and space, or whether it follows instead the incarnate One. The current separation between theological education and land suggests the colonialist mentality may be more operative than we realize.

If Jennings is right, then the division between creation and contemporary theological education emerges in part from our own failures to recognize and welcome the God of the garden, the God of Abraham and Sarah at the oaks of Mamre, the God of Jacob at Bethel, and the God incarnate in Jesus Christ in Nazareth. If Jennings is right, it is possible that we have separated God's identity from the material world and in so doing unwittingly put God and creation in separate and unrelated categories.

The tragedies here are multiple. The vast train of exploited people and lands lies in the wake of this error. This may seem like a distant reality in the contemporary lecture hall or sanctuary, but we should not underestimate the risks. The risk is that theological education fails to live up to its own mission. With the error of dividing identity and land, we risk repeating the tragic cycles of unknowing that plague the colonial imagination. Colonizers never really knew the lands or the peoples they colonized, and that failure of knowledge grew logically out of a failure to rightly know the God they claimed to serve.

The opportunities here are also multiple. If the division between land and identity is false and obscures the identity of the triune God, then what extraordinary possibilities might ensue from a reintegration? What insights about and experiences of God, neighbor, and land might emerge if we find a way through this division—if we seek this God not divided from creation, but rather intimately connected to it? How might we know ourselves and this God anew by rediscovering the intimate interconnections of land, space, place, and identity?

Farminary: An Experiment in Re-Grounding Theological Education

Though I didn't know it at the time, when I arrived as a student at PTS, I was a living example of the division Willie James Jennings describes. I grew up farming in Kansas. After college, I served as a youth pastor for a half-dozen years, and then returned to farming. I loved farming, but I had a problem. While farming, I couldn't shake a sense of call to ministry. Thus, I moved from Kansas to PTS so I could attend seminary. I left the farm convinced that my love of agriculture and my sense of call to ministry were two different things. God calls people away from land, not into it. Or so I thought . . . and so I lived the division that Jennings describes.

By God's grace, seminary challenged the division. A good friend learned that I had been farming before coming to seminary and proceeded to share a dream. What would it look like to integrate fully accredited theological education and small-scale sustainable agriculture? It took the better part of a decade for the seed of that dream to germinate, but it finally did. Along the way, PTS realized it already owned a twenty-one-acre farm, and the farm sat less than three miles from the main campus.

In the beginning, the Farminary grew out of a simple conviction. The skills, proficiencies, and sensibilities of the adept agrarian, farmer, or gardener broadly overlap with the skills, proficiencies, and sensibilities of the adept pastor or church leader. Both know how to tend life, pay attention to seasons, mind limits, and ask for help. Both know how to read a context and assess what it can bear. They recognize both vitality and its lack. They know how to respond in ways that restore vitality. They understand the interconnectedness of life and death.

Thus, we began the experiment. I taught a pilot course at the farm that considered how agrarian thought and practice might impact our understandings of education. The course explored how time working a garden, growing food, and sharing meals might influence the aims, goals, curriculum, methods, roles of teacher and learner, context, and assessment of Christian theological education. In the midst of the pilot course,

PTS committed to officially embarking on the Farminary journey. We have been teaching courses at the farm ever since.

Now, a few short years into the journey, the conviction regarding overlapping skills and proficiencies remains, yet Jennings's work opens possibilities and responsibilities that were not initially imagined. I suspected the farm would transform students' doctrines of creation, Eucharist, and resurrection. I believed it would impact their images of theological education. I did not realize the depth of the division between the seminary community and the land, even as I did not realize the depth of the division within myself. I also could not have anticipated the signs of hope that have emerged along the way.

During one fall semester at the Farminary, I had the privilege of teaching "Text and Terrain," a one-credit Old Testament course, at the Farminary with Professor and Old Testament scholar Jacqueline Lapsley. As part of the course, we read Old Testament texts that were rich in agrarian imagery; we gardened; and we asked two simple questions: How does our time in the text influence our time in the garden, and how does our time in the garden influence our interpretation of the texts?

Naturally, we read Genesis 2–4. Jacq brought the full force of her scholarly proficiency to the exploration. We considered the intimate relationship between humankind and the soil in Genesis 2:7. God forms *adam* (the first human) from the *adamah* (the humus). We also studied Genesis 2:15, where God places the first human in the garden to "till it and keep it," as it is commonly translated. The terms till and keep struggle to convey the full sense of the Hebrew verbs, *abad* and *shamar*. Throughout the Old Testament, scholars more frequently translate *abad*, for example, as work or serve.[7] Furthermore, the Old Testament also uses *abad* to describe humanity's proper posture toward God. "Worship [*abad*] the LORD with gladness; come into his presence with singing" (Ps 100:2).

In other words, the Hebrew uses the same term to describe the posture of humankind to both God and the land. Land and God remain distinct, and worship is reserved for God alone, yet somehow the posture to God and land overlap. Participants in "Text and Terrain" studied all of this, drawing on Jacq's expertise.

Some weeks later, Jacq—who had warned me of her lack of gardening proficiency before the course began—found herself planting carrots in the garden during our class, side by side with students. She knelt on

7. For example, "Six days you shall work (*abad*), but on the seventh day you shall rest" (Exod 34:21).

her hands and knees and meticulously prepared a shallow groove in the soil. She then carefully placed the seeds one by one in the groove. As she worked (*abad*), it hit her. There in the garden, she embodied Genesis 2:15; her posture was that of service. Scripture for the Old Testament scholar came to life in a new way. Interdependence and interconnection came to light. She served the garden in service to the God who could bring about growth in hopes that she might ultimately receive life from both carrot and Creator.

So much could be said about this moment. It represents both the reality of the division between theological education and creation, and also the possibility of healing. Vast economic, political, and yes, theological forces lead teachers and students to identities divorced from the land. If Jennings is right, those forces have been growing roots for centuries, and they will not be overcome in an afternoon in the garden. Even so, I would like to think that something significant shifted in Jacq that day. The division was healed, even if only a little, and she knew herself, God, and creation in a new and more interconnected way. The shift importantly did not exclude rigorous intellectual engagement or scholarly precision. It did not even exclude the lecture hall. Rather, it depended on them. It just happened to also depend on a renewed and intentional relationship with creation integrated into the scholarly and intellectual pursuits.

Conclusion: Honoring Osmer

More than a decade ago, I arrived at Princeton Theological Seminary as a member of a fall cohort of new students. I underwent orientation in the lecture style room within the grand edifice of Stuart Hall. Having attended a very small undergraduate institution where I doubt I ever had a class with more than thirty students, the sheer scope of a teaching space with over a hundred students brought me up short.

To be clear, good things happen in lecture halls. I experienced faith-shaping, knowledge-building, Spirit-inspired lectures in that space. The deepest conviction of this chapter is simply that we cannot let the lecture hall and seminar room be the only spaces where intentional theological education happens. Theological education reduced to such spaces simply cannot sufficiently bear witness to the God in whose name we teach.

The work of Willie James Jennings and the experiences at the Farminary lead to questions about theological education and space or place. They invite us to consider where, exactly, knowledge of God grows. Where does new insight emerge? In what context does faith flourish? Yes, it can happen in a lecture hall, but God forbid it only happens there. There is knowledge and love of God that grows in the field and at the table that is simply not accessible in a lecture hall.

Jacq learned this in the garden. It is a lesson I first learned from Rick Osmer. I don't remember reading it in one of his books, though I suspect that I did. It wasn't an insight that clicked in an instant. As I recall, the insight came together thanks to the combination of two moments. The first moment occurred in a casual conversation, though I don't remember where. It may have been on a class break during a doctoral seminar. It may have been a chance encounter in the library. I don't remember the exact words, but it was something like, "There is knowledge and insight that emerges uniquely in the practice of ministry."

Rick's comment reflected one of his deep practical theological convictions. Practical theology is not merely applied theology. In that model, systematic theologians and dogmaticians do the theological heavy lifting. They discern the convictions about God's life and being. Then practical theologians merely apply their insights out in the world.[8] Osmer, as pastor, educator, and theologian, knew better. He had experienced better. His research and scholarship as a practical theologian convinced him of better, and he insisted on sharing the insight with his students.

His comment stayed with me not because a light went on in that moment, but because it didn't. I wanted to understand what this pillar of practical theology was saying, but in that time and space, it eluded me. The insight—true to Osmer's conviction—emerged later in a second moment. Again, I do not recall the exact time or place. It happened in ministry—while teaching, tending, planting, or maybe composting, and it was a harbinger of Jacq's experience planting carrots. A light went on. New knowledge burst forth in a way that depended integrally on the teaching, tending, planting, or composting. I knew God in new ways in that moment, and that new knowledge of God depended on my practice of ministry. It never could have emerged in a library or lecture hall.[9]

---

8. Note the division between theology and creation explicitly at work in the applied theology model of theological education. In it theology happens in a secluded ivory tower, not in the world.

9. To be perfectly clear, the need for library and lecture hall remains. The point is to recognize their limits.

My memory flashed back to Osmer's comment. "There is knowledge and insight that emerges uniquely in the practice of ministry." And I got it. This was what he meant.

His insight has been guiding me ever since.

I could not foresee anything like the Farminary when I began as a student at Princeton Seminary more than a decade ago. I think it is safe to say that Rick could not foresee it, either. In my mind, the initially unforeseen nature of the Farminary as an expression of vibrant theological education only demonstrates more fully the veracity and vitality of Osmer's practical theological vision. Attentiveness to context, interdisciplinary exploration, courage to act, and the abiding conviction that the whole of life is the locus of theological reflection—the Farminary exists because of the careful interweaving of these things. So also, Rick's practical theological vision.

The future of theological education in the church, academy, and world is much like the Farminary when I first arrived in Princeton in 2007 and sat as a student in one of Rick's classes—completely unforeseen. Yet by God's grace and Rick's generosity of intellect and teaching, a practical theological framework exists that carries within itself the hope that the triune God is still at work throughout the whole creation, and new life and redemption, though presently unforeseen, are already coming into being in our midst.

Thank you, Rick. And thanks be to God.

Bibliography

Jennings, Willie James. *The Christian Imagination: Theology and the Origins of Race.* New Haven, CT: Yale University Press, 2010.

———. "The Colonization of Land." Class Lecture via Skype, EF 1520: Ecologies of Faith Formation, Princeton Theological Seminary, Princeton, NJ, October 10, 2016.

7

The "Double-Pointed Ellipse"

Integrating Spirituality and Mission

BO KAREN LEE

TWELVE YEARS AGO WHEN Princeton Theological Seminary began offering classes in spirituality, it took a risk. It took an even greater risk when it created a degree track that explicitly coupled together spirituality and mission. This second move contained a counterintuitive logic within it, highly unprecedented among theological institutions today. But this instinct has the potential to alter the way seminaries think about their curriculum, and even how the church thinks about itself.

The first risk included the question of whether faculty should teach spirituality-specific courses in an academic setting. At Princeton Seminary, classes on mission were offered since the founding of the institution, but the contemporary turn toward spirituality had not yet been embraced. Our theological forerunners were much more comfortable with cultivating "piety"[1] or teaching various devotional practices, but not with the looser term "spirituality," so prevalent today. Protestants especially worried that "spirituality" might become ingrown, overly focused on a narcissistic "Jesus and me" orientation. Shortly after creating a faculty position in spirituality, however, the faculty in the Education

---

1. See Mikoski and Osmer, *With Learning and Piety.* Prior to 2007, individual classes along the way may have focused on spiritual theology or formation, but an organized curriculum in spirituality had not yet been available to students.

and Formation area at Princeton Seminary decided to link spirituality[2] and mission[3] explicitly in the curriculum, because of the conviction that growth in spiritual formation and missional formation are intrinsically connected to one another. Significantly, it was Richard R. Osmer who led the way in making this innovative curricular connection, a connection rarely made in other seminaries or in the larger culture.

In this essay, I will argue that Osmer's coupling of spirituality and mission has potential to revitalize both of these important aspects of the church's call—namely, the call to follow Christ with passion, *and* the call to follow him into sacrificial service in the world. The *de facto* separation of spirituality and mission in both congregations and the academy has enervated both. Osmer's insistence on integrating these practices not only protects churches and seminaries from becoming enterprises unto themselves; it also enables practical theology to take up its call to empower the church to act in service to the world.

2. For the purposes of this chapter, I am utilizing Arthur Holder's definition of Christian spirituality. He states, "Although the apostle Paul never used the word 'spirituality,' this earnest confession of faith [Rom 8:14–16] suggests that any Christian understanding of that term must necessarily refer to the intimate loving relationship between God's Holy Spirit and the spirit (animating life force) of believers—a relationship that can be characterized both as kinship and communion. The Christian life is always 'life in the Spirit' (cf. Gal. 5:25), in all its variety and unpredictability." Holder adds that much of the literature on Christian spirituality focuses on "lived Christian experience," and that this "complex subject" of spirituality "can only be understood and appreciated when approached from a variety of perspectives, and with careful attention to the particular manifestations in an infinite range of historical and cultural contexts." Holder, *The Blackwell Companion*, 1–2.

3. For the purposes of this chapter, I define mission according to David Bosch's understanding. As Osmer writes in his chapter, "Formation in the Missional Church: Building Deep Connections between Ministries of Upbuilding and Sending," in *Cultivating Sent Communities: Missional Spiritual Formation*: "*Missio Dei*, the mission of God, marks a shift in thinking about mission from an ecclesiocentric to a theocentric perspective. Instead of thinking of mission as activities the church does (i.e. outreach programs, evangelism, sending missionaries overseas), it views mission, first and foremost, as something God does in sending the Son and Spirit into the world. David Bosch puts it like this: 'We have to distinguish between *mission* (singular) and *missions* (plural). The first refers primarily to the *missio Dei* (God's mission), that is, God's self-revelation as the One who loves the world . . . *Missions* . . . refer to particular forms, related to specific times, places, or needs, of participation in the *missio Dei*.'" Osmer continues, "Missional vocation refers to missions (plural), to the particular ways congregations participate in the *missio Dei* in concrete times and places. Congregations find their missions within God's mission." Osmer, "Formation in the Missional Church," 30.

Many scholars have followed Osmer's seminal work in practical theology through his numerous published writings, but few have had front row access to his thought while designing a brand new curriculum with him. Team-teaching with Rick has been a singular joy for me at Princeton Theological Seminary. Working alongside him strengthened my intuitions about the ways in which spirituality and mission invigorate one another, when properly understood and practiced. Osmer has long insisted that Christian mission and spirituality are to remain tightly tethered in a theology of the church. Though he was not the first to recognize the importance of this connection,[4] he has been a pioneer in reintegrating the church's two-fold call in the field of practical theology.

Osmer reinvents this coupling of spirituality and mission in his chapter for Dwight Zscheile's volume, *Cultivating Sent Communities: Missional Spiritual Formation.*[5] Drawing on David Bosch's *Transforming Mission*, Osmer imagines the church as an ellipse with two foci: the edification of the church and sending it forth into the world.[6] The first focal point, or "upbuilding," roots the church deeply in the "source of its life" through the preaching of the Word, Christian education, pastoral care, and spiritual formation. Vital to this upbuilding is the church's growth in fellowship as a spiritual community; spiritual friendships are nurtured, and the church experiences a deeper form of knitting together as the body of Christ. The second focal point represents the sending of the church in evangelism, service, social involvement, and social justice, as the church bears witness to the watching world.[7] And these two foci cannot thrive without the other. The church lives in tension *between* these

---

4. The Mary *and* Martha trope, which *integrates* the contemplative and active life, rather than contrasting the two figures, has a long history in the Christian mystical tradition, for example. And others such as Henri Nouwen, Thomas Merton, Howard Friend, Joan Chittister, Elizabeth O'Connor, Janet Hagberg, and Robert Guelich have also written on this integration, especially as it pertains to combating justice fatigue, or even compassion fatigue. Other religious traditions have stressed this same dynamic, e.g., Buddhist teachers often speak of the interior life's cultivation so that compassion might flow outwards in acts of courage and service.

5. Osmer, "Formation in the Missional Church."

6. Parker Palmer uses the idea of a Möbius strip to express a similar idea—that spirituality and mission are intricately tethered together, mutually informing and illuminating: see Palmer, "Life on the Möbius Strip." Palmer argues that without the cultivation of the interior life, one would all too easily burn out in community organizing efforts and sustained social justice concerns. This insight is also part of Palmer's thesis in his early work; see Palmer, *The Company of Strangers.*

7. For more on the "watching world," see Yoder, *Body Politics.*

two points that are dynamically related to each other: it is formed spiritually as it is built up as the body of Christ and is simultaneously formed in its mission. In fact, "formation is most powerful when deep connections are created between these two foci."[8] Here Osmer quotes Bosch:

> In and around the first [focus] it acknowledges and enjoys the source of its life; this is where worship and prayer are emphasized. From and through the second focus, the church engages and challenges the world. This is a forth-going and self-spending focus, where service, mission and evangelism are stressed. Neither focus should ever be at the expense of the other; rather, they stand in each other's service. The church's *identity* sustains its *relevance* and *involvement*.[9]

Expanding on the way in which spiritual formation serves as a foundation for fulfilling Christ's call to mission, Osmer draws on Darrell Guder's work to develop his theory of evangelism,[10] but also presses beyond those very insights that had informed his thinking. For example, Guder has written that the church's work of evangelism is three-fold, involving 1) saying, 2) doing, and 3) being the gospel. The "saying" of the gospel involves preaching and evangelism, where the gospel is shared in words. The "doing" of the gospel embodies the church's ethical orientation, that is, the manner in which members of the church treat others and act in community, and how they embody the teachings of Christ, both

---

8. Osmer, "Formation in the Missional Church," 49. In the section entitled "Toward a Theological Conceptualization of Formation" (point 4). We indicated above that Osmer imagines the church as an ellipse with two foci: 1) the edification of the church and 2) sending it forth into the world. More precisely understood (even though all visual analogies have their limitations) the church occupies the space *between* the two foci and flourishes when the two points interact with and influence one another.

9. Bosch, *Transforming Mission*, 385. As Osmer explains, "Bosch is drawing here on the missional ecclesiology of the great German theologian, Jürgen Moltmann, who describes the congregation with the bipolar concepts of identity and relevance." Osmer, "Formation in the Missional Church," 50. Also see Moltmann, *The Church in the Power of the Spirit*, and for helpful overviews of Moltmann's writings in English Osmer recommends Bauckham, *The Theology of Jürgen Moltmann*, and McDougall, *Pilgrimage of Love*.

10. Osmer, *The Invitation* (forthcoming). Thanks to Richard Osmer for sharing pre-published versions of his manuscript with me.

toward one another and in the world. For Guder, "being" the gospel primarily means "being and becoming the witness," i.e., Christians who as individual persons and communities grow in sanctification and live out the gospel for others to see.[11]

According to Osmer, the "being" of the gospel (within this threefold paradigm) needs to be developed more fully, and this is the place where spiritual formation must take center stage. The shaping of the heart and of the life, as well as the disposition of the soul before God, are crucial in spiritual formation and invite more cultivation. Our relationships with others involve not only what we say or do for them, but who we are, both in relation to them and to ourselves as individuals. Who are we before God? What is our character, and what is the wellspring of our affections, as well as of our choices?[12] The depth of one's interior life necessarily influences how one lives out the gospel for others to witness.

In addition to focusing on one's individual relationship with God, Osmer stresses the importance of communal formation as a vital ingredient in spiritual formation; we are formed *in* community and *for* community. In *The Invitation*, Osmer even argues that a key part of the call we extend to the watching world is an invitation to participate in authentic Christian community. The church does not lead others first into a conversion experience *per se*, but leads them to a taste of genuine Christian community. Here the church meets a longing that many people in our world experience today, and it sets in motion their desire to learn more about the Christ who holds this community together, eventually leading them to consider becoming a disciple of Christ.[13]

Furthermore, Osmer writes that in "the literature of contemporary spirituality, the language of formation is conceptualized almost exclusively in terms of the pole of identity, as the upbuilding of the members

---

11. Guder, *Be My Witnesses*, 124–28. While chapter six focuses on "Being the Witness: The Equipping Community As Witness" and emphasizes transformation of the community into God's will vs. conformity to the world (Rom 12:1–2), Guder also writes briefly about the "inward dimensions of *doing* the witness" in the next chapter, "Doing the Witness: Christian Action as Witness," i.e., being formed in love for God and one another.

12. Smith, *You Are What You Love.*

13. Osmer, *The Invitation* (forthcoming), chapter one. See also Hunter, *The Celtic Way of Evangelism*, which Osmer used in our introductory course, and which speaks to this kind of approach. Those invited to the gospel of Christ were *first* invited into a sense of *belonging* to the *community* of Christ. In other words, *belonging* comes before *believing*.

of the gathered congregation through spiritual practices and programs." Osmer's ecclesiology broadens spiritual formation to include the second point of the ellipse, namely, that the "congregation and its members are *formed* as they act with and for others beyond the church in partnership, mutual learning, and solidarity with the vulnerable. Missional formation . . . includes, but goes beyond, the typical practices we associate with spiritual formation."[14] The disciple of Christ, then, is formed spiritually *as* she takes up her missional vocation; in following Christ to serve others, the Spirit continues to form her (as well as the church, communally) into the likeness of Christ.[15]

The Double Elliptical Classroom

All of these insights and questions, and the connections between spirituality and mission, even in inchoate form, came into play as Rick and I created our new course. We discussed not only our burgeoning ideas, but practices that would support the ideas and how these practices might be embodied—both in the syllabus and in the way we team-taught the course. We chose Ignatian spirituality as the centerpiece of our teaching and practice in spiritual formation because it is particularly adept at representing the double–pointed "ellipse"—i.e., the importance of nurturing both the inner life in Christ and the outer life of mission.[16] We also opted

14. Osmer, "Formation in the Missional Church," 51.

15. As Osmer further explains, "The primary actor in spiritual formation is not the congregation. It is the Holy Spirit as she builds up and equips the congregation for mission and as she empowers the congregation to carry out in its particular vocation. Spiritual formation, thus, is the congregation 'taking form' in the Spirit, what might be called *primary missional formation*. This includes the relationships, structures, programs, and practices that emerge as a particular congregation lives into and out of its missional vocation. These, in turn, shape the spiritual lives of those who participate in this missional vocation, what might be called *secondary missional formation*." He adds that the Holy Spirit is "the primary actor in formation as a congregation discerns and embodies its missional vocation. A more adequate way of putting this would be to say that the Holy Spirit forms the congregation and its individual members toward the likeness of Christ in ways that are particular to its missional vocation. Christ takes form in the congregation through the Spirit as it embodies its calling in a particular time and place." Osmer, "Formation in the Missional Church," 49, 52.

16. Jesuits are also well-known for the outward focus of their ministry, in terms of mission endeavors, the establishing of schools, and their emphasis on social justice. As a religious order, they are highly mobile, non-cloistered, and integrate daily spiritual practices with active service in the world. For more on Ignatius of Loyola and

for depth in one tradition over breadth in several, which our first course evaluations confirmed was a choice helpful to students' learning.[17] Furthermore, we felt comfortable teaching Ignatian prayer because of our personal training in this tradition.[18]

There were several ways in which our teaching team embodied, organically (and perhaps fortuitously) some of the elliptical ideals that we espoused. First, a sense of genuine spiritual community arose within the teaching team when we gave ourselves permission to teach not only as fellow professionals, but as members of the body of Christ who cared deeply for one another. We also conducted ourselves in the classroom with evident respect and appreciation for one another, celebrating each other's gifts as a team.[19] And we joyfully began our teaching team meetings in prayer, attending to God's Spirit among us, listening together for God's still, quiet voice. This strengthened our understanding of Christ's call, and how Christ might be calling our students into more vibrant service

---

The Spiritual Exercises, see Martin, *The Jesuit Guide*, and Liebert, "Ignatius of Loyola." Another helpful introduction is *Pioneers of The Spirit*, Parish of Trinity Church. An especially helpful volume for personal prayer through *The Spiritual Exercises* is O'Brien, *The Ignatian Adventure*.

17. As one exception, we taught from Hunter's *Celtic Way of Evangelism* in our course, which provided another beautiful embodiment of the integration of mission and spirituality (see also n. 13 above). In Osmer et al., *Spiritual Companioning: A Guide to Protestant Theology and Practice*, Osmer reaches back into the devotional practices of the Protestant tradition. He also taught classes at Princeton Seminary on small group movements, small group Bible studies, and the history of various spiritual movements in the Protestant church and their missional impulses (e.g., Pietism, Puritanism, etc. and how their missionary movements grew out of their deeply rooted devotional practices).

18. Rick was trained in Ignatian spirituality through his program in spiritual direction with the Kairos School of Spiritual Formation, including his work with Marcus Smucker. Though I did most of the classroom teaching on these units, Rick was right on board, encouraging my pedagogical instincts. His gracious support was critical for my own exploration and discovery of new teaching methods, and also in my understanding of how spirituality and mission must remain tightly tethered. And with Rick's sensitivity as a trained spiritual director, it was a joy to witness his skillful guiding of students both in precept discussions and on our class retreat.

19. A hearty thanks to Caleb Maskell, Marcus Hong, Briana Wong and Kelsey Lambright, who were key members of our teaching team over the past several years that we taught this course. In David Bosch's ecclesiology, Christ has given himself for the world, and so we live, as disciples of Christ, in necessary solidarity with the world and with one another. Furthermore, Christ draws us to himself and to one another, in spiritual companionship and fellowship, and we are formed together into the body of Christ by the Spirit of God. See Bosch, *Transforming Mission*.

of others. We also created a class retreat component that was a vital part of the semester's learning. During this overnight retreat at Loyola Retreat House, students joined in spiritual companioning groups (facilitated by trained group spiritual directors) to process their individual prayer times, formed by Ignatian Gospel contemplation, to which I will return.[20] These opportunities to build community reinvigorated individuals in their various calls, and enabled them to process their struggles with that vocation, as well as their wrestlings with the God who called them.

The missional component of the class also informed the focal point of spirituality in several ways. For example, many of our students, while focusing on the academic rigors of a theological education, struggle to discern or deepen their sense of call. Some may have arrived on campus with a clear vision but lose their way when the spring of their interior life dries up. But we saw students, in the very process of grappling with their sense of purpose in the world, reach back into their relationship with God to discover their call afresh.[21] Other questions also emerged for the students: if we are called to bear witness to the gospel, have we ourselves experienced the power of this gospel in our lives? How do we even understand this "good news" on a daily basis? What is it that we are proclaiming?[22] Students realized over time that we cannot preach or give to others that which we have not experienced ourselves. Alongside these wrestlings, the call to love and serve others (with all of its accompanying challenges) compelled students to draw on resources from that deeper internal spring. Often, it was in the very act of reaching out, whether through field education or other venues of service, that their relationship to God was further revitalized.

20. One student on retreat commented that though he was in training to be a pastor in the Presbyterian Church (U.S.A.) he had never once prayed on his own or been taught how to pray. Using Ignatian prayer, he encountered Christ in brand new ways and beamed as he told the story of how he first "learned to pray." Imagine how this practice would transform this seminarian's preaching, teaching, and witness to his future congregations!

21. Several students from our introductory class spoke in subsequent semesters about how they were ready to leave the ministry until the connection between spirituality and mission became clear to them. They even mentioned in student focus groups that had it not been for the integration found in this class, they would have left seminary. This new insight may not have given them specific details on where or how to serve, but it gave them hope that the Christ who called them would also faithfully lead them.

22. See Osmer, *The Invitation* (forthcoming), chapter one, for an excellent exposition of the complexities in how one defines the "gospel."

Truth be told, I did not understand the full potential of this integrative approach when I started teaching at Princeton Seminary. Having taught at Loyola College for three years, Ignatian spirituality became a part of my wheelhouse, but the way in which spirituality and mission were interwoven throughout Ignatius's vision initially eluded me. Despite my training in Ignatian spirituality,[23] I neither conceptualized nor experienced the power of spirituality and mission's integration until team-teaching this new course with Rick. Even the title of the course, "Introduction to Spirituality and Missional Formation," which was birthed in Osmer's vision to integrate spirituality and mission in the curriculum, kept us grounded in this necessary coupling and challenged me to return time and again to the double-pointed ellipse.

Teaching with Ignatius: Elliptical Pedagogy in Practice

Several years ago, a colleague who had been a Catholic priest for thirty years made the startling comment that he had served his parish for all those years without once ever encountering Christ himself—until he prayed through *The Spiritual Exercises*. Until then, his sense of mission was often a reaction to external pressures or feedback. Mission was reduced to another task on the humdrum list of rote duties, rather than the irrepressible fruit of gratitude, erupting from an internal wellspring of passion, motivation, and desire.

Confessions from many of our seminary students revealed to me that they too were preaching a gospel that had become increasingly distant to them during their time at seminary. Their passion for mission and service withered as they lost sight of the one who called them. Several spoke of becoming "dry bones" (Ezek 37) and no longer existentially encountering the God that they had once personally believed, or even loved. As Henri Nouwen admitted of himself in *The Return of the Prodigal Son*, many ministers and theologians in particular, even in proclaiming the love of Christ to others, remain perpetual bystanders to that love—the unhappy plight of the firstborn son in the parable—rather than

---

23. Coursework in graduate school first introduced me to Ignatian spirituality, which I then expanded through spiritual direction training with the Oasis Ministries program, and numerous other Ignatian retreats and training programs (e.g., at the Jesuit Center [Wernersville, PA], Loyola Retreat House [Morristown, NJ], Bethany Spirituality Center [Highland Mills, NY], Morning Star House of Prayer [Trenton, NJ], and Francis House of Prayer [Westampton, NJ]).

knowing themselves to be deeply beloved as the prodigal child.[24] Ignatius illumines a valuable pathway from bystander to beloved, bringing the follower of Christ into a more immediate encounter with the Christ who passionately loves him/her and the world. This then releases the pastor (and seminarian) into a more vibrant and authentic mode of proclamation and lived expression.

This deep integration of spirituality and mission in Ignatius's thought can be found in his *Spiritual Exercises,* the primary prayer manual he bequeathed to the church. Many denominations today, Catholic and Protestant, turn to it to enrich their prayer lives.[25] In this guide, Ignatius walks us through four movements (or "weeks"), each of which is designed to bring us into a lived encounter with Christ, which then brings us back into the world with a strengthened heart for service. In the first movement, retreatants ponder the beauty of the created world alongside its brokenness. We focus our meditation on ourselves as profoundly loved of God. And we bask in the compassion of Christ and learn to love ourselves, extending Christ's compassion to ourselves despite life's severe wounds. This grounding is essential in the life of any minister. Going out into the world to serve others without this foundation sets us up for discouragement, a relentless cycle of people-pleasing or self-judgment, and burnout. The enduring power of mission is lost when the source of life and love becomes distant.

In the second movement, the retreatant meditates on the incarnation, life, and ministry of Christ, and imaginatively walks alongside Christ as he brought healing and life to others. As seminarians hoping to serve in ministry according to the model of Christ, this movement wields great potential for their participation in Christ's very own ministry through imaginative prayer, or gospel contemplation.[26] In the third movement, the retreatant accompanies Christ through his passion, daring to stay with him in his suffering, remembering the way he suffered alongside others. (Again, this practice can generate endurance for ministry in

---

24. Nouwen, *The Return of the Prodigal Son,* 14.

25. See Liebert, "Ignatius of Loyola," for the surprisingly wide circulation of *The Spiritual Exercises* in interdenominational ministries of spiritual direction, community Bible studies, church small groups, etc. See also Dyckman et al., *The Spiritual Exercises Reclaimed.*

26. This form of prayer goes by various names, such as "Gospel contemplation," see Martin, *A Jesuit Guide,* 145–62, or "imaginative prayer." See Silf, *Inner Compass,* 12–24.

pastors.) Finally, in Ignatius's fourth movement of prayer, the retreatant witnesses the resurrection and the power of the risen life and learns to live anew out of that resurrection power. These four movements help to resource the retreatant's return to the world with renewed vigor, determination, and love. Spiritually strengthened in fellowship with Christ, one's mission in the world is revitalized.

One of the innovations in Ignatius's model of prayer is its vivid and powerful use of the imagination.[27] In Ignatian prayer, we are invited to place ourselves within the gospel narrative, almost as if part of a motion picture.[28] With which character did we relate? Where were we, physically, in relation to the character of Jesus? What might Jesus have said directly to us—to me—in this unfolding scene? With the movie rolling forward, were we one of the disciples trying to protect Jesus from being crushed by the crowd? Were we in the crowd, pressing in, desperate for a loving glance or for healing? Or were we—was I, perhaps—the person Jesus touched or addressed?[29]

Several years after I experienced Ignatian group spiritual reading for the first time in my classroom, Rick encouraged me to facilitate this form of prayer in our introductory course of sixty students.[30] I was accustomed to using the exercise in smaller courses, but I did not know how to create a spirit of shared attentiveness to biblical narrative in such a large group. To my surprise, the lectionary text for the day (Mark 4:35–41, "Jesus calming the storm") allowed students to confront various kinds of pain: crushing disappointments long buried, anger at God long suppressed. Many identified with the disciples, furiously pouring water out of the boat and pleading with Jesus, "Do you not care that we are perishing?"[31] Others spoke of a deep disbelief in Jesus' power or questioned his compassion. Still others admitted to personal storms in their own lives, and their yearning for calm in the midst of their studies or ministry and fam-

---

27. For more on the gift of the imagination, see Anderson, *Light When It Comes*, 33; cf. Hooper, *The Letters of C. S. Lewis*, 193.

28. See Busse, "Grace Enough," 42–49, where the actor Andrew Garfield relates Ignatian meditation to the craft of acting and film-making.

29. See Lee, "The Compassionate Christ" (forthcoming), for details on one such prayer experience with Mark 5:21–34 (the story of the hemorrhaging woman). Parts of this essay also appear in that chapter.

30. I offer deep and personal thanks to Richard Osmer for encouraging this experiment in our classroom, thereby helping me to grow further as a teacher.

31. Mark 4:38.

ily demands. A final group of students experienced Jesus speaking peace into their lives through the text, releasing them from the anxieties they had carried into the classroom. Whatever their engagement with the text (and a few indeed struggled to enter the scene at all; imaginative prayer takes some patience and practice), the opportunity to become engulfed by a biblical scene opened up fresh honesty in conversation with Christ and with each other, by unmasking pain, doubt, and hidden hopes.

Integrating Spirituality and Mission in the Education of Christian Leaders

As I came to appreciate how important the integration of mission and spirituality is for the formation of the church, I stumbled upon something else as well. The ancient recognition that endurance in Christian leadership—not to mention endurance in faith itself—utterly depends on this integration, which is why it is so critical for our students who are studying for ministry. Without this kind of honest encounter with Christ, it becomes all the more difficult for pastors to maintain the kind of perseverance needed to sustain their outreach to their parishioners, or to witness Christ's love to our watching world. If I have not first received this love, what can I give?

Seen from the other point of the ellipse, when my relationship to God becomes one of vibrant love where divine grace flows freely, mission and service are not things "I do" but rather grateful responses to that love. Mission is then empowered by the Holy Spirit and impossible to stifle. God enters us as love (we inhale God's breath) and we share that love (exhale into the world). We cannot afford to separate these two. On the other hand, if mission is something that "we do," it can be exhausting before we even start.

Osmer is convinced that the coupling of spirituality and missional formation requires that disciples of Christ, as Guder puts it, *speak, do, and be* the gospel. In *being* the gospel, Osmer stresses that disciples must grow as people of prayer in relation to God. They are also invited into experiences of community, which is one of the church's most important and powerful means of witness to the gospel of Christ. If we model this integration in the theological classroom, more Christian leaders will be encouraged to drink deeply from the wellspring of love in their own lives, so that they can move out into the world to serve others with confidence, passion and vigor. Their service, in turn, fuels their life of prayer, as the world's needs and their own limitations bring them to their knees in a mutually informing ellipse.

Bibliography

Anderson, Chris. *Light When It Comes: Trusting Joy, Facing Darkness & Seeing God in Everything.* Grand Rapids: Eerdmans, 2016.

Bauckham, Richard. *The Theology of Jürgen Moltmann.* Edinburgh: T&T Clark, 1995.

Bosch, David. *Transforming Mission: Paradigm Shifts in Theology of Mission.* Maryknoll, NY: Orbis, 1991.

Busse, Brendan. "Grace Enough: Andrew Garfield on the Ignatian Journey that Led Him Through 'Silence.'" *America* 216 (2017) 42–49.

Dyckman, Kathryn, et al. *The Spiritual Exercises Reclaimed: Uncovering Liberating Possibilities for Women.* Mahwah, NJ: Paulist, 2001.

Guder, Darrell, L. *Be My Witnesses.* Grand Rapids: Eerdmans, 1985.

Harter, Michael, ed. *Hearts on Fire: Praying with Jesuits.* Chicago: Loyola Press, 2005.

Holder, Arthur, ed. *The Blackwell Companion to Christian Spirituality.* Oxford: Blackwell, 2005.

Hooper, Walter, ed. *The Letters of C. S. Lewis to Arthur Greeve.* New York: Macmillan, 1979.

Hunter, George. *The Celtic Way of Evangelism: How Christianity Can Reach the West . . . Again.* Nashville: Abingdon, 2011.

Lee, Bo Karen. "The Compassionate Christ in the Classroom: Ignatian Spiritual Reading." In *The Soul of Higher Education: Contemplative Pedagogy, Research and Institutional Life for the Twenty-First Century,* edited by Margaret Benefiel and Bo Karen Lee. Charlotte: Information Age, forthcoming.

Liebert, Beth. "Ignatius of Loyola: The Spiritual Exercises." In *Christian Spirituality: The Classics,* edited by Arthur Holder, 197–208. New York: Routledge, 2009.

Martin, James. *The Jesuit Guide to (Almost) Everything: A Spirituality for Real Life.* New York: HarperCollins, 2010.

McDougall, Joy Ann. *Pilgrimage of Love: Moltmann on the Trinity and Christian Life.* Oxford: Oxford University Press, 2005.

Mikoski, Gordon, and Richard Osmer. *With Learning and Piety: The History of Practical Theology at Princeton Theological Seminary 1812–2012.* Zürich: Lit, 2011.

Moltmann, Jürgen. *The Church in the Power of the Spirit: A Contribution to Messianic Ecclesiology.* San Francisco: Harper & Row, 1977.

Nouwen, Henri. *The Return of the Prodigal Son: A Story of Homecoming.* New York: Doubleday, 1994.

O'Brien, Kevin. *The Ignatian Adventure: Experiencing the Spiritual Exercises of Saint Ignatius in Daily Life.* Chicago: Loyola, 2011.

Osmer, Richard R. "Formation in the Missional Church: Building Deep Connections between Ministries of Upbuilding and Sending." In *Cultivating Sent Communities: Missional Spiritual Formation,* edited by Dwight J. Zscheile, 29–55. Grand Rapids: Eerdmans, 2012.

———. *The Invitation.* Grand Rapids: Eerdmans, forthcoming.

Osmer, Richard R., and Bo Karen Lee. "Enriching the Love of Learning with a Desire for God." *Hungry Hearts* 17 (2008) 20–21.

Osmer, Richard R., Angela H. Reed, and Marcus G. Smucker. *Spiritual Companioning: A Guide to Protestant Theology and Practice.* Grand Rapids: Baker Academic, 2015.

Palmer, Parker. "Life on the Möbius Strip." *The On Being Project,* February 17, 2016. onbeing.org/blog/life-on-the-mobius-strip/.

————. *The Company of Strangers: Christians and the Renewal of America's Public Life.* New York: Crossroad, 1983.

Parish of Trinity Church. *Pioneers of the Spirit: Ignatius of Loyola.* Worcester, MA: Vision Video, 2005.

Silf, Margaret. *Inner Compass: An Invitation to Ignatian Spirituality.* Chicago: Loyola, 2007.

Smith, James. *You Are What You Love: The Spiritual Power of Habit.* Grand Rapids: Brazos, 2016.

Yoder, John Howard. *Body Politics: Five Practices of the Christian Community Before the Watching World.* Scottdale, PA: Herald, 2001.

SECTION THREE

THE EVANGELIST: SHARING GOD'S GOOD NEWS

8

Practical Theology
and Missional Theology

How Are They Related?

DARRELL L. GUDER

THE EMERGENCE OF THE conversation about "missional theology" and "missional church" can be dated. It began with the publication in 1998 of the study entitled "Missional Church."[1] In that context, the term was a constructive proposal for the theological challenge confronting the Christian movement in the west (see the sub-title: "A Vision for the Sending of the Church in North America"). That challenge is linked to the much discussed and much analyzed "end of Western Christendom." The umbrella concept of Christendom includes complex historical developments like the disestablishment of Western Christianity, the secularization of north Atlantic cultures, and the emergence of religious pluralism replacing the hegemony of the Constantinian *corpus Christianum*. With the decline of Christendom the awareness has grown that the West is now a mission field that presents daunting challenges to the Christian movement. The question driving the discussion is how the church structures and practices of Christendom can become again missionary in their focus and action, since they are now located in such difficult mission fields. As Christendom disintegrates, we are also enabled to recognize God's faithfulness through the centuries of

1. Guder et al., *Missional Church.*

compromise and captivity. That faithfulness is evidenced, for example, in ancient practices of pastoral care from which we continue to learn and by which we are blessed.

The neologism "missional" also articulates a growing awareness of the absence of "Mission" as a major theological theme in Western ecclesiologies for over a millennium.[2] By adding the syllable *al* to the term *mission*, the authors of "Missional Church" were making the case that the church's nature, purpose, and action are defined by God's mission (*missio Dei*): the healing of the nations, the salvation of humanity, the inauguration of the kingdom of God, the expectation that God will complete the good work that has begun—all of which are brought about by the life, death, resurrection, and ascension of Jesus Christ. The missional church serves God's mission as the called, equipped, and sent out witness to Jesus Christ. It is the continuation of God's called and set apart people who, since Abraham, are blessed by God to be a blessing to "all the families of the earth" (Gen 12:3).[3] God's mission expands outward to embrace all of humanity as Jesus "appointed twelve, whom he also named apostles, to be with him, and to be sent out to proclaim the message" (Mark 3:14). The formation of the disciples in the four biblical Gospels is to be understood as the process of discipleship carried out by Jesus during his earthly ministry in preparation for the expanding mission of the church from Easter and Pentecost onwards. Discipleship in the missional church leads to apostolate, to witness, which in turn gathers the community of witness to be equipped and sent. The missional church is then the continuation of the apostolic mission begun in the first century and documented in the New Testament. It is the outworking of the promise made by Jesus on the Mount of the Ascension: "But you will receive power when the Holy Spirit has come upon you; and you will be my witnesses in Jerusalem, in all Judea and Samaria, and to the ends of the earth" (Acts 1:8).

Thus, missional theology challenges deeply engrained assumptions about what the church is and what is its purpose that have emerged in the course of Western Christendom. The church, from the purview of missional theology, is not an end in itself and is not the reason for the gospel. The church exists for God's purposes that have all of creation in view. Because of God's love for the creation, there is gospel. And because there is gospel and the promise of redemption, there is church. That church

2. Flett, *The Witness of God*, 30–34.

3. The Revised Standard Version is cited except where I have offered my own translation.

takes on concrete shape within human history, but its institutional forms are not the reason for its existence. Rather than making its survival its goal, the institutional church serves God's mission as its first fruits, instrument, and agency.

The missional theological discussion has thus been insistent that the challenges facing Christian witness in the West are not merely strategic or institutional. Course corrections, enhanced efficiency, and improved methodologies will not resolve the crisis of Christendom. The issues are profoundly theological. The critique that Western ecclesiologies remain silent about mission constitutes a call to reclaim the fundamentally missional character of the original apostolic movement. The purpose of that movement was the formation and equipping of witnessing communities. This means that the authoritative role of Scripture for the formation of the witnessing church receives central importance. Biblical scholars are responding to this challenge as they investigate how the scriptural witness has served and must serve the formation of faithfully witnessing communities. These investigations coalesce around the task of "missional hermeneutics."[4] That task engages the biblical witness with some version or aspect of the basic question: How did this text continue the formation of faithfully witnessing communities then, and how does it do so today?

The focus upon "faithfully witnessing communities" represents a point of convergence between the missional discussion and the task and scope of practical theology as represented by the work of Richard Osmer. In the missiological exploration of the church's nature, purpose, and action during much of the twentieth century, the gathered community ("the local church") comes to be recognized as the primary instrument of God's mission. The recent emphasis upon the missional church affirms that priority as it explores how such communities are to be formed for this service. Osmer's focus on the form and function of congregations provides guidance for the way in which communities should be formed for their missional vocation as witnesses to the gospel.

It is in the particularity of God working out God's mission through a certain people that missional and practical theologies overlap. Going back to the Abrahamic call and woven through the long and often perilous pilgrimage of God's called people through time, there is this remarkable and pervasive conviction that God is carrying out healing purposes for creation through the chosen and set apart people. That conviction is

---

4 Gorman, *Becoming the Gospel.*

taken up in the apostolic mission whose actual purpose was not just the saving of souls but rather the calling, equipping, and sending of communities of witness into the world God loves. Thus, it is essential for the continuing formation of faithfully witnessing communities that they engage in the theological interpretation of their practice to see if they are in fact leading their corporate life "worthy of the calling to which [they] have been called" (Eph 4:1). Missional theology prompts practical questions.

The missional approach that we envision will not tolerate a view of practical theology that, as Osmer critically comments, "views this field as solely concerned with application, with helpful techniques and skills applied to the life of the church."[5] We suspect that the reclamation of mission as the decisive theological interpretation of the church's nature, purpose, and action, will have a profoundly integrative effect upon theological discourses that have for too long worked in their respective silos—with profoundly problematic consequences for faithful witness. In particular, the division between the doctrine of the church and the disciplines clustered together under the rubric "practical theology" is unworkable if God's mission does, in fact, define the church's nature, purpose, and action. What the church confesses about its vocation becomes observable action as the Christian witness unfolds in history.

The theologian who unites this missional reading and the task of practical theology is Karl Barth. His ecclesiology is both unequivocally missional in its concerted focus upon the vocation of the Christian as witness, and practical in trying to think through the shape and form of that witness in the world today. That Barth's ecclesiology is unequivocally missional is made abundantly clear in his concerted focus that the "vocation of the Christian is witness."[6] This claim comes as the climax of the large and embracing theology of reconciliation which is the theme of volume IV of the *Church Dogmatics* and which reaches its climax in Barth's "missional ecclesiology," especially in paragraph 72: "The Holy Spirit and the Sending of the Christian Community."[7] The gospel of reconciliation is only fully expounded when God's work of justification and sanctification issues forth in the doctrine and practice of the vocation of the gathered and sent community as Christ's witness. It is thoroughly consequent, then, when Barth's argument in paragraph 71 ("The Vocation of Man")

---

5. Osmer, *Practical Theology*, ix.

6. Barth, *Church Dogmatics*, 481–680.

7. Ibid, 681–901.

leads into the discussion in paragraph 72 of "the Sending of the Christian Community."[8] The English-speaking reader needs to be reminded that "sending" is the Germanic equivalent of "mission."

The emphasis upon witness as mission is the theological presupposition for Barth's detailed exposition of the forms of service in which the gathered community carries out its vocation. This exposition happens in the concluding sub-section of paragraph 72, whose title unnecessarily clericalizes the argument.[9] Barth expounds the actions of witness with twelve rubrics that together make up the "service" of the called and sent community. The English translation opts for "ministry" rather than "service," although up until now the German noun *Dienst* has regularly been translated as "service." Be that as it may, the ecclesiological exposition of the Christian vocation as witness becomes practical in twelve actual "forms" and disciplines of service, all of which both equip for and carry out the calling of witness. One could entitle this provocative section of the *Church Dogmatics* a "missional practical theology," as a survey of the forms demonstrates:

1. The praise of God (865–67)

2. The preaching of the Gospel (867–70)

3. The Instruction of the Community (870–72)

4. Evangelization (872–74)

5. Mission (874–78)

6. Theology (879–82)

7. Prayer (882–84)

8. Cure of Souls (885–87)

9. Personal Examples of Christian Life and Action (887–89)

10. Diaconate (889–95)

11. Prophetic Action (895–98)

12. Fellowship (898–901)

In the missional exposition of all of these actions, the gathered community is equipped for the practice of witness in the world. These actions

8. Ibid.

9. Ibid, 830–901. The page numbers of the twelve forms discussed in this sub-section are provided in the text below.

communicate and demonstrate the nature and promise of the new creation which the gospel announces. Following through on the biblical injunction to "disciple the ethnicities" (Matt 28:19) in all their linguistic and cultural diversity, these twelve forms of service are all vehicles for the embodying and disseminating of good news for the world. They can be and should be translated into the languages and cultures around the globe. This centered diversity makes concrete what the catholicity of the church is really all about. These forms all can and should find expression, critique, and application in the disciplined tasks of "practical theological interpretation" as expounded by Osmer. Many, if not all of these forms of service will make up the content of research and instruction in the disciplines of practical theology today. As they form communities for faithful practice, they serve the continuing articulation of missional theology in relevant translation in diverse settings.

What Barth's practical theological formation envisions in his discussion of the twelve forms of service is addressed by Lesslie Newbigin in his magisterial discussion of *The Gospel in a Pluralist Society*.[10] He defines the congregation as "the hermeneutic of the gospel," whose diverse actions and forms of service "equip the saints for the work of ministry" (Eph 4:12).

Newbigin's conclusion could be used as a summary of Barth's discussion of the forms of witnessing service: "The congregation has to be a place where its members are trained, supported, and nourished in the exercise of their parts of the priestly ministry in the world. The preaching and teaching of the local church has to be such that it enables members to think out the problems that face them in their secular work in the light of their Christian faith."[11] If we understand Osmer's approach to practical theology as the discipline that reflects on Newbigin's "preaching and teaching of the local church," and what Barth lays out as the "forms of service," then we have an interactive resource for the exploration of the question of the ways in which practical theology and missional theology might be related.[12]

Have we, then, arrived at least at the beginnings of a response to the query, how are practical theology and missional theology related? Defined by the theology of the *missio Dei*, missional theology contributes

---

10. Newbigin, *The Gospel in a Pluralist Society*, 222–23.

11. Ibid., 230.

12. Osmer, *Teaching Ministry of Congregations*.

the fundamental convictions that determine the church's nature, purpose, and action. These theological convictions center on God's action in gathering a people to witness to the healing of all creation. That healing is accomplished for all generations and times in the event of Jesus Christ as reported in the New Testament Scriptures. In response to the proclamation of that event, the Spirit gathers witnesses and forms them into communities to serve God's mission. The gathered life of witnesses displays, demonstrates, enfleshes the good news by the ways the community communicates the gospel both as narrative as well as action. That communication takes place in and through all the Spirit-empowered forms of service that missionally defined practical theology enables the community to investigate, research, generate, and employ.

The formation of communities for witness takes place through the interaction of all the forms through which God's Spirit works. The list of twelve forms offered by Barth is a helpful and also debatable summary of the church's experience over time, traced back to Jesus' earthly work of disciple formation. The task of rigorous, intentional practical theological analysis is to provide content, structure, and discipline for the formation of such communities, as the process of formation is intentionally addressed. The christocentric focus of missional theology and the practices that constitute its witness determine the cutting edge of the Christian mission in its "sentness" into any cultural context. That christocentric focus replaces the unhelpful dichotomy between theology as theory and practice, as well as the divisiveness of the disciplinary silos of the academy. In their place we encounter in Scripture the many-faceted emphasis upon the integrity of ecclesial action in the world. Centering on God's mission in Christ generates a life of witness in which the doctrines of the faith are embodied and demonstrated by the actions of the witnessing community. The rigid distinction between theory and praxis becomes pointless, if not distorting. This can be persuasively documented by pursuing the question, "What kind of community did Jesus intend?" This was the provocative question which Gerhard Lohfink raised in the 1980s with his book, *Wie hat Jesus Gemeinde gewollt?*[13] This approach demonstrates how doctrine emerges from practice and shapes its continuing exercise. Lohfink identifies basic convictions of the gathered community serving Christ's witness that shape it as a visible witness. These include

---

13. Lohfink, *Wie hat Jesus Gemeinde gewollt?*; the English translation by J. P. Galvin received a title that completely obscured the thrust and promise of this remarkable study: see Lohfink, *Jesus and Community*.

the rejection of all forms of violence, the end of patriarchy as formative of the ecclesial community, the continuing reality of healing within the life of the church, the development of the witnessing community as a "contrast society," and the intentional formation of the community under the rubric "one-anotherness." These convictions expressed in the life and practice of the gathered community are the continuing demonstration of what the early church learned from the example and practice of Jesus as he trained his disciples to become his apostles. The "practical theology" that shaped the apostolic communities was the result of following him and becoming "fishers of people" (Mark 1:17).

Paul's formation of witnessing communities parallels the process of discipleship leading to apostolate in the four Gospels. One can argue that Paul and his missionary colleagues strove to form communities "the way that Jesus intended them."[14] His concern for the faithful witness of the churches he planted is expressed in his constant struggle with the challenges to the integrity of the community's witness. The problems and temptations that the apostolic communities experienced serve the formation of subsequent generations of churches, as they reflect on their practice in light of the mission of God and their commission to "be Christ's witnesses."

For example, at the beginning of 2 Corinthians 3, Paul reflects on the vocation and practice of Christians in Corinth using the image of "Christ's letters to the world": "You yourselves are our letter, written on our hearts, to be known and read by all; and you show that you are a letter of Christ, prepared by us, written not with ink but with the Spirit of the living God, not on tablets of stone but on tablets of human hearts." (2 Cor. 3:2–3).

In this passage, Paul's formation of the Corinthians for their continuing witness in the mission field into which they are sent is very much focused on the integrative character of their lives and practice as witnesses. He has already sounded his concern when he states bluntly in 2 Corinthians 2:17, "For we are not peddlers of God's word like so many." The Corinthians, when they are gathered, are to understand themselves as letters being written by God's Spirit. They are forms of communication sent out in order to be made available to all in their context who might "read" them—they are, in fact, intended "to be read by all." So, they are to be legible, clear, faithful, and reliable transmitters of the gospel they

---

14. Barth, *Church Dogmatics*, 862–64.

are to communicate. It is essential for the formation of faithful witnesses that they are people of integrity whose message and practice are congruent. Paul envisions their life together as the time of their being written as Christ's letters to the world. The corporate practices of formation (Barth's twelve forms!) all serve their composition as gospel letters. Their gathered life is not for their benefit alone, but serves God's greater mission. The life of community formation and witness is characterized by a rhythm of gathering, upbuilding, and sending, to use Barth's ecclesiological triad. The sending cannot actually happen unless it is prepared and equipped in the shared life of the community. But the gathered life of the church is never an end in itself, never self-justifying. It must prepare for and issue forth in the action of witness in a watching and often resistant world.

Another compelling example of missional community formation is found in the Thessalonian correspondence. Paul reminds his Thessalonian friends about the distinctive witness he and his team brought to them. They were experiencing from the outset the kind of community that Jesus intended. "For our appeal does not spring from deceit or impure motives or trickery, but just as we have been approved by God to be entrusted with the message of the gospel, even so we speak, not to please mortals, but to please God who tests our hearts. As you know and as God is our witness, we never came with words of flattery or with a pretext for greed; nor did we seek praise from mortals, whether from you or from others" (1 Thess 2:3–6). Paul's exposition of the gospel of Jesus Christ was communicated to the Thessalonians in such a way that the content of the story was totally congruent with the way it was told, the way in which the Pauline community lived the gospel as its witnesses.

Here again, the community Jesus intended was to be formed in Thessalonica as a gathering whose life and message were congruent. The community was to "incarnate" the story of Jesus, so that his mission could continue through their life and practices. Paul underlines the integrity of their message with its transmission when he writes, "We were gentle among you, like a nurse tenderly caring for her own children. So deeply do we care for you that we are determined to share with you not only the gospel of God but also our own selves, because you have become very dear to us" (1 Thess 2:7–8). Certainly there is nothing greater than "the gospel of God," yet Paul can hyperbolically say "not only the gospel of God" as he reminds them of the new community they had become as a result of the gospel witness.

The formation of the witnessing community takes place as the outcome of practices that shape gospel obedience. Paul describes such conduct with a distinctive phrase that merits much thought as it guides and empowers our response. It occurs five times in the Pauline corpus, first of all further along in 1st Thessalonians: "As you know, we dealt with each one of you like a father with his children, urging and encouraging you and pleading that you *lead a life worthy of God*, who calls you into his own kingdom and glory" (1 Thess 2:11–12).[15] All of the instances in which this emphasis upon worthy conduct is made are plural. This is an admonition directed at the formation of the entire community. The standard of worthiness is multi-faceted: "worthy of the gospel, worthy of God, worthy of the Lord, worthy of the call, worthy of the calling." It has to do with conduct that communicates, which reminds us that Barth looked upon the first six of his "forms of service" as communication that was an event (e.g., praise, preaching, instruction, evangelization).[16] This formative admonition has a dynamic character: all of the instances but one (Phil 1:27) are built upon an imperative of movement: "lead your life" or "walk your walk." The formative imagery to be learned and experienced is that of a pilgrimage, a movement forward towards a goal. The Christian obedience being learned here anticipates growth, discovery, exploration, and risk. The mission is not reduced to a limited range of verbal events. The entire life of the witnessing community serves this communication.

In the reference to worthiness in Philippians 1:27, the emphasis, although related to the other citations, is different in important ways. We translate it, "Live your life in a manner worthy of the gospel of Christ." The opening term needs a greater sense of urgency and emphasis. The apostle is calling his readers' attention to a very important statement, so "listen up now!" The imperative here differs from the other four. It alludes to public life and conduct. One might translate it more freely: "Let the conduct that the world sees be congruent with and properly express the gospel of Christ." Over against all tendencies to make our faith internal, intimate, private, and withdrawn from the world, this injunction summons us to public presence and action. It is commensurate with the use of the Greek term *ecclesia* to designate the assembled church. In the

---

15. See also 2 Thessalonnians 1:11, "that our God may make you worthy of his call . . . "; Colossians 1:10, "to lead a life worthy of the Lord . . ."; Philippians 1:27, "only let your manner of life be worthy of the gospel of Christ . . ."; and Ephesians 4:1, "I . . . beg you to lead a life worthy of the calling to which you have been called . . ."

16. Barth, *Church Dogmatics*, 862–64.

Greek-speaking world, an ecclesia was a public assembly, a town hall meeting, a gathering to do public business in behalf of its constituencies. The forms of service of the witnessing community must have public relevance if they are to lay before the world the reign of Christ to whom "all authority in heaven and on earth has been given to me" (Matt 28:18).

These diverse forms of reflection and practice can, of course, serve other theological or ecclesial masters. But if the missional vocation of the gathered community is to be formed and equipped by its engagement in diverse forms of service, then the prior commitment must be to missional vocation and its practice. Such prior (and constantly reaffirmed) commitment constitutes an open invitation to the practical theologian to engage the vocation of the missional church by equipping the saints for the work of service. As the decline of Christendom continues apace, and the challenges to missional faithfulness become more acute, there is undeniably a profound need for marginalized communities of witness to be more faithfully and rigorously formed for their practice. The resources of missionally informed practical theology are crucial for public Christian witness today. Newbigin has framed the challenge with realism and candor:

> If the gospel is to challenge the public life of our society, if Christians are to occupy the "high ground" which they vacated in the noontime of "modernity," it will not be by forming a Christian political party, or by aggressive propaganda campaigns. Once again it has to be said that there can be no going back to the "Constantinian" era. It will only be by movements that begin with the local congregation in which the reality of the new creation is present, known, and experienced, and from which men and women will go into every sector of public life to claim it for Christ, to unmask the illusions which have remained hidden and to expose all areas of public life to the illumination of the gospel. But that will only happen as and when local congregations renounce an introverted concern for their own life, and recognize that they exist for the sake of those who are not members, as sign, instrument and foretaste of God's redeeming grace for the whole life of society.[17]

---

17. Newbigin, *Gospel in a Pluralist Society*, 232–33.

Bibliography

Barth, Karl. *Church Dogmatics: Volume IV/3.2*. Edinburgh: T. & T. Clark.

Flett, John G. *The Witness of God: The Trinity, Missio Dei, Karl Barth and the Nature of Christian Community*. Grand Rapids: Eerdmans, 2010.

Gorman Michael, J. *Becoming the Gospel: Paul, Participation, and Mission*. Grand Rapids: Eerdmans, 2015.

Guder, Darrell L., et al., eds. *Missional Church: A Vision for the Sending of the Church in North America*. Grand Rapids: Eerdmans, 1998.

Lohfink, Gerhard. *Wie hat Jesus Gemeinde gewollt?* Vienna: Herder Verlag, 1982.

———. *Jesus and Community: The Social Dimension of Christian Faith*. Translated by J. P. Galvin. Philadelphia: Fortress, 1984.

Newbigin, Lesslie. *The Gospel in a Pluralist Society*. Grand Rapids: Eerdmans, 1989.

Osmer, Richard. *Practical Theology: An Introduction*. Grand Rapids: Eerdmans, 2008.

———. *Teaching Ministry of Congregations*. Louisville, KY: Westminster John Knox, 2005.

9

Worshipping, Witnessing, and Wondering

Integrating Proclamation, Evangelism, and Catechesis for God's Mission Today

Thomas John Hastings

Introduction: Preachers and Teachers as Partners in the Mission of God

With some fear and trepidation, I once shared with a well-known New Testament scholar that, based on my reading of Paul's letters and other relevant parts of the New Testament,[1] it seems probable that, while the early itinerant ἀποστόλους (apostles), προφήτας (prophets), and εὐαγγελιστάς (evangelists) travelled from place to place, διδασκάλους (teachers or catechists) were the first "permanent clergy" to settle down in one place. Operating out of the theological conviction that it is "God who gives the growth," the church's first itinerant preachers were "planting" and settled teachers "watering" nascent seeds of faith.

I added that it is easy to overlook the implicit missiological reason these embryonic communities of faith required more settled catechists or

1. 1 Cor 12:28; Gal 6:6; Rom 12:6–8; Eph 4:11; Jude 3; 2 Tim 1:13, 4:3, Titus 1:9; Heb 6:2.

educators. Namely, Gentile converts who had confessed faith in Jesus as the Christ had no knowledge of Israel's Scriptures—the only Bible at the time—so they needed teachers who would commit to the time intensive work of catechesis. In time, a "proto-catechumenate" developed that integrated 1) Study of Scripture and confession of faith, 2) Participation in worship, and 3) Moral teaching and ethical discernment, enabling Christian faith to move beyond its original location in first-century Palestinian Judaism and eventually take root in societies within and beyond the Greco-Roman world. By the time of the third century document called the *Apostolic Tradition*,[2] we know that pre–baptismal catechetical instruction often lasted several years, and it seems this educational practice played a significant role in shaping church doctrine, which found expression in early creedal summaries. J. N. D. Kelly claims, "It should be obvious that a wider background must be sought for *the brief confessions of faith* than the actual ceremony of baptism itself. Their roots lie not so much in the Christian's sacramental initiation into the Church as in the catechetical training by which it was preceded."[3]

I am happy to report that the New Testament scholar enthusiastically agreed with my thesis about the complementary work of itinerant preachers and settled teachers and thought it was a good description of what likely happened in the churches that were a fruit of the Gentile mission. He also confessed that he had never thought of the Jewish-Gentile dynamic in terms of cross-cultural mission, nor had he imagined catechetical practice as an engine driving the development of church doctrine as well as cross-cultural "translation" of Christian faith.

I concluded by telling my New Testament colleague that, had I not spent twenty years as a missionary working with Japanese pastors, congregations, and theologians, I would never have been sensitized to the implicit missional and theological dynamic at work in the communities "in front of" the New Testament writings. That is, I observed in the Japanese churches a missional situation analogous to the churches featured in the New Testament. Initially a result of the efforts of mostly North American missionaries, the 150–year–old Japanese Protestant churches are still struggling to find their distinctive local voice and to put down roots.

2. There are significant textual problems with this work, but generally scholars agree that it was written around 215 and probably reflects practices common to that period; cf. Westerhoff and Edwards, *A Faithful Church*, 50.

3. Kelly, *Early Christian Creeds*, 50.

Canonical "Ways of Knowing"

Since the Protestant Reformers began with the normative *sola scriptura* principle, we will begin there, too. Old Testament scholar Walter Brueggemann shows how Israel's Scriptures embody three distinct yet intimately related ways of knowing which he calls the "disclosure of binding" of the Torah, "the disruption for justice" of the Prophets, and "the discernment of order" of the Wisdom writings.[4] Israel's tripartite canon encompasses epistemic dimensions of continuity (Torah), discontinuity (Prophets), and contemporaneity (Wisdom).

Firstly, in Torah, the intergenerational transmission of Israel's defining story pivots on the *wonder* of a child: "Why is tonight (Passover) different from all other nights?" Torah responds to the identity question of "Who are we?" with a "pre-doubt" confidence, reciting the core narrative of the Exodus and confession of faith (*Shema Yisrael*, "Hear, O Israel: The LORD is our God, the LORD alone"). The Exodus and *Shema* are the received parameters within which each new generation rediscovers its faith identity as a free gift of Yahweh.

Secondly, the Prophetic literature accompanies God's people on a disorienting journey into a far country where they urgently ask, "Is there any word from the Lord?" In response to national calamity, moral corruption, external threat, or punishing exile, Israel's prophets proclaim an unanticipated and subversive Word from the Lord—an "interruption for justice"—that is not easily managed by the priests who guard and teach Torah. The passion of the community is reawakened and renewed by prophets who are called, especially on behalf of the neglected members of the community (i.e., the poor, orphans, widows, and sojourners), to hold fast to the truth of divine justice, even in the face of agonizing experiences of suffering, oppression, marginalization, and loss. Not surprisingly, prophets are often ignored, vilified, or silenced, because they boldly deliver God's Word, not from the sanctioned centers of power, but from the margins of the community. If Torah comforts the afflicted, prophecy afflicts the comfortable on behalf of "the least of these."

Thirdly, as counterpoint and complement to the continuity of Torah and discontinuity of prophecy, Brueggemann calls the Wisdom writings the "most self-consciously educational"[5] material in the Hebrew Scriptures. Characterized by "contemporaneity," these writings treat the

4. Brueggemann, *The Creative Word*.
5. Ibid., 68.

whole gamut of real problems people confront in their lives together. The Wisdom writings explore the relevance of the community's knowledge and test the limits of their understanding, especially when they face liminal situations. According to Brueggemann, in these writings "we are in touch with a mystery that cannot be too closely shepherded, as in the Torah, or protested against, as in the Prophets."[6] Here Israel discerns what may be believed with conviction while humbly acknowledging that some answers are known only to Yahweh.

Within this matrix of Torah, Prophets, and Wisdom, Israel's spiritual life embraces the 1) salvation history taught by priests, 2) disruptive Word of divine justice proclaimed by prophets, and 3) the moral and ethical wisdom of Sage-Kings.

Arising out of Israel's long experience in transmitting a centered yet dynamic faith that can withstand the scope of human experience, the earliest Christian churches took pains to carefully nurture adult converts and their children in 1) the *worship* of the God of Israel—revealed in Jesus Christ—who by the power of the Holy Spirit continues to be present to the community of faith through proclamation of the Word and sacramental enactment, 2) the *witness* of this community called to discern how to live faithfully in the face of variant personal, social, cultural, and political situations, and 3) through the catechetical practices of teaching and learning, the *wonder* of sharing the *evangel* and confession of Jesus Christ as Lord.

While the forms of the New Testament canon, of course, do not mimic Israel's Torah, Prophets, and Wisdom, we can discern—as a heuristic device—an analogous substructure in the *kerygma* (preaching), *parenesis* (moral or ethical guidance or advice), and *didache* (teaching), interwoven within and across the Gospels, Acts, Letters, and Apocalypse. Under the guidance of the complementary work of itinerant preachers and settled teachers, earliest Christian practice recapitulated Israel's tripartite epistemology, but now with a new focus on Jesus Christ as the one who has opened up God's promises to Israel to the whole world. 1) *In the worship of the community of faith, they heard the preaching of the Gospel of Jesus Christ and participated in sacraments he had instituted,* 2) *In their daily lives, they bore witness to Jesus Christ as Lord of life,* 3) *In educational settings marked by wonder, they grew in their understanding of Scripture and confession of faith in Jesus Christ.*

6. Ibid., 71.

Confession of Faith and Catechesis in the Reformed Tradition

Until the late nineteenth-early twentieth century, catechisms were a key feature in the churches rooted in the magisterial reform. As a fruit of the humanist turn to original sources (*ad fontes*), reformers like Martin Luther and John Calvin had some knowledge of the adult catechumenate in the ancient churches. They knew, for example, of the focus on teaching the baptismal creed, participating in liturgy, and offering moral exhortations. Vexed especially by the moral laxity and ignorance of basic Christian doctrine in their own time, they envied the ancient dictum that linked Christian worship (*lex orandi*), life (*lex vivendi*), and belief (*lex credendi*).

Originally written for clergy and male heads of households, the reformed catechisms were expositions of the Apostles Creed, the Ten Commandments, and the Lord's Prayer and sacraments, though not necessarily in that order. These catechisms had an enormous impact on subsequent generations. Even as late as 1959, Scottish theologian T. F. Torrance complained that the overall educational level of the Scottish people had fallen with the demise of the Westminster *Shorter Catechism*.[7]

As we rethink the place of catechisms today, we should also remember that small editions of the Bible were not common until the eighteenth century. Except for churches, schools, and wealthy households, personal possession of a complete Bible was rare until the early nineteenth century, when the practice of private reading became more common among the laity. With the heightened individualism that accompanied the Enlightenment turn to the self, the practice of private reading eventually led to the novel innovation of the private interpretation of Scripture. The worldwide Sunday School and missionary movements further strengthened this trend toward private biblical interpretation.[8] Thus it is hard for us to appreciate that, long before the Bible was in the hands of the faithful, catechisms functioned as an important aid in understanding biblical sermons in worship.

As the Presbyterian *Book of Confessions* shows, there has always been a strong conviction about the relationship between the church's

7. Torrance, *The School of Faith*, xxix.

8. See "The Doctrinal Basis of the Evangelical Alliance, A.D. 1846," Article Two: "The right and duty of private judgment in the interpretation of the Holy Scriptures" in Schaff, *The Creeds of Christendom*, 827.

confession of faith and catechesis in the reformed stream of Protestant-ism. For example, the Second Helvetic Confession's Chapter 25, 5.233, "Youth to Be Instructed in Godliness," integrates careful instruction from the Ten Commandments on *how to live*, the Apostle's Creed on *how to believe*, and the Lord's Prayer and sacraments on *how to worship*.[9]

While the catechism was too often reduced to a litmus test for orthodoxy in the eighteenth and nineteenth centuries, the Protestant Reformers had richer and broader educational objectives in mind when they introduced this new genre as an aid in nurturing a more vibrant public worship of God and witness to the gospel. By analogy with the Old Testament, Calvin emphasized the offices of Priest, Prophet, and King recapitulated in the person, message, and work of Jesus Christ. He also depicted Christ as the singular exemplar for the life of faith lived *Coram Deo* ("in the presence of God").

While much good work happens in congregations today under the heading of Christian education, many churches have lost the sense of the integral connection between Christ's work as Priest, Prophet, and King, or the connection between what Christians learn in more explicit edu-cational settings, what Christians learn in worship, and what Christians learn from being sent forth, again and again, to live out their vocation in the world as Christ's "afflicted but well-equipped witnesses."[10]

Because of the unresolved tensions between the traditional reformed approach to catechesis, the Bible-centered Sunday school movement, and the child-centered religious education movement, the educational ministries of Protestant congregations today are confused, tending to emphasize one of the following: 1) church-centered socialization based on teaching of Bible and/or doctrine, 2) individual-centered conversion or spirituality, or (3) society-centered witness and reform. While each of these emphases embodies an important aspect of the Reformed tradi-tion, there is an unfortunate tendency to focus on one dimension while neglecting one or two of the others. One wonders if this fragmented ap-proach to the Christian life may be one reason for the deep and enduring divisions between traditional, evangelical, and liberal churches today.

9. *The Constitution of the Presbyterian Church*, 110.

10. Barth, *Church Dogmatics IV/3*, 481.

Confession of Faith and Catechesis: A Contemporary Case

In the mid-1990s, the Presbyterian Church (USA) General Assembly authorized the preparation of two new catechisms. *Belonging to God: A First Catechism* and *The Study Catechism* were approved in 1998 as provisional study documents for educational use in congregations and families. These contemporary catechisms, which were prepared by a committee of leading systematic and practical theologians, including Rick Osmer, were intended to strengthen the doctrinal understanding and Reformed identity of Presbyterians.

Here I need to touch briefly on the historical background behind this development. Recognizing that post-World War II America no longer resembled the *republica christiana* ideal of the Protestant Reformers and that the Westminster Standards were no longer functioning as the *de facto* basis of Presbyterian confession of faith or catechesis, in the 1960s the PC (USA) drafted and approved a new confession (*The Confession of 1967*) and expanded its *Book of Confessions* to include the following ancient, Reformation, post-Reformation, and contemporary documents: *The Nicene Creed* (381), *The Apostles' Creed* (second–eighth centuries), *The Scots Confession* (1560), *The Heidelberg Catechism* (1563), *The Second Helvetic Confession* (1561), *The Westminster Confession of Faith*, *The Shorter Catechism*, *The Larger Catechism* (1647), *The Theological Declaration of Barmen* (1934), and *A Brief Statement of Faith* (1983).[11]

The two new catechisms must be situated within these developments. Given the move away from a "Westminster only" stance, there was a sense among some pastors and theologians that we needed new, contemporary catechisms to help guide the faithful. Five years after their adoption, the denomination's Office of Theology and Worship reported, "The catechisms have not yet fulfilled their promise in the life of the church. Misunderstanding of the nature of catechisms (confusing them with rote memorization, for example) and insufficient awareness of possibilities for their use in a wide variety of educational, liturgical, and devotional settings, have restricted the catechisms' use and limited their value in the church. The Office of Theology and Worship urges that renewed efforts be made to incorporate fully the new catechisms into the church's ministry of the Christian formation of disciples."[12] In

---

11. In 2016, the General Assembly also approved the *Confession of Belhar* (1986), which came out of the South African church's struggle against apartheid.

12. Presbyterian Church (USA), MINUTES of the 215th GENERAL ASSEMBLY,

spite of some early enthusiasm, these catechisms are either neglected or completely unknown by most Presbyterians today.

While I think that this renewed interest in catechesis reflects a positive acknowledgment of how the lines between the gospel, church, and culture have become so blurred in North America, this new interest is not an unambiguous development—a point well expressed by postliberal theologian George Lindbeck in the final chapter of *The Nature of Doctrine*. On the one hand, Lindbeck says that "This method [his "cultural-linguistic" view of doctrine] resembles ancient catechesis more than modern translation. Instead of redescribing the faith in new concepts, it seeks to teach the language and practices of the religion to potential adherents." On the other hand, Lindbeck is gravely pessimistic about any practical application of his proposal in North America. "Western culture is now at an intermediate stage . . . where socialization is ineffective, catechesis impossible, and translation a tempting alternative . . . " Lindbeck leaves the reader with the paradoxical conclusion that, while his postliberal proposal has a family resemblance to the catechesis of the early church, a renewal of catechesis today is ruled out because the churches today are so completely enculturated. "In the present situation, unlike periods of missionary expansion, the churches primarily accommodate to the prevailing culture rather than shape it."[13]

By way of contrast, in 2002 a Japanese translation of the new PC (USA) catechisms was published,[14] and they have been used widely in churches and Christian schools. More importantly, in 2004 this translation helped motivate the National Union of Presbyterian Churches to write their own catechism as well as a church school curriculum based on that catechism.[15] Given the very different missional situation of the minority Japanese churches, perhaps their interest in catechesis is not surprising.

When I was appointed to serve as a missionary in Japan, a wise Japanese pastor told me, "Welcome to Rome in A.D. 150." On the surface, the situation of the churches in Japan and the US are very different. We might

---

PART I JOURNAL (Louisville: Office of the General Assembly, 2003), 565.

13. Lindbeck, *The Nature of Doctrine*, 132–33.

14. ヘイスティングス、田中、神代訳、『みなのカテキズム』、一麦出版社、2002年 [*Catechisms for All Ages,* translation by Hastings, Tanaka, and Kojiro].

15 『明解カテキズム』、関川/泰寛と『カテキズム教案』、全国連合長老会、キリスト新聞社, 2004–2011年 [*A Clear Catechism,* Kekikakwa Yasuhiro with the National Association of Presbyterians].

say that Japan is a "pre-Christendom" and the US is a "post-Christendom" context. In spite of significant differences, Christians in Japan and the US share one deep resemblance: we cannot assume spiritual support and encouragement from our societies. This fact distinguishes us from Christians at the time of the Reformation when the *cuius region, eius religio* ("whose realm, his religion") principle held sway, albeit within the smaller unit of nation, principality, or city-state.

Worship, Witness, and Wonder: Integrating Perception, Action, and Thinking Coram Deo

I want to conclude by proposing *worshipping*, *witnessing*, and *wondering* as complementary practices found in communities of faith marked by a turning from self-centeredness to self-giving, "redemptive love" after the kenotic pattern of Jesus Christ and in the power of the Holy Spirit.

Worship as Practice in Loving God

The God revealed in Jesus Christ is glorified in the public worship of communities of faith gathered in the power of the Holy Spirit. As T. F. Torrance says, "when we encounter the Truth in Christ, we discover that we are at variance with the Truth, in a state of rebellion and enmity toward it, so that the way of knowledge is the way of surrender and acknowledgment through self-denial and repentance."[16] The *worship* of the gathered community is accompanied by other spiritual practices such as prayer, meditation, fasting, spiritual reading, study, self-examination, mutual discernment, hospitality, etc. By participation in practices of *worship*, our desire to love, follow, and know God is renewed through confession of sin, singing, the preaching and hearing of the Word, prayer, celebration of the sacraments, and being sent forth into the world as Christ's witnesses. The canonical referents here are prophecy and kerygma, thus the focus in *worship* is on Jesus Christ as Prophet.

16. Torrance, *The School of Faith*, xxxv.

Witness as Practice in Following God

The vocation of Christians as participant witnesses to the ongoing mission of God is formed, renewed, and sustained in self-giving, redemptive interactions with neighbors, especially those in particular need, in and beyond the community of faith. Afflicted witnesses reflect the pattern of "redemptive love" revealed by Jesus as we learn of him in the Gospel narratives. "Redemptive love" may be described in folksy ethical terms in the following way: "You mess up, I clean up your mess, but do not assign any blame."[17] By participation in liberating practices of witness, our determination to follow, know, and love God is renewed by welcoming, loving, forgiving, standing with, and caring for others in the way of Jesus. As St. Francis purportedly said, "Preach the gospel, and if necessary, use words." The canonical referents here are Wisdom and parenesis, thus the focus in *witness* is on Jesus Christ as Sage-King.

Wonder as Practice in Knowing God

Scripture, confession of faith, church history, theology, literature, and devotional writings are studied, interrogated, and personalized in the company of other pilgrims and in an awareness of "the great cloud of witnesses" who have come before. By participation in educative practices of *wonder*, our longing to know, love, and follow God is renewed through sustained study, conversation, and reflection. Here, "wonder" is not simply the sense of "pre-doubt" awe with which the people of Israel approached Torah, but it also embraces the modern sense of interrogation, suspicion, and doubt, as when we say, "I wonder if that is really the case." The canonical referents here are Torah and didache, thus the focus in *wonder* is on Jesus Christ as Priest.

It is easy to see how the practices of *worshipping*, which accent perception, *witnessing*, which accent action, and *wondering*, which accent thinking, flow into and support each other over a lifetime of discipleship.

For Jesus Christ to become the center of a person's or community's life, that person or community will be transformed in relation to the triune God revealed in Jesus Christ, commitment to God's mission in the world, and grounding in Scripture and confession of faith. This distinctively

17. This view of "redemptive love" is indebted to the work of Kagawa Toyohiko. See Hastings, *Seeing All Things Whole*, 48–105.

Christian epistemology embraces loving, following, and knowing Jesus Christ, and while *loving, following, and knowing* may seem like unrelated activities, Israel, the church, and other long-surviving religious traditions have intuited from long ago that human perception, action, and thinking are deeply intertwined. In spite of the "disembodied" epistemology of the modern West, which, for the sake of clear, rational, scientific analysis, sought to disassociate thought from feeling and action, ancient peoples knew what contemporary neuroscience is rediscovering, which is the irreducibly embodied confluence of thought, feeling, and action.[18]

The "ways of knowing" specific to Christian faith are participatory and holistic, encompassing all dimensions of life. Intuiting that the practices of loving, following, and knowing Jesus Christ are deeply interconnected, worshipping, witnessing, and wondering communities engage in proclamation, evangelism, and catechesis[19] as fitting responses to God's mission. Keeping the focus on God's self-emptying mission in Jesus Christ and in the power of the Holy Spirit, Christian practices of proclamation, evangelism, and catechesis are never seen as ends in themselves and always conducted with humility and assurance.

In our own time, while the settings for *worshipping, witnessing, and wondering* may be distinct, it is important to reconceive these practices as a unified whole. To do this, it is helpful to see these practices christologically, i.e., in analogy to the unity of Word, person, and act in the God/person Jesus Christ.

What might congregations do in their response to the ever-sufficient grace of God in Jesus Christ to help nurture and sustain a community of *worshipping, witnessing, and wondering* disciples across a lifetime? While the church's ministries will embrace all three of these movements, it is important to remember that our efforts are always contingent on Christ who comes to us "clothed with his Gospel" (Calvin) and the mediation of the Holy Spirit. While God's people may be divided and broken—sometimes desperately so—Christ's Word, Person, and Act are always inseparably one.[20] Since he is the singular focus of our loving, following, and knowing, the church's preachers and teachers need not obsess about achieving some balance between the various modes of knowing. As we keep the focus on Jesus Christ as he comes to us in the Gospel narratives,

18. Johnson, "Embodied Understanding," 875.

19. These days, evangelical traditions use the term *discipleship* and mainline Protestants opt for *spiritual formation,* but we have chosen the classical term.

20. Torrance, *The School of Faith,* xxxii.

we discover that worship is not limited to feelings, witness is not just about moral exhortations to right action, and wonder is not limited to our cognitive function.

We can only touch briefly here on the key question of divine agency. In an article entitled "Practical Theology and Theological Education," James Fowler pointed out the following "two deep sources of concern and reservation" regarding the leading contemporary approaches to practical theology: 1) Their failure to account for divine agency; and (2) their imprisonment in an Enlightenment rationality.[21] Under the sway of the modernist epistemology, practical theologians have been reticent to say much about the decisive role of divine agency in the church's practices of proclamation, evangelism, and catechesis. Seeking to address this significant omission, James E. Loder wrote, "In practical theology the disciplines that will help us understand human action must be put into a constructive relationship with the disciplines that enable us to understand who God is from God's self-disclosure. The systematic task of practical theology, then, is to preserve the integrity of such disciplines and . . . relate them so as to gain a more comprehensive understanding of the phenomenon in question than any one such discipline may be able to provide by itself. At the same time, such a relation should enrich both sides of this interdisciplinary endeavor."[22]

Theologically, the ordering of the intersecting spheres of worship, witness, and wonder picks up on the ancient pattern of *lex orandi est lex credendi et vivendi* ("The rule of prayer is the rule of belief and of life"). While we may be reluctant to say too much about divine agency in relation to these ecclesial practices, we must not be silent by saying less than is warranted by Scripture. By refocusing our practices of proclamation, evangelism, and catechesis on the completed work of Christ as Priest, Prophet, and King, we not only keep before us an exemplar of how these ways of knowing interpenetrate and complement one another, but we may also expect the Holy Spirit to lift us continually beyond our natural capacities to seek "our spiritual lives not in ourselves but in Christ, and so find the real truth of our own personal being in union with our Lord and Savior."[23]

---

21. Fowler, "Practical Theology and Theological Education," 56.
22. Loder, "Normativity and Context in Practical Theology," 359–81.
23. Torrance, *The School of Faith*, xxxvii.

Bibliography

A Clear Catechism. Sekikawa Yasuhiro and the National Association of Presbyterians. Tokyo: Kirisuto Shinbumsha, 2004–2011.

Barth, Karl. *Church Dogmatics: Volume IV/3*. Edinburgh: T & T Clark, 1962.

Brueggemann, Walter. *The Creative Word: Canon as a Model for Biblical Education*. Philadelphia: Fortress, 1982.

Catechisms for All Ages. Translated by Thomas John Hastings, et al. Sapporo: Ichibaku, 2002.

Fowler, James W. "Practical Theology and Theological Education: Some Models and Questions." *Theology Today* 42 (1985) 43–58.

Hastings, Thomas John. *Seeing All Things Whole: The Scientific Mysticism and Art of Kagawa Toyohiko (1888–1960)*. Eugene, OR: Pickwick, 2015.

Johnson, Mark. "Embodied Understanding." *Frontiers in Psychology* 6 (2015) 875. https://www.frontiersin.org/article/10.3389/fpsyg.2015.00875.

J. N. D. Kelly, *Early Christian Creeds*. London: Longman, 1972.

Lindbeck, George. *The Nature of Doctrine: Religion and Theology in a Postliberal Age*. Philadelphia: Westminster, 1984.

Loder, James E. "Normativity and Context in Practical Theology: The Interdisciplinary Issue." In *Practical Theology: International Perspectives*, edited by Friedrich Schweitzer and J. A. van der Ven, 359–81. New York: Peter Lang, 1999.

Presbyterian Church (USA). MINUTES of the 215th GENERAL ASSEMBLY, PART I JOURNAL (Louisville: Office of the General Assembly, 2003), 565.

Schaff, Philip. *The Creeds of Christendom (Volume III): The Creeds of the Evangelical Protestant Churches*. New York: Harper and Brothers, 1877.

Torrance, Thomas F. *The School of Faith: The Catechisms of the Reformed Church*. London: James Clarke and Company, 1959.

The Constitution of the Presbyterian Church (USA), Part I: The Book of Confessions, in The Second Helvetic Confession, Chapter XXV, "Of Catechizing and Comforting and Visiting the Sick." Louisville, KY: Office of the General Assembly, 2002.

Westerhoff, John H. and O. C. Edwards, *A Faithful Church: Issues in the History of Catechesis*. Wilton, CT: Morehouse-Barlow, 1981.

10

Meaning, Belonging, and Being Open

Missional Theology and the Evangelization of Emerging Adults

DREW A. DYSON

IN THE SPRING OF 2011, Richard Osmer delivered an important series of lectures, the Princeton Lectures on Youth, Church, and Culture, entitled "Evangelism in an Age of Religious Diversity" and "Interreligious Dialogue in an Age of Diversity." In the first lecture, drawing on the work of Karl Barth, he defines evangelism as "the ministry by which the Holy Spirit uses the members of the church to awaken others to the gospel, to the good news of God's gracious love toward the world in Jesus Christ."[1] He uses a missional framework for his interpretation of evangelism, noting that evangelism is not about "promoting one pattern of religious experience or gaining new church members," but is centered in "giving witness to the gospel" following the prompting of the Holy Spirit.[2]

In developing this definition, Osmer draws on the work of Karl Barth, particularly a section of *Dogmatics* called "The Awakening to Conversion." On Osmer's view, Barth emphasizes Christ's representative nature, noting that "In turning away from sin and toward his Father in

---

1. Osmer, "Evangelism in an Age of Religious Diversity," 8.
2. Ibid.

faith and obedience, he is doing what humanity cannot do for itself."[3] Christ is able to do for humanity what humanity is unable to do; namely, to break the power of sin and death, turning to God in a restored relationship through grace alone. Conversion is therefore our participation in the conversion of Christ—awakening and reawakening from the slumber of sin to new life and restored relationship with God through Christ.

This definition of evangelism leads Osmer to offer three practical implications for the church's ministry of "awakening" others to the gospel. First, Osmer contends that the ministry of evangelism can no longer be focused solely on those "out there," beyond the walls of the church.[4] The notion of awakening—and reawakening—faith in Christ leads to the important notion that evangelism is a continuing act in the life of the Christian. In a diverse cultural milieu, Osmer contends, there is no single program or method for effective evangelism. Rather, faithful Christians and communities of faith must be open to the leading of the Holy Spirit in order to identify opportunities for witness and discern an appropriate approach. Finally, Osmer challenges the church to be open to the ministry of witnessing to its faith in Christ because of the church's need for conversion, not solely for the "other."[5] The church needs itself to experience an awakening to fresh insights into the gospel that derive from being in ministry with those who are newly awakened to life in Christ.

The insights that arise in Osmer's work are particularly important for the church contending in the midst of such a diverse context as in North America. Osmer's work serves as a challenge to the church to "awaken" itself to the ministry of evangelism, and to experience the Holy Spirit's awakening and empowering movement to engage people—especially young people—beyond the church's walls. At the same time, one is left to wonder, what does this holy engagement look like in practice? In addition to requiring the church to be open to its own conversion under the Spirit's guidance, *how* does a community of faith go about engaging young people in the current cultural milieu in order to "offer them Christ"?

---

3. Ibid., 7.

4. Ibid.

5. Ibid., 10.

Effective Evangelism with Emerging Adults

This essay examines Osmer's challenge to reclaim evangelism as a congregational practice in mainline congregations, by exploring the evangelization of emerging adults in three local congregations in radically different contexts. Ample empirical evidence underscores the commonly held assumption that young adults are churches' "invisible generation."[6] But churches do not need empirical data to know they have a problem with emerging adults. The evidence for emerging adult faith drift is borne out anecdotally every Sunday morning in mainline churches whose pews are filled with older congregants wondering where all the young people have gone.

The truth is that most young people simply do not care that mainline Protestant denominations are rapidly declining, or that congregations struggle to remain connected and influential in their lives. Our goal as church leaders , therefore, must not be to salvage our institutions, but to become the communities of authentic belonging and missional engagement that emerging adults crave—and in so doing create an approach to evangelism that effectively engages them. To better understand this kind of evangelism, I went in search of congregations who effectively practiced it. I then completed qualitative case studies of three of them—congregations recognized by regional leaders as having successful ministries of evangelism with emerging adults.[7] The question I sought to answer was what made these churches successful in addressing emerging adults within and beyond the church community? What did these congrega-

6. The moniker "invisible generation" refers to the rapidly growing cohort of younger adults who have disengaged from active involvement in the Christian life in and through mainline congregations. See Martinson, "Spiritual but not Religious." Also see Wuthnow, *After the Babyboomers;* Hoge et al.,"Determinants of Church Involvement of Young Adults"; Barna, "Most Twenty Somethings Put Christianity on the Shelf"; Willits and Crider, "Church Attendance and Religious Beliefs"; and Grossman, "Young Adults aren't Sticking with the Church."

7. According to Creswell, "a case study is an exploration of a 'bounded system' or a case (or multiple cases) over time through detailed, in-depth data collection involving multiple sources of information in rich context." This research project began as three distinct "within-case analyses," investigating the particular cases and creating a thick description of emerging themes. From there, it expanded into a "cross-case analysis," linking themes that emerge from these exemplary cases and examining similarities and differences in order to provide different lenses through which to view the driving research question. Case studies allow the researcher to paint a picture, to tell a story that illuminates how a given phenomenon plays out in a given context. See Creswell, *Qualitative Inquiry and Research Design,* 61.

tions do that called emerging adults into the life of Christian faith, and integrated them meaningfully into the life of the faith community?

By exploring three "best practices"[8] congregations, it is not my intent to offer you three models of ministry with young people to be tweaked and cloned to fit other situations. In fact, a clear danger in case study research is highlighting a few specific cases and making broad theoretical generalizations or applications.[9] Instead, we can make "petite generalizations" that offer insight into how these communities, in their specific contexts, have effectively connected emerging adults with a life of faith and life in community. The pages that follow highlight how three communities wrestled to discern unique, contextualized ministry pathways that effectively engage disconnected young adults with faith and a faith community.

Young People with Passion: Outreach Red Bank (The ORB)

Outreach Red Bank (ORB) began as a ministry reaching out to un-churched youth in the shore community of Red Bank, New Jersey. Many of the members of the founding group of ORB were young adults that were serving as volunteer youth leaders for a large mainline church in the neighboring town. A conflict arose in that ministry about the leaders' desire to reach out to youth who weren't already a part of the church. Many of the parents of the church kids resisted their outreach efforts and the interim pastor supported the desires of the parents for a more internally focused ministry. As a result of the conflict, some of the leaders and other interested adults began to meet and pray about how God was calling them to be in ministry with the unchurched youth in the community and to discern God's leading for that ministry.

After several months of prayerful discernment, this group of adults began a ministry reaching out to youth on the streets of Red Bank. They spent time in skate parks, coffee shops, and malls getting to know the youth in their natural environments. Eventually, they began a Bible study

8. "Best practices" research enables the qualitative researcher to investigate cases that have proven exemplary in a given area to discern what empowered their success. In a cross-case analysis, best practices research identifies the "threads" that run through multiple cases to develop *petite* rather than *grand* generalizations. See Eglene, "Conducting Best and Current Practices Research."

9 "The real business of case study is particularization, not generalization." See Stake, *The Art of Case Study Research*, 7–8.

in one of the skate parks and about fifteen youth joined four leaders in the first ORB event. From there, an intergenerational worshipping community developed as youth began inviting their parents and other adults in their lives to experience God's grace as they had through this vital ministry.

Through observation and interviews, three distinct theological commitments of Outreach Red Bank emerge as central to their life and ministry: sin and grace, missional vocation, and hospitality. When asked about the theological commitments of the congregation, the founding pastor responded, "It begins with a clear understanding of our sinfulness and our desperate need for God's grace. We truly believe that our need for grace levels the playing field. When every member of the community understands the depth of our own sin and our utter reliance on God's grace, then there is truly a place for everyone." Mandy, another emerging adult participant in the young adult group, concurs: "We learn here that God loves the real you, sins and all, not the fake person that you show yourself to be."

Another key theological commitment framing the ministry of Outreach Red Bank is a deep awareness of individual and corporate missional vocation. For Christian, the lead pastor, missional vocation is at the heart of this community. "The heartbeat of this ministry is a sense that God is up to something here in Red Bank and has given us—as individuals and as a community—a role in carrying out God's mission. It is the *missio Dei* that drives us to receive grace, live in grace, and extend grace. That's our center." The missional shape of the church inherently transmits an understanding that Christians are not here for themselves—but for a world in need of God's grace. Thus, when youth begin to understand God's grace and come alive to their identity in Christ they seek ways to be in ministry and carry out the mission of God in the world. Youth experience God's grace and catch a fire to be a part of the ministry of ORB, not for institutional survival but because of a call to be a part of God's mission in the world.

Finally, ORB is clearly marked by a deep theological commitment to divine hospitality. It is striking when one visits any of the ministries of Outreach Red Bank that there is a wide array of people from varied social, economic, and age cohorts. The basement during a Thursday night youth gathering, led entirely by emerging adult leaders, is filled with young people from myriad social clusters interacting freely among themselves and with the leaders. In a typical American high school these groups would be deeply stratified. Chris, one of the older youth in the group and a self-described "skate rat," says freely, "This is the place where I came to love myself, to be okay with who I am and not be ashamed of who I am. When I came for the first time, the leaders and even the other kids, they just, well, embraced me. This place is so amazing because people are able to come and just be who they are."

In their love for one another and their profound acceptance and welcome of all people, Outreach Red Bank stands as a contrast community within an area deeply imbued with economic stratification, social group stigmatization, and an active drug culture. At the same time, the alternative community experienced at ORB does not lead to impermeable boundaries that define the church as over and against the prevailing culture. Rather, in a beautiful and poignant way, the contrast community of Outreach Red Bank shines as a beacon of God's radical welcome extended to all humanity.

A Church Willing to Lay Down Its Life: The Wine Cellar

The Wine Cellar, an outreach ministry of the Bloomsbury and Asbury United Methodist Churches in rural New Jersey, came into existence when a small, struggling congregation challenged themselves to invest significantly into the future of the church in the face of their pending closure. Facing the prospect of closure, the pastor of the church challenged the congregation to pursue life in the face of death. "I put the question before them," she offered, "as to what type of legacy they wanted the church to leave and whether or not they wanted to go out swinging." She invited a small group of key leaders to join her in dreaming of what the future might hold. They met together at the church for several months and dreamed together about possibilities for ministry in their community. Within a few months, the young people and the pastoral leaders approached the leaders of the congregation with a bold plan for a new ministry.

With the blessing of the church leadership and a commitment of significant financial and physical resources amounting to the majority of the church's savings, the team secured additional funding and began converting the lower level of the church building into a "high-tech, low-key" facility complete with satellite television, high-speed internet, printing and computer services, café tables, comfortable seating areas, and a full-service kitchen. The transformation of the space was amazing in its own right, but the loving care of parishioners who donated additional funds, purchased furniture, painted walls and doors, laid new flooring, renovated the kitchen, made curtains and pillows, and prayed regularly in the space long before it opened, was even more striking. This new venture was not only the mission of a pastor and a few young people, it was truly the mission of two congregations, one of which knew that the birth of this ministry may very well lead to its own closure.[10]

The first theological pillar holding up the foundation of The Wine Cellar is a profound appreciation and awareness of God's grace active in the lives of the young people in the community.[11] For the pastor, an emphasis on prevenient grace lies at the heart of this vital ministry.[12] "This ministry begins from a real awareness that God is already present and active in these young people's lives. God is nudging them, and loving them, and stirring in them, long before they walk through the cellar doors. We see our role in this ministry as nurturing their awareness of this grace, and opening clear pathways of invitation leading to their acceptance of God's gift of love poured out for them."

The community of The Wine Cellar is also marked by a thorough commitment to a Wesleyan notion of sanctification as the growth in holiness of heart and life.[13] As young people awaken to God's activity in their lives, and open themselves up to receive that grace, there is an emphasis on learning to live as missional witnesses to that grace. That includes, for these young people, being formed and transformed through Scripture,

10. Eventually, the Wine Cellar closed its doors. Rather than pointing to a failed ministry, however, this serves to illustrate the fluid nature of ministry among emerging generations.

11. As a United Methodist ministry, The Wine Cellar is deeply rooted in its Wesleyan theological heritage and the distinctive way John Wesley understood the Christian doctrine of grace. See Rakestraw, "John Wesley as a Theologian of Grace."

12. Prevenient grace, on Wesley's view, was the critical doctrine that enabled him to affirm the total depravity of human kind. Essentially, prevenient grace is an expression of God's grace that surrounds and indwells all of humanity prior to, and regardless of, their own awareness of that grace. It is the presence of God in the Holy Spirit that gently, and sometimes relentlessly, moves humans towards an awareness of their own sin, and into a saving relationship with Jesus Christ. Ibid., 196.

13. Wesley's notion of sanctification as the growth of holiness of heart and life constitutes a "faith-response to God's grace-initiative," meaning that good works do not produce holiness, but rather God's grace works in the person of faith through the means of grace to gradually form her in holiness on the road to Christian perfection. See ibid., 200.

prayer, and corporate worship and being sent into the world and empowered to live out our faith."

It is clear that while a holistic Wesleyan understanding of grace runs throughout The Wine Cellar, prevenient grace lies at the heart of the ministry in its current form. This emphasis on prevenient grace, with a concentrated effort to invite all young people into the community to experience an awakening to the presence of grace that is already present in their lives, leads to a complementary theological pillar of the community, namely, divine hospitality.[14] When asked to identify the one central feature of The Wine Cellar, most young people emphasized in different ways the profound acceptance one experiences when they walk through the basement doors. "From the moment I walked in," Brandon offered, "I was accepted and welcomed. There was no judgment. There was no fear. There was no hatred. I was loved and I just felt it. Being gay, I haven't really felt that way in church before."

A Bishop with a Vision: Saint Laurence

In 2000, Anglican pastor Chris Russell received a call from the bishop of the Diocese of Oxford that changed his life and gave new direction to his ministry. Chris recalls, "The bishop called to ask if I would pray about a vision that God had laid on his heart for a revitalized parish church in Reading focused on building church with the young people of the community." After significant prayer, encouragement from his peers and family, extended conversations with the vicar from another parish in the community, and further discussions with the bishop and archdeacon, Chris accepted the invitation and the ministry of St. Laurence in Reading was reborn with a vision "to see young people come to faith and build new forms of church with them."[15] Along with a small team of leaders, Chris moved to Reading and opened the church in 2001 under this new mandate.

Similar to Outreach Red Bank, St. Laurence's is an intergenerational faith community that understands its missional vocation as living the gospel among young people in the community, calling young people to

14. Following Amy Oden, I use divine hospitality to refer to God's welcome extended by communities of faith to all people as a means of welcoming people into God's gift of abundant life, not simply a warm and fuzzy welcome into a community of friends. See Oden, *God's Welcome*.

15. "Mission," St. Laurence, Reading.

faith in Jesus Christ, and finding ways to build "fresh expressions"[16] of church with them. While the primary focus of the church's outreach efforts is with young people from the primary and secondary schools in Reading, numerous emerging adults have partnered with St. Laurence in living out this missional identity. The emerging adults participate in this mission as staff people of the church, volunteer leaders in the youth ministry, worship leaders and musicians, administrative personnel, and more.

There are three key theological commitments guiding the work of St. Laurence: invitational witness, missional vocation, and a theology of place. The ministry of St. Laurence is marked by a continual invitation for young people to respond to the love of God offered in Jesus Christ. "We want to always be clear," Chris opines, "Christianity is more than just a worldview. It is a response to what happened in and through one person, Jesus Christ. It is not our intent to simply do youth work that serves the young people of Reading, it is our intent to see young people come to faith in Jesus Christ. What we do here is invitational at its core." The invitation to follow Christ permeates the ministry of St. Laurence, from the Wednesday afternoon lunchtime club that meets in the public high school to Monday night youth club at the church.

The missional vocation of the church is centered in its ministry with youth in the community of Reading. Every member of the parish church understands and embraces the centrality of this mission in the church's life and witness. The leaders of St. Laurence understand that the church is a living response to the work of God in Jesus Christ, and that the call of the faith community is to continue this story of God's inviting, incarnational love.

The renovated twelfth century building standing in the heart of Reading at the gates of the Abbey serves as a central element of the church's ministry. "We have a deeply rooted theology of place, to use John Inge's term,"[17] the Vicar explains. "In an age when so many people argue against the significance of buildings, we believe that the incarnational presence of the church and its history in Reading is truly significant to

16 Fresh Expressions is a term coined by the Anglican Communion to call forth "new forms of church for a rapidly changing world." See "Fresh Expressions Homepage," http://www.freshexpressions.org.uk/

17. Inge puts forth the notion that the biblical paradigm for the sacramental human encounter with God occurs at the nexus of "place, people, and God." See Inge, *A Christian Theology of Place*, x.

our ministry with young people." As the largest provider of youth work in the city, St. Laurence's location in the center of the town square provides young people with a clearly identifiable safe haven from the complexities and challenges of life.

Meaning, Belonging, and Being Open: Theological Commitments and Ministry Directions

Emerging from these case studies are three key threads of theological commitment weaving throughout each story that bind these communities together: a clear understanding of individual and corporate Christian vocation, or purposeful work; a strong sense of identity and belonging within the community of faith; and a posture of radical openness and hospitality to the community beyond the church.

Meaning and Purpose

It was interesting to discover in this research that all three ministries representing different theological heritages claim missional vocation as the guiding principle for the formation of their respective congregations, not simply for their ministries with emerging adults. Darrell L. Guder asserts that the missional nature of the church is chiefly to make known the joyful message of salvation to the world. "That is how God's mission now continues. The center or core of the *missio Dei* is evangelization: the communication of the gospel. Carrying the good news across all borders and into all the world is an essential part of the kingdom message which Jesus brought and embodied."[18] Each of these communities calls emerging adults to be active agents of missional transformation rather than passive recipients of the church's ministry programs.

Outreach Red Bank was developed as a missional community that understands its particular vocation as reaching out to unchurched youth in Red Bank; from the outset the stated mission was "becoming a community of grace where *youth* can come to know Jesus Christ." In that way, they saw themselves forming a community that was striving to live faithfully as disciples of Jesus Christ and making the story of salvation known to the young people in their sphere of influence. The Asbury United Methodist Church wrestled with the question of how God was

18. Guder, *The Continuing Conversion of the Church*, 49.

calling them to participate in God's mission in the face of their immi-nent closure. Through an intentional process of prayer and discernment, the small congregation decided to invest a significant portion of their remaining savings as well as their limited people resources in the devel-opment of The Wine Cellar. At St. Laurence, the missional vocation of the congregation is bound in its preferential option for young people as they seek to be a parish church for the youth in Reading. The vicar explains, "While we are a parish church and serve an intergenerational commu-nity, we are clearly outward focused and we ask everyone in the church to support our ministry with the young people, whether in leading, serving, giving, or praying. This is our vocation as a church and it is what we have heard God calling and sending us to do in the world."

Belonging in Community

All three congregations have worked hard to develop communities within which emerging adults can experience true belonging and from which a clear identity as members crystallizes. The words of Sidney, a self-identi-fied "member" of the Wine Cellar, echo across each story: "Before I came here, I was sort of lost, you know? I knew . . . or at least thought I knew . . . that I wasn't wanted anywhere near a church. But when Isaiah brought me here, I immediately felt like I belonged . . . like I was always meant to be here." Whether sitting around the warm fireplace in the basement of the Wine Cellar, the old couches and comfy chairs in Red Bank, or the contemporary loft of an ancient building in Reading, England, scores of emerging adults have discovered authentic community and religious belonging. These churches have countered the trend that emerging adults do not experience authentic belonging in the church.[19]

A salient feature of the Christian identity formed through participa-tion in the community of faith, as evident in all three cases, is a willing-ness to extend the grace received to others. Jill recalls her first meeting with Pastor Gina: "When I first met Gina, I was a mess! My life was falling apart and she welcomed me without judgment or condemnation. Through her, the church embraced me and I came to really put my life back together . . . Now my ministry here is to do the same thing for other kids who were a mess like I was."

19. Smith, *Souls in Transition*, 152.

Radical Hospitality and Genuine Openness

This conspicuous presence of God's deep welcome for all young people has clearly left a mark on the faith community of Outreach Red Bank. There is no doubt that this congregation understands its primary mission as being living witnesses to God's grace so that all people can experience that gift of grace—regardless of who they are, where they have been, or what they have done. For the leadership of St. Laurence, radical hospitality stems from the longing to see young people come to faith in Jesus Christ and the continual invitation extended. Through invitational witness, the emerging adult leaders offer a message of acceptance and invitation for the youth of the community to join them in following Christ. Hospitality in this community is also deeply rooted in their theology of place, in the identification of the church as the parish church for the young people of Reading. As an incarnational presence in the community, and through the witness of the building's restoration, there is a clear message to the young people of Reading that they are welcomed by the church, and by God.

In all three settings, there is a deep openness and receptivity of the people, particularly young people, who do not identify themselves as Christians. In their practice of welcome at the beginning of every corporate gathering, someone from the community of Outreach Red Bank will step forward and announce something like, "This is a place where we want you to feel and experience a deep sense of belonging. Here, you can be who you are and know that you are loved. Here, some of us are Christians, and it is our hope that you come to experience God's love and grace as we did. But you don't have to be a Christian to be here . . . or to belong here. You just have to be you."

Stories of congregations such as these that are effectively reaching emerging adults and engaging them in community life fall like buckets of rain on the parched, dry land offering hope to struggling churches. Strikingly, the programmatic ministries offered in the three congregations we have explored do not differ greatly from other congregations who have attempted to effectively engage emerging adults. One cannot look here for "tricks of the trade" for effective evangelism with young people. What we can discern, however, is the work that led each of these congregations and their leaders to create such ministries. By undertaking the painstaking work of contextualization, by learning the unique developmental needs of emerging adults taking shape in their communities, and by identifying the particular gifts and resources that their congregations offer, these churches have effectively lived out their missional calling with and for young people. Not coincidentally, every church found bridge-building connective tissue between the congregation and emerging adults in their theological DNA, especially in Christian teaching around meaning, belonging, and openness to others.

Each of these case studies tells a unique story about a particular people who discerned that God was calling and equipping them to participate in the *missio Dei* by developing ministries that would invite young people into lives of faith and life in community. Once they discerned that calling, they each set about the difficult task of contextualization and developed ministries that flowed from their gifts and resources and were reflective of their unique context. The missional heartbeat of these congregations underscores the importance of recovering a revitalized and robust missional ecclesiology as the starting point for developing a faithful ministry of evangelism with and among emerging adults. Standing alone, each story is a powerful witness to God's work of grace in and through a community of faith that offers hope for church's attempting to reach "the invisible generation." Seen together, these stories can point congregations towards more holistic, effective ministries of evangelism with emerging adults.

Bibliography

Arnett, Jeffrey Jensen. *Emerging Adulthood: The Winding Road from the Late Teens through the Twenties*. New York: Oxford University Press, 2004.

Barna, Geroge. "Most Twenty Somethings Put Christianity on the Shelf Following Spiritually Active Teenage Years." *The Barna Update*, September 11, 2006. http://www.barna.org/barna-update/article/16-teensnext-gen/147-most-twentysomethings-put-christianity-on-the-shelf-following-spiritually-active-teen-years.

Creswell, John C. *Qualitative Inquiry and Research Design: Choosing Among Five Traditions*. Thousand Oaks, CA: Sage, 1998.

Emmerson, Michael O., and Christian Smith. *Divided By Faith: Evangelical Religion and the Problem of Race in America*. New York: Oxford University Press, 2000.

Eglene, Ophelia. "Conducting Best and Current Practices Research: A Starter Kit." SUNY Center for Technology Research Center. https://www.ctg.albany.edu/media/pubs/pdfs/conducting_best.pdf.

"Fresh Expressions Homepage." Fresh Expressions, July 2, 2010. http://www.freshexpressions.org.uk/.

Guder, Darrell. *The Continuing Conversion of the Church*. Grand Rapids: Eerdmans, 2000.

Grossman, Cathy Lynn. "Young Adults aren't Sticking with the Church." *USA Today*, August 6, 2007. http://www.usatoday.com/news/religion/2007-08-06-church-dropouts_N.htm.

Hoge, Dean R., et al. "Determinants of Church Involvement of Young Adults Who Grew up in Presbyterian Churches." *Journal for the Scientific Study of Religion* 32 (September 1993) 242–55.

Inge, John. *A Christian Theology of Place*. Burlington: Ashgate, 2003.

Martinson, Roland. "Spiritual but not Religious: Reaching an Invisible Generation." *Currents in Theology and Mission* 29, (2002) 326–40.

"Mission." St. Laurence ReadingAugust 21, 2010. https://www.stlreading.org/who-we-are-1/.

Oden, Amy. *God's Welcome: Hospitality for a Gospel-Hungry World*. Cleveland, OH: Pilgrim, 2008.

Osmer, Richard R. *Practical Theology: An Introduction*. Grand Rapids: Eerdmans, 2008.

————. "Evangelism in an Age of Religious Diversity." Paper presented at the Princeton Lectures on Youth, Church, and Culture, Princeton, NJ, 2011. http://www.ptsem.edu/lectures/?action=tei&id=youth-2011-02

————. *The Teaching Ministry of Congregations*. Louisville, KY: Westminster John Knox, 2005.

"Millennials: A Portrait of Generation Next; Confident. Connected. Open to Change." Pew Research Center, February 24, 2010. http://assets.pewresearch.org/wp-content/uploads/sites/3/2010/10/millennials-confident-connected-open-to-change.pdf.

Rakestraw, Robert V. "John Wesley as a Theologian of Grace." *Journal of the Evangelical Theological Society* 27 (1984) 193–203.

Smith, Christian. *American Evangelicalism: Embattled and Thriving*. Chicago: The University of Chicago Press, 1998.

————. *Souls in Transition: The Religious and Spiritual Lives of Emerging Adults.* New York: Oxford University Press, 2009.

Stake, Robert E. *The Art of Case Study Research.* Thousand Oaks, CA: Sage, 1995.

Willits, F. K., and D. M. Crider. "Church Attendance and Religious Beliefs in Adolescence and Young Adulthood: A Panel Study." *Review of Religious Research* 31 (1989) 68–81.

Wuthnow, Robert. *After the Babyboomers: How Twenty- and Thirty-Somethings are Shaping the Future of American Religion.* Princeton, NJ: Princeton University Press, 2007.

SECTION FOUR

THE PRACTICAL THEOLOGIAN:
LEGACY AND PROMISE

11

A *Fundamental Practical Theologian: Karl Barth*

BLAIR D. BERTRAND

Every Seven Days

FOR THE PASTOR, SUNDAY comes with grinding regularity. Every seven days, whatever has happened during those seven days, the preacher mounts the pulpit and attempts to speak a word from God. For some, this regularity can be one of the less enjoyable aspects of being a preaching practical theologian. Few are the pastors who didn't wish that people could die at more convenient times. Or that crises might unfold in a timely manner. Or that other important ministry tasks weren't as time consuming. The routine of weekly preaching gets disturbed by important and necessary responsibilities such as funerals, counseling, and teaching.

Routine is another word for methodology. Each preacher configures their week differently but all have a method of arriving on Sunday morning with a sermon. To use Richard Osmer's language, sermon preparation includes a descriptive, interpretative, normative, and pragmatic moment. When a routine gets disturbed, the method must accommodate. All parts remain but in attenuated form. There is a process of evaluation that happens: does this news item demand a response? Does this article add to my understanding of what is going on? Do I have enough time to read this commentary? Do I need to revise this manuscript one more time? Preaching is always the art of the good enough and we constantly evaluate our method against that standard, fitting our method into the time that we have.

While the pressures of time force an ongoing evaluation of method, they have the opposite effect on some more fundamental material assumptions that all practical theologians make. No matter what is going on, a preacher can't rework an understanding of revelation through Scripture every single week. There isn't enough time. When things change those things that are foundational become even more important. The freedom to evaluate and change our method comes from the fact that we have a foundation of material assumptions.

This reality, that there are fundamental assumptions that every practical theologian makes that are separate from the method of our work, often gets missed when discussing Osmer's work. This is true both of what Osmer calls "second level of methodological reflection"[1] or "the metatheoretical level of research and theory-construction"[2] and of his work itself. This chapter proceeds in two steps. First, it gives an account of these second level assumptions common to all practical theologians. Second, it demonstrates how Osmer's late career shift towards Karl Barth makes sense in light of these assumptions. Osmer's shift to Barth points to ways that Barth might fund other practical theologians, including the preacher caught in a time crunch on Saturday night.

Fundamentals of Practical Theology

Osmer first articulated his second level reflections in the epilogue to *The Teaching Ministry of Congregations* and confirmed them in "Practical Theology: a current international perspective." There are four second order assumptions:

1. the theory-praxis relationship

2. sources of justification

3. models of cross-disciplinary work

4. theological rationale

1. Osmer, *The Teaching Ministry of Congregations*, 306.

2. Osmer and Nel, "Practical Theology," 1–2.

Osmer's description of these second order assumptions is relatively sparse. Definitions are outlined but not detailed. Examples of these categories at work are more general or autobiographical. For instance, Osmer offers the example of Elaine Graham's work that "hang[s] together" into a cohesive paradigm or interpretive framework because she is consistent across all four categories.[3] In practice, Osmer and others such as Graham work out the relationship between these four constitutive parts but he has not done so theoretically.

At a minimum, "hanging together" requires consistency. Answers within one category are mutually exclusive; it is very difficult to understand the theory-praxis relationship in both neo-Marxist and neo-Aristotelian terms. This exclusiveness then bleeds into other answers. Neo-Marxists should tend to find experience more authoritative while neo-Aristotelians will usually find tradition more compelling, causing them to justify their theological projects with different arguments. Making a certain decision in one category will generally lead to complementary answers in other categories. This begs the question, "Is there a primal category that determines the rest or is it inconsequential which category a practical theologian begins with?" If there is a primal category that has logical precedence, it follows that there is actually some kind of third order reflection foundational to the first (the four moments) and the second (the four categories).

It is my conviction that when it comes to doing practical theology there is a primal category, namely the theological "tradition" from which one comes. I am moving beyond what Osmer might argue. In saying that Osmer's category "theological rationale" is primal and logically prior to other considerations, I assume that theological traditions have both a historical component, collective and individual, as well as a material component. Each of us inhabits a historical space that we receive without having any agency in its creation. Just as no single individual created a language, no single individual created a particular way of construing the world theologically. At the same time, like language, every theologian uses the received heritage in unique ways. Collective history has a dynamic relationship with our individual history. No individual is the perfect embodiment of a particular tradition. Rather, each individual molds it and adapts it according to particular contexts. This vision of a dynamic relationship between tradition and individual agency is important to

---

3. Ibid., 4.

ward off the two-sided temptation of either pigeonholing individuals or despairing of any common language to describe ourselves. To pigeonhole is to give too much weight to some theoretical and static vision of a tradition. We then can dismiss someone simply by saying, "Oh that person is just a _____" and not engage in their particularity. To despair of common language is to deny the traditions that each of us operate in. While each of us exerts agency, we do so in conversation with our own tradition and therefore descriptive phrases such as Reformed or Roman Catholic can partly point to the reality of a given individual.

This understanding of tradition in relation to an individual does not exclude the fact that each tradition is made up of material content. We are bequeathed answers to commonly held theological questions. I have in mind the various treatments of doctrines captured in typologies used to differentiate traditions. Whatever we may think of Gustav Aulen's atonement typologies or H. Richard Niebuhr's Christ/culture framework there is no doubt that they describe different traditions from a material perspective. A practical theologian standing within a tradition which supports penal substitutionary atonement differs from one who supports a moral exemplar view. Further, these answers are tied together with other doctrinal questions. To support a moral exemplar view is to hold a particular kind of Christology which further necessitates a specific doctrine of God that is grounded in a specific doctrine of revelation and so on. This constellation of theological decisions that is both given shape and expressed within a tradition, is materially required before determining other stances such as sources of authority or interdisciplinary dialogue.

While this moves beyond what Osmer described, I believe there are good reasons to do so. Our theological tradition is the only specifically "theological" category. It should be self-evident that a practical "theologian" must include a concept of theology as a constitutive part of their work. This is true even of traditions that may take their cue from outside traditional "Christian" theology. For instance, those who operate with a "critical" understanding of theology differentiate themselves from their philosophical counterparts by making some appeal to a specific theological understanding. While I am not attempting to erect a hard and fast boundary or test for orthodoxy, there is some sense that those who self-identify as practical theologians must, to some extent, appropriate a particular understanding of theology.

The theological tradition offers a normative orienting hermeneutic for answering the other three second order questions. For instance, in determining how one might answer the question of inter-disciplinary dialogue, there is a presumed ontology at work. This ontology comes from a sense of what is real and what is real is determined by our theology. Here the connection that Margaret Archer makes between ontology and methodology is illuminating. We can only ask questions and get answers (methodology) concerning individuals and society if we already have a basic understanding of what constitutes reality (ontology). If the individual is the base unit of reality then I will exclude questions that point to causal agency rooted in structures; if I do not conceive of the individual as the base unit of reality I will only ask questions that concern structure. Working within sociology and navigating the debate between individual agency and social structure, Archer rejects both the strong individualists and the hard structuralists on ontological grounds, thus rejecting their methodologies as well.[4] To consider how a theorist approaches the individual-collective question is to first answer the deeper and broader question, "What is basic reality?" Likewise, a practical theologian must answer some questions concerning the nature of reality before considering methodological concerns such as how inter-disciplinary dialogue will take place within a particular work. Our sense of basic reality, which is found in our basic sense of what constitutes theology, orients and determines valid methodological paths for us to follow as practical theologians.

There is also a sense that to justify our conclusions we depend on argumentation and rhetoric justified by our theological tradition. Certain sources of justification carry more weight, are more persuasive, than others depending on the theological tradition we operate out of. As Osmer notes in his inaugural lecture at Princeton Theological Seminary, practical theology is part of a communicative model of rationality that employs different argumentation depending on context and uses various forms of rhetoric to persuade.[5] Osmer makes the connection between epistemic values, those ideas that undergird our communication, and our arguments and rhetoric. As preachers, we design a sermon depending on what we think the telos of worship is. We construct an argument, use particular forms of rhetoric, depending on what we as preachers believe is important and what listeners need to hear. The same logic applies to much of our work as practical theologians. We accept certain arguments and employ particular rhetoric because of what we believe to be

4. Here I am drawing on the first two chapters of Archer, *Realist Social Theory*.
5. Osmer, "Practical Theology as Argument."

true. Because sources of authority are contextual and rhetorical they are derivative from some larger tradition.

In arguing for the primacy of the theological rationale I am well aware that some may see this as a Barthian hegemonic move; because Barth assumes a primacy for "theology" and I am a self-identified Barthian, I must show that all others must do the same. The line between description, what I am attempting here, and norm, what I could possibly be accused of, is admittedly thin but still, I believe, distinct in this argument. I am not proposing some kind of litmus test that determines what is properly "theological." All that I am arguing is that those who self-identify as "practical theologians" are making theological assumptions and that those assumptions have a logical priority over other assumptions that they make. This is true whether the practical theologian operates within the academy or some other context like the fictitious preacher caught in a time crunch. The theological in this case can interact with the other categories as much or as little as an individual practical theologian might deem warranted.

I am not advocating a naïve purity for theology that determines the boundaries for other categories, as should be clear from my understanding of tradition. For instance, a practical theologian might arrive at the task with deep commitments to American pragmatism, commitments which give shape to their understanding of theory-praxis interaction (likely in some kind of mixture of tradition, community, and new circumstances), determine their sources of authority (likely experience), and their stance vis-à-vis other disciplines (likely open provided it helps the community in the moment). The American pragmatism will even shape their theological understanding of God, excluding certain traditions and including others, perhaps favoring a more open or process or moral view of God than some traditions allow for. In this case, a prior commitment to a philosophical tradition has been given normative and regulative authority to all categories. Still, once the practical theologian approaches a practical theological task, there is a logical priority acceded to these assumptions taken as a whole in relation to whatever we might conceive of as theological.

Consider how Osmer's work "hangs together." His theological commitment informs his interdisciplinary methodology, which in turn shapes his understanding of theory-praxis interaction and is based on his sources of justification. More specifically but still in broad categories, Osmer is committed to the Reformed understanding of God's revelation in Jesus Christ, which is mediated to humanity through the enlightening work of the Holy Spirit acting upon us as a community and our interaction with Scripture. From there Osmer bases his arguments in Scripture first then tradition, reason, and experience (likely in that order of priority), understands inter-disciplinary dialogue as an ongoing conversation about the really real (transversally) and the theory-praxis relationship to be an interaction between human/divine interaction that takes place pneumatically.

My argument to this point is simple: all practical theologians operate at three distinct levels and there is a hierarchical relationship between them. The fundamental level is the theological tradition or rationale, the second order level includes theory-praxis relationship, sources of justification, and inter-disciplinary conversations, and the first order are the four moments.

Karl Barth

It follows that which theological tradition and what parts of that rationale practical theologians operate from makes a great deal of difference to their work. Given that Osmer has always operated out of the Reformed tradition, the late career shift to Karl Barth that he has made makes sense. From the very beginning of his academic life he engaged in substantive conversations with neo-orthodox "practical" theologians like James Smart and Shelton Smith, both of whom had significant interactions with Barth. One of the founders of the Reformed tradition, John Calvin, influenced Osmer for years. Arguably one of Barth's major contributions to theology is his reformulation of Calvin's doctrine of election, thus connecting the two. In working through the legacy of practical theology at Princeton Seminary, Osmer engaged with Elmer Homrighausen, an early translator of Barth. Finally, Osmer's academic home, Princeton Theological Seminary, is also the home to Barth scholars Darrell L. Guder, George Hunsinger, Bruce McCormack, Daniel Migliore, and the Barth Centre. Osmer's interaction with Barth was not determined by all of these things but they explain why Barth was a possibility.

"Making sense" is a long way from a "good idea." Just as the fictitious preacher does not change theological rationales each week, there is no practical reason why Osmer had to reexamine which part of the Reformed tradition he wanted to operate from. Quite the opposite. There are many reasons why practical theologians shy away from Barth. The dominant co-relational approach to practical theology has no time for Barth. Browning's dismissive evaluation, "[In Barth] there was no role for human understanding, action, or practice in the construal of God's self-disclosure," is typical.[6] Following Browning, the field of practical theology has privileged certain understandings of human freedom, autonomy, and experience, understandings that by definition exclude Barth because of his arguments regarding the human-divine relationship. When practical theologians have engaged with Barth, such as Osmer's colleagues James Loder and Deborah Van Deusen Hunsinger, they have often done so in a limited way. From different perspectives, Loder and Van Deusen Hunsinger use the Chalcedonian logic present in Barth. As valuable as this engagement is, there is much of Barth's corpus that remains untouched by sympathetic practical theologians.[7] In other words, Osmer's engagement with Barth goes against the field that he has helped to define and into a corpus of work that has largely been unexplored to this point.

Osmer's shift to Barth happened within his Reformed tradition but against some formidable obstacles. The tipping point was likely circumstantial. Jack Stewart, who held the Ashenfelter chair, retired. This left the Princeton Seminary faculty with no professor whose title included evangelism. Out of a faculty of forty-five, there were a few that had "mission" in their title but no one focused on one of the most basic aspects of the church, evangelism. Simultaneously, Darrell Guder also retired, leaving a hole in the theology department for an explicit missional focus.

This kind of insider baseball discussion is important, because if we return to the fictitious preacher at the beginning of this chapter, there must be some motivation for the preaching practical theologian to reconsider their theological rationale. The tyranny of the urgent will not be sufficient. In fact, the immediate crisis forces the preacher to rely more on their foundational assumptions because they need some stability to deal with the change. What Osmer sensed was a deeper change than just staffing. With Stewart and Guder retiring, there was a need for Osmer to consider how to remain true to the gospel as understood in the Reformed tradition. His previous interlocutors, such as Calvin and Moltmann, were good but did not fund the same engagement with evangelism and

---

6. Browning, *A Fundamental Practical Theology*, 5.

7. There is likely a third group of practical theologians who are appreciative of Barth and use him generative ways for their projects but in a critical way. Root, for instance, in Christopraxis, would be an example of this. Ray Anderson and John Swinton might also fit this category.

mission that Barth did. The challenge that Osmer took upon himself was threefold: to answer the criticisms of his colleagues like Don Browning, to build upon the work of colleagues such as Van Deusen Hunsinger and Loder, and to construct a positive engagement with Barth around evangelism. To do this required a rereading of Barth's magnum opus, the *Church Dogmatics*.

From the outset of the *Church Dogmatics*, Barth makes an argument very similar to the one that I made earlier in this chapter, namely that material theological claims have priority over formal claims and are determinative of methodology. From the start, Barth rejects one of the main claims of the liberal theology dominant in his day. He cannot countenance its positive assessment of the human condition and our ability to know God through means other than God's self-revelation in Jesus Christ. This rejection is not made from the confines of a comfortable academy. World War I shattered faith in a progressive and positive assessment of human nature. Good liberal Christians massacred other good liberal Christians. The *Church Dogmatics* took shape in the wake of this disillusionment but then came into full force as World War II raged.[8] Here the total depravity of humanity was on display in Auschwitz, Stalingrad, and Hiroshima. Here the horror was compounded; in addition to killing other good Christians, so-called Christians massacred millions of humans of other faiths.

Even in this rejection of humanity as the starting point for any theology, Barth explicitly includes practical theology. Humans gathered as the church do not drop from sight. Drawing on the Reformed tradition, Barth argues that God reveals God's self through Jesus Christ, the Scriptures as they witness to Christ, and the verbal proclamation of the gospel. Theology is the discipline of the church that helps respond to this revelation. For Barth,

> the criterion of past, future and therefore present Christian utterance is thus the being of the Church, namely, Jesus Christ, God in His gracious revealing and reconciling address to man [sic]. Does Christian utterance derive from Him? Does it lead to Him? Is it conformable to Him? None of these questions can be put apart, but each is to be put independently and with all possible force. Hence theology as biblical theology is the question

8. *Die Kirchliche Dogmatik I: Die Lehre von Wort Gottes 1* was first published in 1932 and the final volume, *Die Kirchliche Dogmatik IV: Die Lehre von der Versohnung 3* was published in 1959.

> of the basis, as practical theology the question of the goal and as
> dogmatic theology the question of the content of the distinctive
> utterance of the Church.[9]

God reveals God's self in the Word incarnate, written, and proclaimed. Revelation is not a static once-and-for-all moment. Instead, it is ongoing and is found in event and encounter. This dynamism creates a need for theology for there is a continual need to reflect on the event and encounter. This reflection calls forth three distinct forms of theology: systematic, biblical, and practical. Systematic considers the current church's witness; biblical the basis of that utterance as witnessed to in Scripture; practical in the telos of the response to that revelation in word and deed.

From these opening pages of the *Church Dogmatics*, Barth signals that there is an integral role for practical theology. This role is determined by material claims that affirm part of the Reformed tradition but go on to push that tradition to new places. In rejecting any human source for revelation and asserting a strong christological understanding of God's self-revelation, Barth affirms total depravity and the sovereignty of God. By introducing the dynamic nature of event and encounter he makes the discipline of theology free to reformulate a faithful understanding of God. These are material claims that fund a much different approach to practical theology than the dominant co-relational methods. Human action happens in response to divine action for Barth. Practical theology attempts to discern the most practical way to proclaim that response. Because the encounter with God happens through Christ, Scripture, and proclamation, and is therefore event, Barth rejects any attempt to formulate universal principles. Co-relationalists like Browning cannot recognize these two moves as practical theology because they assume very different material claims. Namely, they have a different theological anthropology that places a higher value on human agency and autonomy, and a different understanding of revelation that can formulate universal principles.

This logic of systematic, Biblical, and practical theology appears throughout the *Church Dogmatics*. As expected of a systematic theologian, Barth makes extensive use of the theological tradition. He is in constant conversation with the great (Augustine, etc.) and Reformed (Calvin, etc.) traditions. Less predictable is the volume of Barth's exegetical work. Long sections of fine-print scriptural interpretation, including

---

9. Barth, *Church Dogmatics* I/1, 4–5.

engagement with the best of contemporary biblical scholarship, fill the *Church Dogmatics*. As well, Barth includes ethics in every volume and intersperses practical notes on almost every aspect of Christian life throughout. George Hunsinger describes this logic as "dialectical inclusion."[10] The relationship between the three is not sequential but concurrent. There is a dialectic between distinct forms. Simultaneously, each contains the whole of the other. Each part includes the entirety but does so from a different perspective. Dialectical inclusion has its ground in material claims but issues forth into methodological practice. For instance, a Barthian practical theologian will necessarily include engagement with systematic theology and biblical studies. This necessity is in contrast to other practical theologian's assumptions that might lead to the necessary inclusion of the human sciences. Neither the Barthian or the non-Barthian by definition excludes various conversation partners but by logical force of their assumptions both will privilege different methodological patterns.

This Barthian pattern was present in Osmer's work long before he made a conscious move towards Barth. All his major books include significant engagement with both systematic theology and biblical studies. In this, Osmer's engagement with Barth is only an affirmation of his existing practices. This makes sense given that Osmer has always operated out of the same Reformed tradition as Barth did.

Saturday Night Preacher

There are three areas that Osmer's shift has significance both for him and for our late-night Saturday preacher. First, Osmer's turn to Barth gives Reformed practical theology a new theoretical grounding. Reformed theology has had an uneasy relationship with the dominant co-relational approach. With this turn to Barth, Osmer offers a comprehensive way of connecting the Reformed tradition to the tasks common to all practical theologians. Practical theology, both the guild and discipline, dismisses more conservative Reformed voices such as Tim Keller in part because there seems to be a disconnect between their sixteenth-century Calvinist theology and the twenty-first-century context. Despite the fact that these voices seem to hawk an anachronistic practical theology, they are very popular because, I believe, there are few compelling alternatives. If our Saturday night preacher wants to stay Reformed, they are more likely to take their cues from the Gospel Coalition rather than the *Christian*

10. Hunsinger, *How To Read Karl Barth*, 58.

Century. In moving to Barth, Osmer offers a practical theology that is both Reformed and contemporary. He gives the Saturday night preacher a viable alternative.

Second, this kind of theoretical clarity helps in making methodological decisions. For instance, Osmer has always held that inter-disciplinary dialogue is an essential component of practical theology. There have been Barthian approaches previously but in laying out a fuller picture of a Barthian practical theology, Osmer has opened up alternative possibilities. It also opens up a new and productive conversation between the theological disciplines. Rather than silos within separate guilds, systematic, biblical, and practical theology contribute to the unity of knowledge about God's past, present, and future action in the world. There have been moves within each field towards the dialectical inclusion that Barth envisions, such as the theological interpretation of Scripture movement within biblical studies. This unity is aimed at witness and the Saturday night preacher, as the one giving witness on Sunday morning, now has a method that "hangs together" with their theology.

Finally, Osmer's shift opens up a new area for critical reflection. One of the signs of a good scholar is not only that what they say has relevance today but that it is generative. Osmer's shift occurred in conversation with his colleagues, most notably Darrell Guder, but also with students such as Patrick Johnson, Theresa Latini, and Nathan Stucky. Those identifying as "missional" have a way of moving past theory to practice through Osmer's work; those invested in areas such as preaching, pastoral care, and youth ministry can relate their practice to their theological tradition. The Saturday night preacher will benefit from the work of these practical theologians. The grinding regularity of Sunday morning does not go away but through Osmer's shift to Barth there are now companions along the way for the Saturday night preacher.

Bibliography

Archer, Margaret Scotford. *Realist Social Theory: The Morphogenetic Approach*. Cambridge: Cambridge University Press, 1995.

Barth, Karl. *Church Dogmatics: Vol. I/1*. Edited by G. W. Bromiley and T. F. Torrance. London: T&T Clark, 2004.

Browning, Don S. *A Fundamental Practical Theology: Descriptive and Strategic Proposals*. Minneapolis, MN: Fortress, 1991.

Hunsinger, George. *How To Read Karl Barth: The Shape of His Theology*. New York: Oxford University Press, 1991.

Osmer, Richard R. "Practical Theology as Argument, Rhetoric, and Conversation." *The Princeton Seminary Bulletin*, 1997. http://commons.ptsem.edu/id/princetonsemi na1811prin_0-dm007.

———. *The Teaching Ministry of Congregations*. Louisville, KY: Westminster John Knox, 2005.

Osmer, Richard R., and Malan Nel. "Practical Theology: A Current International Perspective." *HTS Teologiese Studies/Theological Studies* 2 (2011) 1–2.

12

Regulating the Empirical in Practical Theology

On Critical Realism, Divine Action, and the Place of the Ministerial

ANDREW ROOT

Confession of Introduction

I THINK I DID it wrong![1] This is my confession. Back when I was Rick Osmer's student he encouraged—gently demanded—that I include an empirical moment. My shortcomings are no reflection on Osmer. I actually believe my method was correct (enough). But nevertheless, I believe the interviews that made up the end of part one of my dissertation (published as *Revisiting Relational Youth Ministry* [InterVarsity, 2007]) were askew. The misalignment is, no doubt, my own responsibility (which is why this is a confession), but the field of practical theology itself also, in part, led me astray.

When it came to my empirical work I was unfortunately able to separate my qualitative methodological pursuits from my concept of divine

---

1. A longer version of this chapter was published as an article. See Root, "Regulating the Empirical in Practical Theology." *Journal of Youth and Theology*, 15, 2016. pp. 44-64.

action. I turned to the social sciences to give my fieldwork direction, but unbeknownst to me, these methods actually made it difficult for me to speak of divine action. They made it much harder to do theology.

In this chapter I explore how empirical methods run the risk of reducing reality, upholding the immanent over the transcendent. I then turn to critical realism as a way to avoid this reduction, making space for the theological, showing how a regulating of the empirical under a realism *can* make the theological a possibility. My overall objective in this chapter is to show how Rick Osmer was right: the empirical is important, but might be pushed to move deeply to connect to divine action, linking empirical work with a theological vision of ministry.

Empirical Obsessions

It has become nearly paradigmatic for dissertations, monographs, and academic papers in practical theology to begin with, or totally consist of, empirical research studies. And there has been good reason for this; practical theology seeks to reflect on lived and concrete experiences. It examines how practices in church and society impact communities and individuals. Practical theology must describe how ecclesial or cultural practices shape lived commitments, and explicit or tacit theological conceptions. Empirical research studies describe these phenomena. This is all very important.

Since the work of Don Browning, Mary McClintock Fulkerson, and Johannes van der Ven, practical theology has claimed its own distinct research program. Practical theology is not the handmaiden of the other theological disciplines, seeking to turn others' best academic work into applied performative procedures. Rather, practical theology has its own academic soul, which is to examine lived situations, contexts and episodes with the best of empirical methods borrowed from the social sciences. Fowler uses developmental psychology and structured interviews to examine stages of faith; Browning uses anthropology-inspired congregational studies to analyze the shape of practical wisdom and ethical actions (like sheltering illegal immigrants). Johannes van der Ven turns to the University of Chicago's late-nineteenth-century push for empirical theology and creates a practical theology that is fundamentally empirical, turning *most* of Continental practical theology in this direction.[2]

---

2. If there was actually someone that was a forerunner to these field-defining

The Rise of Immanence

Because the practical in *practical theology* has been most directly defined through taking on social science's empirical operations, the *theological* nature of the field has been obscured. Empirical methods, by nature, reduce reality to describe it, seeking immanent causations and descriptions, and therefore making little room for transcendence.[3]

Charles Taylor, in the 874-page *A Secular Age*, describes how 500 years ago the Western world saw reality as stratified, making belief in God and transcendence near impossible to deny. Yet, by the year 2000, the Western world is now overtaken by an immanent frame, possessing social imaginaries that understand the world as fully and completely natural and material. The reasons for this cataclysmic shift are numerous, but no small part of the story is the methodological pursuits of the sciences.[4]

This reductive move is legitimate as long as it remains a methodological move to get a better grasp on a greater reality. A problem arises when the reduction gets confused as the total reality. But this confusion is exactly what occurred, according to Taylor. The methods of social sciences rationalized transcendence through "nothing but" stories, and explained experiences of transcendence inside the methodological reduction of immanence. Conversion became nothing but social conditioning, experiences of Jesus nothing but psychological transference. Coupled with economic and technological transitions, the social sciences played a part in reducing reality to such a level that the world was no longer assumed to be enchanted or mysterious, only natural and material.

In the midst of this radical transition, Schleiermacher redefined theology, addressing the cultural despisers and calling practical theology the crown of the theological tree. Schleiermacher viewed practical theology as the expression of theology's life because it most directly gave attention to religion in the immanent frame. In Schleiermacher's mind a Western world without transcendence still needed theology, most particularly practical theology because society, for its own good, needed well trained, professional ministers, just as it needed lawyers and doctors. Practical theology was the crown of the theological tree, I believe, because it was the most immanent, setting practical theology up some 250 years later

---

scholars it was Seward Hiltner.

3. For more on this see Hart, *The Experience of God*, 319.

4. See Taylor, *A Secular Age*, 362.

through Browning, Fowler, van der Ven, and others to link hands with the methods of the social sciences and their empirical pursuits. This linkage makes discussions of transcendence (and therefore theology) more difficult.

Dumb to Transcendence

Sociologist Margaret Archer, in her book *Transcendence,* has shown how the fathers of the social sciences (Marx, Freud, Durkheim, and Weber) had a bias due to an absence in their own experience. Archer illustrates this by using Max Weber's own words; Weber was known to say that he was "dumb to religious [transcendent] experience." Archer argues that because of their own limited experience of reality the fathers of social sciences imagined the social sciences outside of transcendence, taking the methodological shape of attending to only the natural and material realities (immanence) of existence. This bias directed the social sciences to believe that their methodological reduction of reality into only social, cultural, societal, and psychological frames was the totality of reality itself.

Marx, Freud, Durkheim, and Weber were dumb to religious experience; they assumed the results of methodological was reality itself. Transcendence was flattened by the explanations of the natural and material. It is true that these methods of empirical study in the social sciences seek to complicate and nuance the immanent realm. They give detailed interpretation to cultural, gendered, economic, and ideological seams of immanence. But there is little room to actually consider the possibility that the experience of transcendence is real, and not simply reduced to a hiccup in the immanent frame. The empirical methods in practical theology are of great benefit; they allow the practical theologian to delve deeply into forms and shapes of human action. But this becomes problematic for practical theology when these beneficial methods reinforce the immanent frame, making divine action (as a distinct ontological reality) appear illogical.

Taking the methodological shape of the social sciences, much of practical theology has followed the social sciences in believing that to do the empirical is to attend to a world without transcendence; it is to examine and study *only* the natural or material realities of culture and society. In this view, practical theology makes no assertions about the nature and action of God experienced by human agents in concrete situations, but focuses exclusively on human religious actions bound in immanence. Of course, many practical theologians desire to say something theological. But without a reworking from the start of the practical theologian's relationship with the methods of empirical study, there will inevitably be a flattening of reality, making transcendence difficult to speak of.

Returning to a Kind of Realism

To break free from the reduction of all human experience to immanence we must tentatively and carefully return to a realism in practical theology. I say that we must do this tentatively because forms of realism that start outside human experience and claim foundational knowledge are deeply problematic in their own sense. Forcing all knowledge onto a predetermined foundation, whether scientific, philosophical, or theological, leads to a kind of violence. Foundational realism contends that reality is stratified, but also possess-able, because a human knower is able to climb to an objective peak and know all of reality. Practical theology since its renaissance in the 1970s has sought, correctly in my mind, to be non-foundational.

The kind of realism that practical theology needs is *post-foundational* critical realism. This realism acknowledges the hermeneutical nature of reality. It claims that reality is stratified with human beings existing somewhere in the middle of the layers of reality. There is much about reality that the human mind cannot possess or know (even in its best methods); layers above and below that resist empirical observation. Because we cannot reduce reality to our sensory experience, there are ways other than empirical scientific methods that lead us to understand the depth and width of reality. Against the backdrop of a stratified reality we might admit that empirical methods of the social sciences help us to say something reasoned and specific about the immanent layer of reality, but these very methods may be completely blind, reductive, and therefore inappropriate to spotting a person's experience with transcendence. *Practical theology is challenged with needing a critical approach to concrete and lived experience and a way of remaining open to the act and being of a transcendent God.*

Therefore, with this kind of critical realism, we claim that empirical methods are helpful, maybe even necessary, but we also must admit from the start that social scientific approaches can never possess the fullness of reality. Reality will always escape any humanly constructed method of observation; naturalism and materialism do not exhaust reality. This means that ontology precedes epistemology. This ordering of ontology over epistemology has not often shaped empirical methods; rather we usually reverse it and have epistemology swallow ontology. We have assumed in our immanent age that only what can be provided by the reductive methods of empirical science can be real, privileging epistemology over ontology. This tentative walk back into realism acknowledges that reality is stratified, *all forms* of human knowledge are incomplete, and reality itself is more than even the best of human epistemological systems can ever know.

Such a post-foundational realism that claims ontology over epistemology allows, from the start, for divine action to be *possible*. We are freed from the heavy straightjacket of naturalism and materialism to hear people's experience with reality. And because this is a post-foundational realism, it is only through human experience that we can grasp the layers of reality. While ontology precedes epistemology in critical realism, it also acknowledges that human epistemologies are relativized. We find our way into the fullness of reality not through a foundation such as positivist science or biblicism, but through our personal experience. We indwell reality and therefore have personal experiences of reality, even transcendent layers. These personal experiences may correlate to the ontological shape of reality or they may *not*, but experiences of transcendence have not been ruled out from the beginning.

If we begin with this critical realist starting point, that ontology precedes epistemology and therefore people may have real experiences of transcendence, then our empirical research methods must create space for people to testify about such transcendent experiences.[5] Empirical research, then, in practical theology seeks to create space for testimony, for it is through these distinct research program of testimony that we take on a disposition apt to explore the stratified nature of reality. Practical theology begins by inviting people to articulate their experiences of transcendence, seeking observations in ethnographic spaces, not simply of practices that give people meaning. How certain actions and experiences draw people into higher layers of reality becomes the question. These

5. For more on this see Smith, *What is a Person?*, 153.

personal and communal experiences of testimony must always be heard as *possibly* true even as we submit them to scrutiny.

Reality *may* very well have a higher layer(s) of transcendence, but people's experience of this is always from a lower layer, and therefore there is no way to conclusively claim such experiences as unquestionably true (this is why it is testimony). Paul himself has a transcendent experience that takes the concrete shape of the living Christ coming to him (Acts 9; in 2 Corinthians 12: 1–7, Paul speaks of layers and levels of reality). But having this experience was insufficient. Paul must continue, for the remainder of his ministry, to provide rational reasons why this experience was real. Paul gives intelligible explanations for why this experience was one with transcendence and not something else. The intensity of this experience forces him to justify himself through discourses, debates, and distinct research systems (the Torah and the prophets) intelligible to those around him.

Embracing a critical realist conception of reality means that the tradition lives. With this realist commitment, the tradition is neither a static documentation of rituals and practices nor the socially constructed tradition of a people bound in an immanent construction called the church. Instead, tradition is a resource that has and continues to give insight on an individual's and community's experiences of transcendence. Because the tradition is not seen as the foundation but the medium that helps mediate and discern transcendent experience, it too must be reinterpreted next to our new experiences.

But Critical Realism Can Only Take Us So Far

Critical realism allows us to see that reality is stratified, thus making it possible to create a space for transcendence in our conception of the world. This move is invaluable if the empirical methods of practical theology are to escape reduction of all reality into immanence, and if theology (as the articulation of the experience of divine act and being) is ever to be a possibility within the field.

But while taking us this far, critical realism does not solve the heart of the problem for practical theology when it comes to the empirical. Critical realism makes a space for transcendence, but gives us no direction on how empirical methods might attend to divine action itself. In other words, how can we use empirical methods, not to reduce reality, but instead to open us up to the breadth of reality. Critical realism as a philosophy argues that reality always spills over and cannot be captured by human minds. On its own, critical realism cares little for the divine. So, while critical realism gives us a philosophical way of avoiding the reduction of reality by demonstrating that reality is always more than human minds can possess and thus making transcendence a possibility, it tells does not tell us what the structure of this transcendent reality might be.

The Shape of Divine Action

It is here that the shape of divine action itself must lead us. Instead of practical theology taking its empirical shape from the immanent-bound social sciences, we must ask if there *is a way for our empirical pursuits to take the shape of divine action*. If practical theology shares with the social sciences a desire to speak of lived and concrete realities, it nevertheless, as a theology, believes that these concrete and lived realities encounter the act and being of God. Given this, we must adapt, shift, and regulate our empirical methods to put ourselves in a position to see the possibility of divine action within and next to the depth of human experience. We must evaluate scholars' empirical studies in practical theology against our normative commitments about the shape of divine action itself and not against the normative immanent assertions of social sciences. We claim these normative commitments in and through our experience of higher layers of reality, drawing from trusted research systems that give us intelligible and rational conceptions of our experience. Normativity then draws from the rhetoric and practices of a tradition, but this tradition is trusted because it, at least in part, resonates with the experience of reality itself.

There are obviously numerous ways to articulate the relation between divine and human action and therefore numerous ways for organizing the empirical within practical theology. I'll provide my own *only* as an example of how the theological might shape the empirical from the start.

Divine Action as Ministry

The shape of divine action, which I believe leads to an adapting, shifting, and regulating of empirical study in a generative way, is as ministry. Divine action takes the shape of ministry, and as such, divine action is not a frozen tradition but a living and concrete reality that encounters us in the depth of our experience. We experience God's action, not as a heavy metaphysical force but as an experience of ministerial encounter in and through our concrete and lived experience. We are pulled into transcendence through the concrete and practical action of ministry taking place in the immanent. We experience God as an encounter of ministry, and this encounter makes our lived and concrete experience central, and therefore able to be described and empirically observed, while not diluting the transcendent encounter of divine action itself.

If our empirical methods take their shape from divine action, what does it mean to claim that God's act and being comes to us as the experience of ministry? This is to contend that God's being is given in God's act and that God's act is the revealing of Godself for the sake of ministry. So, we can know God (epistemology) only through the priority of encountering God (ontology) as revealed in the act of God's ministry to humanity.

This ministerial action is not something incidental to God, as if God's action is some kind of hobby. It is not naively asking, "What is God up to?," as if it were an obvious catch phrase or trivial knowledge. Rather, ministry as the act of God is the event of God's being coming to humanity; this being is always becoming, because this being is always moving and active. It is, then, the event[6] of God's moving that makes ministry an ontological encounter of the divine with the human. God's being as coming to us is God's very ministry, it is God's giving of Godself to humanity so humanity *might be with God*. So, from the level of divine action, ministry is not clerical or institutional but the act(s) of sharing in the life of another, for the sake of love, mercy, and new possibility. We take the form of the divine being not in the way of ontology but through action. By becoming ministers, we join God's being not through shared essence, but through shared action of ministry. (Matthew 25, again, seems to point in this very direction; the text articulates a direct encounter with revelation, with event of Jesus present, but it happens through ministering to another, sharing in their hunger, homelessness, and imprisonment). Practical theology is a form of human *ministerial* action that, by reflecting on and

6. See Jungel, *God's Being is in Becoming*, 30.

moving into ministry, attends to the very being of God through God's own ministerial action.

Ministry from both the divine and human side is not functional or clerical. For instance, God does stuff, but it is not really the stuff, the functions, that are important, but the unveiling of God's self (be-coming) for the sake of salvation. It is ontological, shattering trivial knowledge, because having God's being in ministry is for humanity. God gives God's very self, and gives it to us at the level of our own ontological person-hood, becoming the ministering Christ, who reveals God (revelation) to humanity and transforms this humanity back into union with Godself (reconciliation) through the work of the Spirit (given the salvation of be-ing in Christ). Human forms of ministry too seek to share in the life of their neighbor, sharing in the depth of their experience (homelessness, hunger, and imprisonment) as witness to and participation in the divine being itself. We share in the being of God by taking on the action of God and joining in ministry, led by the Holy Spirit.

All knowledge of God, all theology, is gleaned from encountering the event of God's ministry; we have theological knowledge because we have been the recipients of God's ministry. God's practical act of minis-try precedes all formal knowledge we might have. Theology can *only* be practical, because its epistemological object is God's ontological state of ministering to creation. Theology is practical because its subject is the practical action of God's self. This action is practical because it ministers to particular and real persons. Ministry allows us to give attention to di-vine action as a transcendent reality that nevertheless encounters us at the level of our concrete and lived experience.

Theology as reflection on a transcendent reality, and the empirical as attention to the concrete and lived, are held together through this con-ception of ministry. Ministry is a divine reality that nevertheless is bound in human experience. Any empirical method must be regulated under the claim of God's ontological state as minister and any thick description of human experience must be adapted to our call to join the being of this God as ministers.

Therefore, from my perspective empirical research in practical theology can never take the disposition of a scientist, objectively com-mitted to their field and method more than concrete personhood. The practical theologian must see his or her move into the empirical as an act of ministry, which opens up the possibility of transcendence, as an act that joins the very being of God as an ontological reality. We use models and approaches from the social sciences, *transforming them through the disposition of ministry*, recognizing that inviting others to express their experiences to be ministered to and ministering to others. The invitation to give testimony to the ministerial action of God regulates our empirical methods, transforming research into an act of ministry itself, which takes both interviewer and interviewee into very act and being of God.

The empirical has a place within practical theology, but only through the regulation and adaptation of the theological reality of God. Practical theology is not an empirical form of theology, but is a form of theology that attends to ministry as divine and human reality. It uses the empirical only so far as the empirical methods help us create a space where we might participate in the depth and beauty of human agents as they share their experience of the presence and absence of God in and through their concrete experience. Our invitation for them to share such experiences is itself an event of ministry; their stories of God's presence and absence minister to us as much as the invitation to share is a blessing to them. So being shaped by seeing divine action as an event of ministry, empirical research can itself be transformed into an act of ministry and therefore must be evaluated as such.

Back to My Confession

Reflecting ten years later on that research, I believe that while it was sound from a social scientific perspective, it was flawed from a theological one and I confess it as so. I had violated the very heart of my theological commitment in the research itself. I was claiming that relationships (ministering to another's personhood) was not a tool for ministry, but the very act of ministry itself. And yet I went into this research looking for data, seeking proof for a thesis. I was blind to the fact that my act of gathering data needed to be regulated by the possibility that the event of encounter with the humanity of those I was researching would itself bring forth the possibility of ministry, telling me something surely about the actions, perspective, and positions of these people. But also, because this was an event of ministry, the research could reveal the act and being of God. I was blind to the fact that if I invited these people to speak of their experience of God, I was walking into the deepest waters, where proclamation of the Word was wrapped tightly around their most profound experiences of joy and suffering. I was asking them to testify and reflect with me on how their very being experiences the being of God.

At the time, I had no conception that the research itself needed to be framed by the ministerial act of God; the social sciences just asked me to reflect enough to be ethical, leading me to ignore how these people were experiencing the ministerial action of Jesus. I didn't see that my own empirical approach, if it lacked a disposition of ministerial action, would neglect the depth and breadth of these people's concrete and lived experience of divine action. I needed to ask questions that would give these people a chance to speak of high layers of reality, not assuming that I could reduce them into cultural categories of immanence (which I did). It, of course, was not my responsibility to see myself as their pastor; I needed to be honest that I was an academic doing research. But, as a theologian I needed to enter this encounter anticipating that their stories might minister to me, that my questions and the ethos of interviews needed to be a blessing to them. I never conceived of my own person or the organizing of my study around the disposition of the event of ministry, and because I didn't, I would remain always blind to divine action, reducing people's experience to something solely immanent. If I saw my research as first and foremost an act of ministry (bound in the being of God's very self that comes to us as the revelation of the ministering Jesus), I believe it would have taken me into deeper insights and maybe even into the privilege of encountering the act and being of God with those I interviewed.

Bibliography

Hart, David Bentley. *The Experience of God: Being, Consciousness, Bliss*. New Haven, CT: Yale University Press, 2013.

Jungel, Eberhard. *God's Being is in Becoming: The Trinitarian Being of God in the Theology of Karl Barth*. Grand Rapids: Eerdmans, 2001.

Root, Andrew. "Regulating the Empirical in Practical Theology: On Critical Realism, Divine Action, and the Place of the Ministerial." *Journal of Youth and Theology* 15 (2016) 44–64.

Smith, Christian. *What is a Person?* Chicago: University of Chicago Press, 2010.

Taylor, Charles. *A Secular Age* Cambridge, MA: Harvard University Press, 2007.

13

The Teacher as Practical Theologian: A Trinitarian Kenotic Praxis of Love

Shin–Geun Jang

In congregations of the Korean Protestant church, Christian teaching has been often considered an individualized and privatized form of praxis, a one-way transmission of Christian tradition from teacher to learner, and a specialized skill employing pedagogical rationality. The result? Members of the Korean church usually hold a corresponding individualized and privatized faith. Current critique about the Korean churches' loss of significance in the public square deeply relates to the privatization of Christian faith, which in turn contributes to a loss of communal Christian identity, leaving Christian pedagogy to emphasize human reason at the expense of divine love.

This chapter critiques individualized, privatized teaching in Korean Protestant churches, and seeks a foundation for pedagogy grounded in the divine praxis of love. Richard R. Osmer's approach to practical theology will guide us, especially as it contributes to a new approach to the teaching ministry of Korean Protestant churches.[1]

---

1. Kathleen A. Cahalan and Gordon S. Mikoski pose eleven major concerns or features of contemporary practical theologians: 1) attentive to theory-practice complexity, 2) practice and performance oriented, 3) oriented to multidimensional dynamics of social context and embodiment, 4) holistic, 5) interdisciplinary, 6) open-ended, flexible, and porous, 7) theologically normed, 8) hermeneutical, 9) interventionist and critically constructive, 10) teleological and eschatological, and, 11) self-reflective and self-identified. This article reflects those features of contemporary practical theology

Osmer's practical theological perspective on teaching emphasizes: 1) a strong theological foundation, 2) theo-praxis as normative for human praxis, 3) three tasks of the teaching ministry for congregations drawn from biblical theology (catechesis, exhortation, and discernment), 4) globalization as a new context for Christian teaching, and 5) a transversal approach to interdisciplinary dialogue. Given the limits of one chapter, these five points—while all important to teaching in Korean Protestant churches—cannot be explored fully here. Instead, I will focus on Osmer's second emphasis, the normative role of divine action for human action, and specifically will explore trinitarian kenotic praxis as a normative for Christian teaching in Korean Protestant churches.

Theo-Praxis as Trinitarian Kenotic Praxis

Many practical theologians, critical of drawing the norms for Christian praxis from social scientific or other secular sources, have explored the concept of theo-praxis (or divine action) as a basis for guiding human praxis. James Fowler, for example, draws on theologian Sally McFague's feminist metaphors for a triune God, proposing God as a Mother or Parent, the Son as a Lover, and the Holy Spirit as a Friend. In these metaphors, the trinitarian theo-praxis is respectively revealed as "the Creating praxis," "the Saving praxis," and "the Sustaining praxis."[2]

In dialogue with Jürgen Moltmann's trinitarian theology, Osmer presents Christopraxis as normative for the teaching ministry of congregations, understood as *marturia, diakonia, doxology, didache,* and *koinonia.* These correspond to Christ's fivefold offices: the prophetic, the priestly, the transfigured, the royal, and the open fellowship of Christ's praxis, or Christopraxis.[3] Following Osmer's lead, this chapter also presents the Trinitarian kenotic praxis as a norm for Christian teaching. Thus, Christian teaching as the trinitarian kenotic praxis of love is considered here to be fulfilled through active participation, a view which stands in agreement with Fowler and Osmer's theo-praxis approach.

---

and loosely employs Richard Osmer's four tasks of practical theology: 1) descriptive-empirical task, 2) hermeneutical task, 3) normative task, and 4) pragmatic task. See Cahalan and Mikoski, "Introduction," 1–7.

2. Fowler, *Weaving the New Creation,* 67–82.

3. Osmer, *The Teaching Ministry of Congregations,* 221–25.

To understand teaching as a praxis of love that reflects the trinitarian kenotic praxis of God, we must first unpack what that means. Though kenotic theology was traditionally thought to originate from the self-emptying of Christ proclaimed in Philippians 2:5–11, both testaments bear witness to the idea. In the Old Testament, the literal meaning of the word *kenosis* is directly related to the Greek verb *kenō*, meaning "to empty" and "to pour out." Its Hebrew equivalents are shown in passages such as Genesis 24:20 and Isaiah 32:15. In Genesis 24:20, Rebekah *poured out* the water from her pitcher into the trough. Isaiah 32:15 uses the Greek verb *exekenōsen* (LXX): "Until a spirit from on high is *poured out* on us."[4] In the New Testament, the Christological hymn of Philippians 2:5–11 is a representative passage that proclaims the incarnation of Christ as the kenosis of God. In this case kenosis is understood as "Christ's voluntary renunciation of certain divine attributes, in order to identify himself with humanity."[5]

Some theologians assert divine kenosis within the inner life of the Trinity itself. Russian Orthodox theologian Sergious Bulgakov claims that, in the perichoretic relationship among the three divine persons, each person of the Trinity gives itself to the others kenotically, in sacrificial love:

> The Father pours himself out, empties himself in the begetting the Son. The Son, on his part, empties himself by submitting to be begotten from the Father and by being obedient to the Father. The eternal kenosis of the third person of the Trinity consists in divesting himself of his hypostatic self (*samost'*) and serving as a "bond" (*sviazka*) or a "bridge of love" between the Father and the Son.[6]

In Moltmann's view, each member of the eternal Trinity makes room for each other through this love-inspired action of self-emptying:

> . . . the divine persons of the Trinity become habitable for each other in their mutual perichoresis, giving each other open life-space for their mutual indwelling. Each trinitarian person is then not only subject but also room for the other. In the perichoresis

---

4. McCall, "Kenosis of the Spirit into Creation," 2.

5. Ibid., 3.

6. Gavrilyuk, "The Kenotic Theology of Bulgakov," 255–56.

of the eternal Trinity we find therefore not only three persons but also three "broad rooms."[7]

Other theologians discuss the kenotic nature of the Trinity in light of God's actions towards creation. These theologians describe the divine kenosis as the act of creation, incarnation, and pouring out of the Holy Spirit as motivated by God's sacrificial divine love for all creation:

> In creating, God enters into relationship, with creatures by granting them their own being, integrity, autonomy—an authentic existence which is theirs alone . . . Creation is thus an act of the profoundly generous divine love which calls the other into being and sustains it in its particularity and otherness.[8]

Triune God's kenotic love is self-limiting as well as self-donating. In creation, God the Father limits divine omnipresence, omnipotence, and omniscience to make room, give time, and grant freedom for God's creatures. Moltmann links the kenosis of God the Father with the Jewish concept of *Shekinah*, God's indwelling or self-humiliation. God's *Shekinah* originates from God's covenant with the Israelites: "I will dwell in the midst of the Israelites."[9] Later the *Shekinah* was understood as God's presence with captured people in the Babylonian exile and with suffering and oppressed people.

In the incarnation, God the Son also demonstrates self-giving, self-limiting love. According to Gordon Fee, the incarnation "presupposes some form of self-limitation on Christ's part in his human life on earth," and notes that in Hebrews 5:7–9 the Son "expresses utter dependence on the Father in prayer, and then submits to his will in full obedience—an obedience he *learned* through suffering."[10] The Son's kenosis reaches its peak on the cross. "Because of the cross, the meaning of Christ's self-emptying is qualified in such a way that it is understood to entail radical *involvement* and *identity* with . . . human existence in its totality, including its extremes of brokenness and death."[11]

The kenosis of the Spirit is shown as she pours herself into the world. The Spirit imparts herself into Creation and shares herself with Creation in perichoretic ways. In John 16:14, the Spirit empties herself

7. Moltmann, "God's Kenosis," 140.

8. Linahan, "Experiencing God in Brokenness," 173–74.

9. Moltmann, "God's Kenosis," 142–43.

10. Fee, "The New Testament and Kenosis Christology," 36.

11. Linahan, "Experiencing God in Brokenness," 172.

by glorifying Christ over herself. But for the Spirit, divine kenosis also can mean being poured into or achieving actualization. The Spirit of God even poured into the ministry of Jesus. "Indeed, the Spirit was *poured into* Jesus so as to empower Jesus for his crucial ministry of imparting life to the masses, which resulted in Jesus' own temporal and bodily death."[12] In Jane Linahan's words, the Spirit is the creative power, saving power, and prophetic power, as well as a kenotic power.[13] As a kenotic power, the Spirit allows, empowers, and supports the actualization of the other:

> It is the Spirit of God who brings otherness into being, who sustains and empowers otherness, who enables it to stand in the freedom of relationship . . . before its creator. This is the kenotic power of the Spirit: a self-emptying love so profound and generous that it gives everything, it risks its very self for the sake of the authentic being of the other.[14]

In short, the trinitarian praxis of kenosis results from the triune God's profound, endless, sacrificial, and self-giving love for one another and for creation. But thanks to the trinitarian praxis of kenosis as creation, incarnation, and actualization, God invites and encourages us to participate in this self-giving, mutually interpenetrating (periochoretic) life in an analogous way. As God's people, we are called to join in the Father's praxis of creation, in the Son's praxis of incarnation, and in the Spirit's praxis of actualization, which for humans evokes thanks and praise. In fact, the most fitting response to the trinitarian praxis of kenosis is doxology. The question is, how shall Christian teaching reflect this?

Christian Teaching as Trinitarian Kenotic Praxis of Love

This section presents Christian teaching as participation in a Trinitarian kenotic praxis of love, an idea that refers to Osmer's Trinitarian and dramatological approach to the teaching ministry of congregations. Osmer sees the three tasks of teaching ministry (catechesis, exhortation, and discernment) as participating in "the triune God's creating, redeeming, and glorifying of the world."[15] So what does Christian teaching look like that is rooted in a trinitarian kenotic praxis of love?

12. McCall, "Kenosis of the Spirit into Creation," 3.

13. Linahan, "Experiencing God in Brokenness," 173.

14. Ibid., 173–74.

15. Osmer, *The Teaching Ministry of Congregations*, 236.

We can begin by saying this much: teaching that participates in God's trinitarian kenotic praxis of love is experienced as self-sacrifice, self-emptying, and self-limitation that is motivated by love. More specifically, we can understand this kind of teaching as a lifelong interpretive process in which mutual caring by both teacher and learner, whether individual or communal, is enacted through practices of room-making/time-taking, embodiment/modeling, and actualization/involvement. (One point we need to keep in mind is that teachers and learners may be either individual Christians or faith communities—and as we will see, the roles of teacher and learner constantly shift.) These practices help teacher and learner alike live into God's eschatological reign, while at the same time enacting God's love in the world.

1) Christian teaching is a lifelong praxis that helps learners live into the eschatological reign of God.

From an eschatological perspective, teaching that participates in a praxis of love is not a short-term process, but a life-long commitment or devotion to the learner. Nor is it confined to the personal or inner lives of the teacher and the learner; participating in a praxis of love means attending to the cultural, social, political, public, and ecological dimensions of learning as well as the inner life of the learner. Christian teaching is thus not an act of domination, enforcement, or invasion by the teacher, but expressed through waiting, inviting, accompanying, empowering, and persuading so that the learner can live under the eschatological reign of God in the power of the Spirit.

Christian teaching does not pretend to generate faith itself. Faith is rather a gift from God through grace, not human enterprise. As Osmer points out, Christian teaching is viewed as an attempt "to create a context in which faith can be awakened, supported, and challenged" by maintaining the eschatological tension of our redemption—faith is both "already" given and "not yet" fully achieved.[16] As teachers help learners taste the reality of the reign of God in their daily lives in an anticipatory manner, they also entrust the learner to the Power of the Spirit, referred to as the stage of "release" in Maria Harris's words.[17]

---

16. Osmer, *Teaching for Faith*, 15.

17. Harris, *Dance of the Spirit*, 74–75.

2) Christian teaching practices mutual caring between teacher and learner.

Like the periochoretic relationship of the three divine persons of the Trinity, mutual caring between teacher and learner is another essential dimension of Christian teaching. This understanding of teaching corrects the misunderstanding of education as unilateral transmission from the teacher to the learner. In a perichoretic relationship, the three divine persons are mutually dwelling within each other in unlimited divine love. Similarly, trinitarian kenotic teaching views the relationship between the teacher and the learner, whether the learner is an individual or a community, as bilateral and cooperative. The teacher does not always lead, and the student does not always follow. They lead and at the same time are led by each other in the process of teaching-learning, following the perichoretic dance of the three divine persons.

Christian teaching as a process of mutual caring also includes the mutual caring made possible by communal relationships formed within congregations, including relationships between generations. As John Westerhoff argues, Christian faith can be shaped and inherited through the process of continuing interaction or care among three different generations: the generation of vision, the generation of the present, and the generation of memory.[18]

3) Christian teaching practices room-making/time-taking for presenting and becoming obedient to the subject matter of teaching.

Parker Palmer defines teaching as creating "a space in which obedience to truth is practiced."[19] Yet, while sympathetic to Palmer, trinitarian kenotic teaching differs from Palmer's understanding in that it emphasizes the divine perspective more explicitly, and lifts up time-taking and time-consuming as equally distinctive aspects of Christian teaching.

Following the Father's kenotic praxis of creation as room-making, Christian teaching makes physical, psychological, conceptual, spiritual space for the learner. Christian teaching makes physical space inviting and hospitable, psychological space welcoming and safe; conceptual

18. Westerhoff, *Will Our Children Have Faith?*, 53.
19. Palmer, *To Know as We are Known*, 69.

space is characterized by sharing the subject matter in a sympathetic and dynamic way, and spiritual space leaves room to be filled and activated by the Spirit.

Just as creation by the Father is a praxis of self-limitation as God's inserts the divine self into time, Christian teaching practices time-taking to present the subject matter and become obedient to it. Both the praxis of room-making and the praxis of time-taking are processes of self-limitation, as teachers grant learners their own being, integrity, and autonomy. They call the learners into being and sustain them in their particularity and otherness.

4) Christian teaching embodies and models the subject matter it's teaching.

Just as the incarnation of the Son embodies divine redemptive love, Christian teaching embodies Christian faith's subject matter and content. More than simply transmitting information, trinitarian kenotic teaching engages the learner's lives and personifies a life shaped by God. At the same time, Christian teaching remains in dialogue with various human developmental theories, such as the psychological, moral, social, spiritual theories, exhibiting (as Osmer suggests) a posture of "priestly listening."[20] This posture of listening requires the practical theologian's gift of creative interdisciplinary dialogue with various human sciences.

5) Christian teaching actualizes otherness and engages in mutual empowerment between the teacher and the learner.

As seen through the Spirit's actualizing outpouring of the divine self into creation, Christian teaching also shares power and empowers others through the kenotic love of actualization. As Maria Harris suggests, Christian teaching nurtures: 1) the power to receive, 2) the power to rebel, 3) the power to resist, 4) the power to reform, and 5) the power to love.[21] These five kinds of power have two fundamental elements: receiver and agent:

---

20. Osmer, *Practical Theology*, 31–78.

21. Harris, *Teaching and Religious Imagination*, 89–96.

First, power is capacity and ability to act as *receiver*, in the sense of being receptive, attentive, and aware of the address of Being. Thus power is a capacity schooled by the contemplative and ascetic imaginations, with their attitudes of listening, watching, waiting, and seeing. But secondly, power is also capacity and ability to act as an *agent*, schooled by the creative and archetypal imagination, with their attitudes of crafting, forming, making, and symbolizing.[22]

Christian teaching as a process of mutual empowerment is thus based on the kinds of power that actualize the other. Harris describes the relationship of these five kinds of power as dancing, a dance that is essentially perichoretic. We can step into any stage of the dance and be swept up into the next step. As the incarnate Son's kenotic action favored the poor, the oppressed, and the suffering, the Christian dance of actualization likewise favors the powerless and marginalized. According to Jung Young Lee, incarnation is "a divine marginalization." He claims, "To be the Son of the living God does not mean to be at the center of centrality. It means to be at the margin of marginality, the servant of all servants."[23] In this sense, Christian teaching participates in a divine marginalization of both the teacher and the learner in order to "remember the dismembered," as Mary Elizabeth Moore puts it, through core educational practices of loving, truth-telling, mourning and repenting, and reconciling.[24]

6) Christian teaching is missional praxis.

Christian teaching is inseparable from missional praxis. As stated above, Christian teaching as a praxis of room-making/time-taking, embodiment/modeling, and actualization/involvement not only has personal, individual, and existential dimensions, but also social, political, ecological, and public facets. Teaching that takes part in a trinitarian kenotic praxis of love is not restricted to speculating about the inner life of the Trinity. The kenotic God is a missional or sending God. Correspondingly, Christian teaching participates in the trinitarian kenotic praxis of creation, incarnation, and actualization, through which the triune God sends (*missio*) God's people both individually and corporally into the world. Darrell

---

22. Ibid., 80–81.

23. Lee, *Marginality*, 25.

24. Moore, *Teaching as a Sacramental Act*, 79–88.

Guder warns against the "the mission-benefit dichotomy"—namely, separating "[t]he benefits of salvation . . . from the reason for which we receive God's grace in Christ: to empower us as God's people to become Christ's witnesses."[25] Avoiding this dichotomy requires Christian teaching to approach room-making/time-taking, embodiment/modeling, and actualization/involvement as missional praxis.

Doxology as the Crux of Christian Teaching

The crux of Christian teaching goes beyond a simple formation of ethical lives, transmission of Christian knowledge through instruction, or faith enculturation. It does not disparage these processes, but encourages the learner to participate in the praxis of giving thanks and praise to the trinitarian God's kenotic praxis of self-sacrifice, self-limitation, and self-emptying love. According to Osmer, *doxology*, including *marturia, diakonia, didache*, and *koinonia*, is the core praxis of the congregation. Rooted in Christ's event of transfiguration, doxology participates in "the transfiguration of the risen Christ through the praise and enjoyment of God,"[26] giving both teacher and learner a foretaste of an eschatological future in the trinitarian kingdom of God.

In this sense, Christian teaching distinguishes itself entirely from secular or general education. If doxology is the crux of Christian teaching, neither education nor practical theology itself cannot be reduced to a means to an end. Christian teaching in Korean Protestant churches (or any church) cannot be a vehicle to achieve self-actualization, cognitive maturity, or even salvation. If doxology is the crux of Christian teaching, then teaching grounded in trinitarian kenotic praxis of love is a good unto itself, a way to praise God. Learning is not restricted to the cognitive level. Instead, the learner might give thanks and praise to the triune God through various artistic, bodily, corporeal, and performative forms, such as singing, dancing, performing, or drawing. All the characteristics of teaching as trinitarian kenotic practice point to doxology because the relationship between knowledge and worship is inseparable. To know God is to worship God.

25. Guder, *The Continuing Conversion of the Church*, 120.

26. Osmer poses 1) Sabbath keeping, 2) praise of God, and 3) recreation as three core practices of doxology. Osmer, *The Teaching Ministry of Congregations*, 223–24.

Bibliography

Cahalan Kathleen A., and Gordon S. Mikoski. "Introduction." In *Opening the Field of Practical Theology: An Introduction*, edited by Kathleen A. Cahalan and Gordon S. Mikoski, 1–7. New York: Rowman & Littlefield, 2014.

Fee, Gordon D. "The New Testament and Kenosis Christology." In *Exploring Kenotic Christology: The Self Emptying of God*, edited by C. Stephen Evans, 25–42. New York: Oxford University Press, 2006.

Fowler, James W. *Weaving the New Creation: Stages of Faith and the Public Church*. San Francisco: Harper San Francisco, 1991.

Gavrilyuk, Paul, L. "The Kenotic Theology of Sergius Bulgakov." *Scottish Journal of Theology* 58 (2005) 251–69.

Guder, Darrell L. *The Continuing Conversion of the Church*. Grand Rapids: Eerdmans, 2000.

Harris, Maria. *Dance of the Spirit: The Seven Steps of Women's Spirituality*. New York: Bantam, 1991.

———. *Teaching and Religious Imagination: An Essay in the Theology of Teaching*. San Francisco: Harper San Francisco, 1991.

Lee, Jung Young. *Marginality: The Key to Multicultural Theology*. Minneapolis: Fortress, 1995.

Linahan, Jane E. "Experiencing God in Brokenness: The Self-emptying of Holy Spirit in Moltmann's Pneumatology." In *Encountering Transcendence: Contributions to a Theology of Religious Experience*, edited by Lieven Boeve, et al., 165–84. Leuven: Peter, 2005.

McCall, Bradford. "Kenosis of the Spirit into Creation." *Crucible: Theology & Ministry* 1 (2008) 2.

Moltmann, Jürgen. "God's Kenosis in the Creation and Consummation of the World." In *The Work of Love: Creation as Kenosis*, edited by John Polkinghorne, et al., 137–51. Grand Rapids: Eerdmans, 2001.

Moore, Mary Elizabeth Mullino. *Teaching as a Sacramental Act*. Cleveland, OH: Pilgrim, 2004.

Nouwen, Henri J. *In the Name of Jesus: Reflections on Christian Leadership*. New York: Crossroad, 1989.

Osmer, Richard R. *The Teaching Ministry of Congregations*. Louisville, KY: Westminster John Knox, 2005.

———. *Practical Theology: An Introduction*. Grand Rapids: Eerdmans, 2008.

———. *Teaching for Faith: A Guide for Teachers of Adult Classes*. Louisville, KY: Westminster John Knox, 1992.

Palmer, Parker J. *To Know as We are Known: Education as A Spiritual Journey*. San Francisco: Harper San Francisco, 1983.

Westerhoff III, John. *Will Our Children Have Faith?* New York: Seabury, 1976.

14

Intelligible Reasons for Practice

Osmer's Contribution to Practical Theology at Princeton Theological Seminary

GORDON S. MIKOSKI

WHEN NOT IGNORING THE past for the sake of the present and the future, practical theologians struggle to nail down the precise origins of their field. One could argue that it has its origins in the mists of time prior to the first scribe who put stylus to clay tablet. One could also point to theologian-practitioners in the medieval period who held out against the rise of Aristotelian scholasticism and the rise of disinterested knowledge in the university. Yet another line of argument would point out that Protestant leaders like Luther and Calvin were consumed by theological passion for the life of faith and the church and had no interest in theological reflection on theological questions of an impractical or speculative nature. The most common line of historical lineage in practical theology connects the rise of the discipline with the arguments that Schleiermacher made for including the three interrelated branches of theological study in the first modern university in the early years of the nineteenth century in Berlin.[1]

A "right" answer to the question of the origins of the field of practical theology is unlikely to exist. Perhaps the complexities of definition and distinction at play when looking back to the field's elusive origins

1. Schleiermacher, *Brief Outline of Theology as a Field of Study.*

make a grand, definitive history of practical theology impossible to discern. In lieu of such a comprehensive narrative, focusing on particular institutions and key figures offer another angle from which we can make out some of practical theology's defining characteristics, current issues, and future possibilities.

Osmer's Place in Practical Theology at Princeton Theological Seminary

Richard R. Osmer has been in dialogue with and an innovator within the long tradition of practical theology, at Princeton Theological Seminary. Since 1812, Princeton Theological Seminary has served as one of several key loci for the unfolding of the story of practical theology in the modern era.[2] In the mode of "applied theology," the founding patriarchs of the seminary regularly brought biblical, theological, and historical insights to bear on the practice of pastoral ministry in their lectures to third-year students on their way to becoming pastors of Protestant churches. Combined with a robust commitment to the practices of prayer, testimony, and preaching on campus, their erudite lectures and pastoral wisdom born of years of leadership experience established the school as a matrix of practical theology for generations of students. Princeton Seminary was nothing if not a theological school utterly devoted to the theological formation of leaders for the church whose pastoral practice would be informed by the best and highest principles of the church's theological inheritance—all of which functioned in the mode of "applied theology" until the midpoint of the nineteenth century.

A remarkable change occurred in the fall of 1854 when Alexander Taggart McGill delivered his inaugural lecture. As the first explicitly designated practical theologian at the seminary, McGill laid out a comprehensive vision for the newly conceived field of practical theology as a consciously thematized intellectual enterprise. McGill observed:

> The man of right conduct for himself, is not always the best man
> to explain even his own conduct, for the benefit of others. In
> daily intercourse, we often find an incapacity of practical men
> to give intelligent reasons for the success with which they direct
> their own business, and meet the challenges and emergencies of

2. For more on Princeton Theological Seminary's influence on the field of practical theology, see Mikoski and Osmer, *With Piety and Learning.*

life; and in the most elevated spheres of magisterial vocation, the same ineptitude has been frequent and striking.[3]

In other words, expert practitioners are not always in the best position to explain why they do what they do. They can usually demonstrate expertise in practice and can provide useful tips and rules of thumb for responsible or even creative practice. Providing a theoretical framework within which such expert practice makes theological sense, however, can elude the expert practitioner. When teaching toward the development of pastoral expertise, McGill argued, a rigorous intellectual framework that can situate expert practice in relation to theological and philosophical principles empowers the practitioner to move beyond mere imitation of the virtuoso instructor toward becoming a practical theologian-in-residence. Theory is needed in order to support, correct, situate, or recreate practice.

A little more than half a century later, Elmer Homrighausen joined the Princeton Seminary faculty with an appointment in Christian education. One of the first translators and promoters of Karl Barth in the American context, Homrighausen continued lines laid down in practical theology by McGill and developed theological vision and normativity of practical theology at the seminary in a vigorous way. The vision and norms arising from the gospel message and the centrality of the church formed the backbone of Homrighausen's approach to Christian education and to the wider field of practical theology within which Christian education functioned.[4] For Homrighausen, careful attention to human experience and the use of insights from various secular fields of study had to be set within a theological framework that gave priority to the destabilizing and transformative power of divine revelation, particularly as manifested in the coming, life, death, and resurrection of Jesus Christ. Homrighausen articulated an approach that gave substantive neo-orthodox definition to the theological dimension of practical theology in the middle decades of the twentieth century.

At mid-century, Seward Hilter brought compelling engagement with human science to the enterprise of practical theology at the seminary. Hiltner went further than McGill and Homrighausen in his serious

---

3. McGill, "Pastoral Theology: An Inaugural Discourse," 55. McGill's groundbreaking work in theorizing practical theology came to light as part of the research that Osmer and the author conducted for their jointly authored work, *With Piety and Learning.*

4. See, for example, Homrighausen, *Christianity in America.*

and sustained engagement with the social sciences, particularly psychology. On the basis of his deep engagement with the complexities of human experience, Hiltner claimed that practical theology could bring about a needed rethinking of established doctrines, if not occasionally new theological insight.[5] His rigorous use of social science research and clinical experience to bring critical perspective to traditional theological conviction brought a newfound appreciation for empirical research in practical theology to Princeton Seminary.

While far from an exhaustive inventory of key practical theologians preceding him, even this brief consideration of the contributions of McGill, Homrighausen, and Hiltner provide context for what has made Osmer's work so important at Princeton Seminary since his arrival in 1989. In his research and teaching, Osmer developed a dynamic theoretical framework for practical theology that provides rich and varied ways to explain pastoral and spiritual practice. Like McGill, Osmer has consistently sought to develop a conceptual framework for practical theology and its related disciplines sufficient to both explain the logic of ecclesial practices and to provide guidelines or something akin to Schleiermacher's "rules of art" for them.[6] As a skilled practitioner of pastoral skills, pedagogical methods, and spiritual practices himself, Osmer has never been content solely to be a practitioner. Instead, he developed a theoretical perspective that makes it possible to understand, explain, reflect theologically upon, and improve practice. Over the years of his critical engagement with Don Browning's "revised correlational" approach, Johannes van der Ven's "empirical theology" approach, or James Loder's "transformational approach," Osmer developed a way to do practical theology that provides an optimal, yet flexible balance between diagnosis and prescription on the one hand and engagement with social science and theological disciplines on the other hand.[7] As an indication of his intellectual humility as well as his considerable analytical abilities, Osmer claims that the conceptual approach he articulated represents more of an "overlapping consensus" of current thinking in the field than his own trademarked or proprietary contribution.

The model that Osmer hammered out in his landmark *Practical Theology: An Introduction* calls for a coordination of four key dimensions

5. Hiltner, *Preface to Pastoral Theology*.

6. See Schleiermacher, *Brief Outline*, 100.

7. See Browning, *A Fundamental Practical Theology*; van der Ven, *Practical Theology*; Loder, *The Logic of the Spirit*.

or moments: the descriptive, the interpretative, the normative, and the pragmatic. Osmer holds that these four moments—while constitutive of work in practical theology—need not be carried out in a strictly linear fashion. Instead, he argues that one could begin in principle with any one of the key moments and engage in practical theological work as long as one systematically works through all four moments.[8] In practice, students of Osmer often miss this point and treat his approach as a four-step linear process—though often with useful effect. Osmer's argument that the four moments do and should function in a dynamic, circular process points to the creativity and flexibility of his conceptual framework and demonstrates how far his approach exceeds that of earlier practical theologians like McGill.

Osmer has made it clear that the theological work of practical theology cannot be relegated solely to the normative moment of his schema. In point of fact, each of the four key moments in Osmer's approach are suffused with theological commitments, insights, and implications.[9] In other words, his framework functions theologically in a fulsome and pervasive sense. Within this more pervasively theological understanding of his approach, Osmer has also made it a priority to ensure that the explicit theological task of reflecting on well-described and deeply-understood human phenomena actually occurs as part of work in practical theology. In both the pervasive and the focused sense, Osmer's approach to practical theology makes it abundantly clear that this field is not "social science light" nor sociology, which aim at describing and understanding human phenomena without holding them up to the light of revelation and without always moving toward constructively faith-ful intervention.

Beyond providing a credible and creative way to coordinate social science and theology into a dynamic interdisciplinary endeavor, Osmer's attentiveness to theological normativity locates his work as distinctive among the pantheon of approaches to practical theology. By taking the complexities of human experience seriously and using the best available tools to get a handle on that experience, Osmer signals that he has great resonance with Hiltner, Browning, van der Ven, and several other European approaches to the field. Yet, his theological perspective arising from the Reformed tradition, especially his deep engagement with the theological work of both Jürgen Moltmann and, more recently, Karl Barth,

8. Osmer, *Practical Theology*, 11.

9. Personal conversation with the author.

moves well beyond the limits of Hiltner's correlationalism, Browning's Niebuhrian moral monotheism, or van der Ven's post-Vatican II liberal Roman Catholicism. This means that human experience, though taken with utmost seriousness, can never finally overpower or subordinate divine communication and disclosure in the person and work of Jesus Christ in practical theology conducted according to Osmer's vision.

This weightiness of revelation pushes Osmer more in the direction of the view of one of his predecessors and former colleagues, James Loder. Like Osmer, Loder strongly affirmed a Reformed commitment to the transcendence of God and the radical disruption of the hiddenness of God in the incarnation, death, and resurrection of Jesus Christ. Osmer, however—much more than Loder—seeks a balance between theological normativity and the contours of human experience. The problem with Loder's heavily-laden theological normativity lies precisely in the fact that it underplays the complexities and vagaries of lived human realities, particularly in relation to social context. This is not to say that Loder ignores human experience; far from it. Yet—unlike Loder—Osmer never allows the theological to overwhelm human experience to the extent that it is merely a foil for divine action. For Osmer, the theological has priority, but not at the expense of the fully and sometimes confoundingly human.

A Singular Voice: Osmer Goes Beyond his Predecessors

Like Homrighausen, Osmer's theological approach has continued to develop over the course of his career at Princeton Seminary. Both of these Princeton Seminary practical theologians began in the field of Christian education and worked from robust theological commitments, gradually expanding the scope of their work and migrating into other areas of practical theology. Yet Osmer's recognition of practical theology's unifying internal logic, his insistence on the importance of qualitative research to elucidate human experience, and his appreciation for practical theology's global context set him apart from his predecessors, and mark him as a practical theologian shaped by his own moment in history.

The Internal Logic of Practical Theology

While never abandoning his commitment to Christian education, Osmer eventually moved beyond education and formation into the fields of spirituality, evangelism, and church development. Osmer recognized in the concrete particularity of the practical theologian's work a deep internal logic connecting multiple practices and disciplines. Christian education—like all forms and modes of practical theology—only occurs in specific times and places with particular groups and individuals. There is no abstract educational ministry that hovers above the ground in a pristine atmosphere of unchanging, universal truths. Instead, context and embodiment matter decisively. In order to work effectively in educational ministry and spiritual formation, the academic or ecclesial practical theologians has to use an array of empirical research tools in order to develop a clear and deep read on the context in which one seeks to form people for Christian faith in light of the gospel. Contextualizing the effort to foster faith and mature discipleship eventually leads to broader thinking about the vicissitudes of congregations' situatedness, and what it takes to help a body of believers in a particular place and time engage the gospel with energy, respect, and commitment.

More than that, this line of thinking leads to disciplined, empirical explorations of the needs and interests of people in a given congregational context who are not currently engaging the gospel in community. For Osmer, and by extension for the rest of us, the ministries of Christian education and spiritual formation, congregational development, and evangelism are indissolubly connected. Indeed, Osmer's work and vocational development bear witness to the internal logic binding together practical theology's various subareas, whether in a department of a theological school or in the ministries of a local church. These arenas of practice are not siloed endeavors so much as they are different aspects of one calling: the invitation to people in particular places and times to hear and engage the gospel message of grace, healing, and hope.

If expertise involves the development and coordination of theory, know-how, contextual awareness, and self-awareness as a practitioner, then Osmer is probably responsible for teaching more pastors, educators, and academic practical theologians how to think about practical theology and to move towards pastoral and academic expertise than anyone else in the history of Princeton Seminary.[10] As a teacher, Osmer has consistently brought innovation and creativity into the classroom by requiring students to engage in empirical research and then equipping and coaching them as they carry it out. He also has helped students to

10. For a discussion of the different elements or kinds of knowing that make up expertise, see Ericsson et al., *The Cambridge Handbook*.

develop sophistication in interdisciplinary methods that can be readily transferred to a wide range of ministry settings and portfolios. In the same way that Osmer saw the logic of practical theology at play in multiple theological practices, he also saw fruitful interaction between the practical theologian and multiple fields of inquiry. Moving beyond practical theology's traditional engagement with psychology and sociology, Osmer's teaching routinely created dialogues between practical theology and fields like communication, organizational theory, and young adult fantasy literature, to name a few.

The role of empirical research in practical theology

To have maximum credibility, a theory of practice, or a theory of the complexity of theory-practice interplay, requires the one articulating the theory to practice what is being preached. More than any of his predecessors, Osmer promoted both quantitative and qualitative empirical research as integral dimensions of practical theology. His commitment to attending closely to people's own accounts of their experience—forged while he was still a graduate student at Candler collecting faith histories for James Fowler's "stages of faith" project—made empirical research increasingly prominent in his work. Osmer designed and carried out dozens of qualitative research projects on three continents, exploring Christian education, spiritual formation, confirmation theory and practice, evangelism, church development, and the problem of evil by using qualitative methods like focus groups, semi-structured interviews, ethnography, and participant-observation. He also worked with a team of practical theologians to develop a five-denomination quantitative empirical study of confirmation practices in the United States that involved thousands of participants.[11] Furthermore, Osmer prioritized teaching pastors, educators, and academics the importance of carrying out their own empirical research in context, while encouraging church leaders and academic practical theologians in South Korea, South Africa, and North America to appreciate the importance of responsible empirical research for theology.

11. See Osmer and Douglass, *Confirming Faith.*

Recognizing Practical Theology's Global Context

More than any practical theologian at Princeton Seminary to date, Osmer has helped internationalize the field of practical theology, and worked to globalize the thinking of students, pastors, and academics alike. He played a central leadership role in bringing together a group of practical theologians from around the world to Princeton Seminary in 1991 to found the International Academy of Practical Theology. Along with Riet Bons-Storm, Don S. Browning, Camil Menard, Karl Ernst Nipkow, Dietrich Rössler, Friedrich Schweitzer, and Hans van der Ven, Osmer established the institutional instrument that for nearly three decades has provided the setting for sharing ongoing research in practical theology for theorists and practitioners from every continent except Antarctica.[12] No longer a geographically and culturally isolated field of study limited to Germany, the Netherlands, the United Kingdom, or the United States, dynamic work in practical theology today can be found among researchers and practitioners alike in South Korea, Norway, Thailand, South Africa, Brazil, Canada, Belgium, Australia, Finland, India, and Croatia. Meeting every two years for several days, practical theologians in the International Academy of Practical Theology share research, develop professional and social networks, and explore a key theme relevant to the host country. While undeniably rooted in a particular institutional context, Osmer's work has nonetheless helped catalyze a global network of creative research and engagement in practical theology.

Future Prospects in Light of Osmer's Contributions

Osmer's work points toward the future development of the field of practical theology in three ways. One of the most important contributions Osmer has made at Princeton Seminary and to the wider field has been an explicit and vigorous commitment to foregrounding theological reflection in practical theology. Osmer resisted pressure from within the field that he felt would cause practical theology to devolve into a form of merely descriptive social science of religious phenomena, encouraging students, pastors, and academics to implicitly and creatively engage theological norms while explicitly urging academics to wrestle with normativity in practical theology. Mere description of lived realities,

12. International Academy of Practical Theology, "History."

however rich and deep, can never be the whole of practical theology. Considering those lived realities in relation to divine revelation, as attested by Scripture and with guidance from ecclesial tradition, provides both interpretive power and leverage for constructive intervention. Said another way, practical theology cannot be reduced to the sophisticated use of social science perspectives and tools; instead, there needs to be at least rough parity in the strength of the use of social science perspectives and theological perspectives.

Methodologically, Osmer's work helps practical theologians of all kinds to remain open to the use of new tools and frameworks. He never limited his toolkit to traditional psychology and sociology, though he used these tools frequently and well. His work opened out to philosophy, communications studies, and literature as examples of interdisciplinary engagement. The challenge that Osmer places before theologians is one of finding the optimal relationship in interdisciplinary work between theological and non-theological resources.

Finally, the international scope of Osmer's work points forward in some specific ways. For example, his comparative work with Friedrich Schweitzer on religious education in the United States and Germany opens up many possibilities for coordinated work across two or more cultural contexts, while suggesting the complexity of the current practical theological task.[13] The comparative approach helps to bring clarity to the participating contexts, illuminates common themes and insights, and lays the groundwork for collaborative contextual practical theological research. Yet in a global, instantaneously interconnected universe, comparative work alone cannot suffice. As new technologies, forms of social media, and challenges and opportunities in human communal life emerge, collaborative work in practical theology must address new levels of complexity, starting with how individuals and communities navigate the nexus of the global and the local in relation to religious meaning making, as well as the insidious tendencies of market forces to amalgamate, poach, and bastardize authentic indigenous cultures.

Osmer's toolkit for practical theology continues to expand. As practical theology confronts hard theological questions about how the interface of the human and the machine shapes human experience; how biotechnology and the possible emergence of cyborgs challenges our notions of life, death, and humanity itself; how shifting climates and

---

13. See Osmer and Schweitzer, *Religious Education*.

migration patterns shape our understanding of, and our physical experience of, earth and neighborhood, there will need to be serious theological reflection around issues like theological anthropology, divine and human agency, and the practice of stewardship, just to name a few. As one who never shrinks from intellectual challenges associated with the engagement of human experience and the gospel, one can easily imagine Osmer rolling up his sleeves and getting to work on such challenges, engaging in practical theological reflection, and providing intelligible reasons for practice.

Bibliography

Browning, Don S. *A Fundamental Practical Theology: Descriptive and Strategic Approaches*. Philadelphia: Fortress, 1991.

Ericsson, K. Anders, et al. *The Cambridge Handbook of Expertise and Expert Performance*. New York: Cambridge, 2006.

Hiltner, Seward. *Preface to Pastoral Theology*. New York: Abingdon, 1958.

Homrighausen, Elmer G. *Christianity in America: A Crisis*. New York: Abingdon, 1936.

International Academy of Practical Theology: History. http://www.ia-practicaltheology.org/history/.

Loder, James E. *The Logic of the Spirit: Human Development in Theological Perspective*. San Francisco: Jossey-Bass, 1998.

McGill, Alexander T. "Pastoral Theology: An Inaugural Discourse." In *Discourses at the Inauguration of the Rev. Alexander T. McGill, D.D., as Professor of Pastoral Theology, Church Government, and the Composition and Delivery of Sermons, in the Theological Seminary at Princeton, N.J., Delivered at Princeton, September 12, 1854, Before the Directors of the Seminar*, 6–64. Philadelphia: C. Sherman, 1854.

Mikoski, Gordon S. and Richard R. Osmer. *With Piety and Learning: The History of Practical Theology at Princeton Theological Seminary: 1812–2012*. Zürich: Lit, 2012.

Osmer, Richard R. *Practical Theology: An Introduction*. Grand Rapids: Eerdmans, 2008.

Osmer, Richard R., and Katherine M. Douglass, eds. *Confirming Faith: Faith Formation as Practical Theology*. Grand Rapids: Eerdmans, 2018.

Osmer, Richard R., and Friedrich Schweitzer. *Religious Education between Modernization and Globalization: New Perspectives on the United States and Germany*. Grand Rapids: Eerdmans, 2003.

Schleiermacher, F. D. E. *Brief Outline of Theology as a Field of Study*. 3rd ed. Translated and edited by Terrence N. Tice. Louisville, KY: Westminster John Knox, 2011.

van der Ven, Johannes A. *Practical Theology: An Empirical Approach*. Translated by Barbara Schultz. Kampen: Kok Pharos, 1993.

Conclusion

Theology's Place in Practical Theology

ANDREW ROOT WITH KENDA CREASY DEAN

GRANDIOSE? WE KNOW. BUT when we think of those early days of practical theology's renaissance, as the work of Browning, Fowler, and van der Ven took shape around a journal and academy, we can't help but imagine Rick Osmer as the Athanasius to these older men's Alexander. Just as Alexander was the leading voice at the Nicene council, and Athanasius his young secretary, soon to be the great theological mind of the Nicene movement, so we imagine Rick Osmer. In our imagination we can see Osmer sitting through meetings, making points, and working through logistics, at that famous 1991 meeting held in Princeton. Osmer may have been in the shadow of the more established practical theologians back in early 1990s. But as the decades would go on Osmer, would become the great theological mind among them.

We don't say this just because Osmer was our teacher (though we will admit our bias on that score), but rather because no one in theorizing about practical theology has as consistently and richly drawn from theological voices as Osmer. Osmer has an acute sense that practical theology would lose its center and soul if it lost the ability to speak of God. As Osmer himself observes in his concluding reflections on this book, "Moving beyond correlational models of practical theology and discovering how to engage the other theological disciplines is one of the most important challenges facing practical theology today."[1] As a good student of Fowler, Browning, and van der Ven, Osmer was intent on speaking of human

---

1. Osmer, "Consensus and Conflict," 220.

action through the social sciences. But without a distinct theological moment (or method) in which the practical theologian does more than just repeat dogmatic ideas—but instead risks speaking directly and freshly about God—practical theology would be hampered.

In this chapter, in honor of Osmer, we'll explore the need for this deep theological attention to God's concrete (and real) action in the world, attending particularly to why, as a field, practical theology has often neglected to follow the model that Osmer embodied. This chapter seeks to contribute to Osmer's legacy by exploring why the theological moment in practical theology (i.e., the speaking directly and specifically about the act and being of God)—which Osmer dubbed *the normative moment*—is necessary for robust practical theological reflection. To be clear, Osmer does not consider normativity a point in time as much as an existential posture of the practical theologian, who brings a normative lens to every practical theological consideration. In that light, every moment in practical theological reflection may be properly considered a normative moment, since theologians look for different things when they describe, interpret, and respond to a situation than, say, politicians or plumbers or statisticians. In the spirit of Osmer, the chapter will attend to the role of divine action in practical theology, even pushing the edges of Osmer's own consensus model to more fully embrace practical theology as a vehicle for noticing and naming ways in which divine action and human action intersect.

The Conundrum of the Core Problematic

As students of Richard Osmer, we (Kenda and Andy) were forced to grapple with what Osmer's colleague and fellow practical theologian James Loder liked to call "the problematic of practical theology." God's Spirit and the human spirit call to one another; they interact. It was therefore the task of practical theologians, Loder believed, to discern the steps in this ongoing divine dance while joining it.[2]

---

2. By the time Kenda knew Loder, who served on her dissertation committee, he functioned as the Princeton Seminary faculty's *de facto* mystic. He insisted on the Holy Spirit's presence in any deviation from the norm of human existence, which he believed—except for regular divine interruptions—was hurtling toward entropy. Entropy finally caught up with him: James Loder died unexpectedly of a brain aneurysm in 2001.

Loder died in 2001. The following year, in a doctoral seminar that I (Andy) took, Osmer assigned a chapter Loder had written. Osmer credited Loder with seeing something clearly that few in the field of practical theology had recognized. In the chapter Loder writes, "Practical Theology is the generative problematic of divine and human action."[3] We agree— but many do not. In fact, Loder's definition and mission for the field of practical theology appears to be a minority position among the major branches of the discipline. Yet overlooking the intersection of divine and human action as the primary nexus of the practical theologian's work has a steep cost. Practical theology has been able to create rich projects on human action in relation to church life, society, and pastoral practice. But these fruitful articulations have not always sailed practical theology into the deep waters of exploring divine action, and therefore miss the generative and problematic nature of practical theology.[4]

Contemplating divine action next to human experience and agency offers deeply generative possibilities to those interested in studying the "text" of the lived Christian life. And yet it *is* "problematic," in Loder's words—for even if we are to contend that divine action is real, it remains a transcendent mystery. How are we to reflect on mystery from the concrete standpoint of human existence?

This is the possibility and peril in practical theology as we voyage into the waters of divine action. We must contemplate how potentially incongruent forms of action can and do relate, even though they exist in different layers or dimensions of reality (e.g., heaven and earth, eternity and history, omniscience and finitude, etc.). To identify the intersection of divine/human action as practical theology's core problematic is to confess the possibility of the event of God encountering us in our concrete and embodied lives. It is a statement of purpose. It is a statement of faith.

Two factors contribute to our inability to discuss divine action in practical theology. The first is practical theologians' erroneous view of divine action as *impractical*. This is especially true where academic practical theology must function within the scientific norms of the university setting ("a degree in make believe" is how one colleague described my [Kenda's] PhD in practical theology). Practical theology's commitment to the lived and embodied realities of concrete persons and communities seems to draw practical theology like a magnet toward conversations

3. Paraphrased from Loder, "Normativity and Context in Practical Theology."

4. Some of the material that follows is an adaptation from part one of Root, *Christopraxis*, 3.

with the social sciences and forms of empirical research. The discourse within these fields and disciplines has given practical theology language and dialogue partners that yield reasoned and reflective approaches to human action.

Divine action, on the other hand, is by definition non-empirical; to mix the metaphysical with the physical is a category error from which there is no return, from the standpoint of the scientific paradigm. Thus, with some exceptions, most practical theological perspectives overlook, underplay, or simply seem disinterested in divine action or transcendent reality—which has made it harder for practical theology to attend to the theological.[5]

The irony is that this perspective flies in the face of Christian theology itself, which confesses God's radical investment and interaction in concrete, lived human experience. Another possibility exists, therefore, for practical theology: to approach divine action as a *deeply* practical and lived reality. People who testify to encounters with God experience these encounters as lived realities, either interwoven into the fabric of daily life or interrupting it with decisive force. These encounters have concrete, observable consequences: they direct human life in formative ways, moving people to do one thing or another in their practical life: join a faith community, quit a high-powered job, forgive oneself for parenting failures, adopt a different outlook on life, etc. These very human experiences are bound in a reality that seems beyond the people who report them. They have been to a "thin place," as the Celts say: they have glimpsed a reality that transcends them, but which is nevertheless *real* to them in the most practical way.

Of course, even scientific observation is no stranger to "impractical" observations; inference and indirection are accepted means of developing hypotheses. We do not observe the wind; we observe its practical effects. Social science owes much to developmental theorists who—long before modern neuroscience could photograph the brain—inferred cognitive development by observing how younger and older children explained their experiences differently. Likewise, denying practical theology's practicality just because it attends to the transcendent risks failing to attend to the truly "practical" (i.e., missing the depth of people's practical experience).

---

5 For an examination of specific projects in practical theology that do this see chapter four in Root, *Christopraxis*, 47–62.

Meanwhile, as a double whammy, overlooking the practical in practical theology has led to a "theological" deficiency as well. As president of the International Academy of Practical Theology in 2011, Bonnie Miller-McLemore wondered aloud about the normative theological nature of the field, even questioning what is theological about practical theology: "For decades, practical theologians have argued that attention to practice as a yield for theology but specifying this or even getting around to it has been difficult."[6] She called discussions around theological normativity a necessary growing edge for the field.[7] Practical theology has rightly started with human experience, but it has been uneasy with the possibility that human experience can be bound up with the divine. This failure to acknowledge people's experiences with God as *real* prevents practical theologians from wading into conceptions of divine action that would move toward unique and substantive theological contributions. These are big claims. How did the practical and theological deficits in practical theology come to be? To find out we'll have to step back and examine practical theology's birth.

Theology's Bastard

Practical theology has experienced a revival of relevance. Born in the ferocious winds of the arrival of enlightenment modernity, practical theology was the bastard child of another radical transition of theological education: a momentous shift in the location of theological education

---

6 "Of course, we must have something interesting to say: "'The primary justification for inclusion is the ability to produce an interestingly different angle on life.' This is where practical theologians face a challenge. No one says practical theology is not normative, constructive, or Christian. But do we have something theologically interesting to say? For decades, practical theologians have argued that attention to practice has a yield for theology but specifying this or even getting around to it has been difficult. If practical theology has been partly about transforming academic theology, then it has to show what it has contributed to theology as theology." Miller-McLemore, *Misunderstanding About Practical Theology*, 58.

7. "Reformulating the final misunderstanding—that practical theology is largely, if not wholly, descriptive, interpretive, empirical—sounds a little like stating the obvious: practical theology is in fact theology. However, there are benefits of a more explicit correction as follows: As theology, practical theology is normative. It makes demands on those who practice it to live by the sacred and transcendent convictions it professes. Greater clarity about our theological and not just our practical contribution is one of our challenges but success in this realm will advance the discipline and its value for religious communities and the common good." Ibid., 59.

from monasteries, abbeys, and humanist classrooms to modern research universities. This shift uprooted theological education from places of formation and repotted it in the soil of empirical science. Because of its new environment, practical theology was pushed beyond the church's protected cloisters into the world.[8]

But its arrival was never celebrated. Until quite recently, in the ethos of the modern scientific research university, theology reigned as queen. Yet practical theology had no claim to royalty; its bloodlines were too mixed with experience and practice—with the practical as opposed to the theoretical—to claim a place before the throne of science. Belittled and ignored, practical theology was the theological encyclopedia's bottom feeder that gathered up intellectual crumbs that fell from the table shared by Bible, systematics, and history.[9] Practical theology was intended to use these scraps to *apply* the noble scientific theories of the university's high table to the peasants out in the practice of ministry. It was believed that if budding pastors had the scientific theory (the true meal) of the classic theological disciplines (dogmatics, history, and Bible), topped off with a few concluding courses (a little sweet and fluffy dessert) on management and liturgical organization, they would be properly nourished and ready to lead.[10]

This perspective held for centuries. With theological education housed in the brick buildings of universities and the church itself

8. Richard Osmer, following Edward Farley and others, has made the point that before the modern research university all theology had a practical edge. Osmer calls such heroes of the faith as Luther, Calvin, Catherine of Sienna, Augustine, and Paul proto-practical theologians, explaining that for them all theology was embedded in concrete communities and was never imagined outside of the lived experience of a people.

9. See Gisbertus Voetius's seventeenth encyclopedia for an example.

10. Duncan Forrester explains, "In both Protestantism and Roman Catholicism this tradition has continued almost up to the present with little or no critical theological reflection or suggestion that the subject is or may be a systematic and rigorous discipline in volume after volume of good advice to ministers, and in hints and tips on how to perform traditional functions of ministry. F. D. Schleiermacher's suggestion that practical theology was the completion and 'crown of theological study' indicated the possibility of a better integration between practical theology and the other theological disciplines. But Schleiermacher saw practical theology as no more than the craft of church management, the channel through which the theories of biblical and systematic theology flow to nourish the life of the church. The present structures of church and ministry were accepted uncritically, as was the assumption that the subject addressed itself exclusively to the practice of clergy." Schweitzer and van der Ven, *Practical Theology—International Perspectives*, 18.

protected by the castles of nobles in Europe and the mono-cultural socialization of North America, the "university" system of theological education was firmly protected from any storm that might blow through.

Winds of Change

But after a few centuries, and leading into the last decades of the twentieth century, the friction created between positivist empiricism and cultural pluralism eroded the brick walls of the university, and the winds of transition began to penetrate the halls of the theology department. These winds brought a bitter chill: empirical fields like the hard or social sciences began to wonder why a university needed a theology faculty at all. As the church lost cultural relevance and faced the challenge of living in a context in which pluralism and doubt met it at every turn, new students—already raw from the winds of transition—stumbled into the cold lecture halls and seminar rooms, shaking their heads as learned professors spoke with little acknowledgment of the state of change, and little concern for how these winds had frozen "applied" theory-to-practice perspectives into irrelevance.

In the 1970s and 1980s a handful of the very scholars teaching in universities made a push for a renewed understanding of practical theology. They would eventually gather in Princeton to stage a renaissance in practical theology. Recognizing the winds of transition and the erosion of the theological encyclopedia, and bolstered by the recovery of practical philosophies (from Aristotle to Marx to American pragmatism to postmodern deconstruction), people like Don Browning, James Fowler, Edward Farley, Mary Elizabeth Moore, Lewis Mudge, Thomas Groome, and Richard Osmer sought to turn the bastard discipline into a prince (or at least mutual sibling).

Arguing that all theology needed to make a turn to the practical, these scholars sought to move practical theology out of the basement of theological education and into a more constructive and essential place within the endeavor. Making a convincing case that concrete communities of practice (whether congregations or other social forms of concrete/lived practice) are the very text of practical theological reflection, they raised the flag on communities as places of embodied theology, contexts where practical wisdom is practiced.

This push gave practical theology a new relevance. Those buffeted by the stiff winds of transition are quick to point to practical theology as a way forward, as a way of connecting theory and practice, theological education and ministry, Christian practice and public engagement. After all, if North American religious institutions are waning, there is nevertheless a potent (though maybe chaotic)[11] spiritual propensity—which suggests strongly that theological education would do well to turn toward these concrete organic communities of experienced practice to learn from them as well as shape them.

More Complicated Than It Seems

Thanks to all those Alexanders, practical theology has been ushered out of its basement room, and—if it is not at the pinnacle of theological prestige, it has nevertheless found fresh air. Moving to the concrete, lived contexts and lived theology—leaving behind the stuffy for fieldwork and questionnaires—practical theology has gained ground both in terms of its significance for churches and for theological scholarship. This push, positively, has not been done simplistically. But because it has not been done simplistically, it has not been free from confusion on what exactly practical theology is and how it goes about its work.

While many standing in the squall of transition have pointed to practical theology as a helpful way forward, these very advocates in seminary administrations or denominational offices have often found it hard to actually say what practical theology is and who does it. Is it something done by pastors, professors, or lay people? And what makes a practical theologian different than, say, a biblical scholar who is concerned for the practice of preaching or bible study in her classroom? Is she a practical theologian as well as bible scholar? And what exactly is a practical theologian? Practical theology's turn to the concrete and lived is essential (and something we deeply affirm), but how is this done?

Moving into Divine Action within Practical Theology

Osmer has provided what he calls his "reflective equilibrium model of practical theology."[12] He explains that this not a method *per se*, though

---

11. Charles Taylor calls this the Nova Effect. See Taylor, *A Secular Age*, part III.

12. For a critical exploration of Osmer's perspective see Hastings, *Practical*

some have used it that way. Rather, it is a model that seeks to explore the shared operations of those calling themselves practical theologians. While Osmer's model seeks to provide some traction on what practical theologians do, we think it shows the importance of attention to the theological.

As this book has shown, Osmer describes four tasks of practical theology: the descriptive, interpretative, normative, and pragmatic. Broadly speaking, these four core tasks articulate what practical theology is and does.[13] The descriptive task asks the question, *What is happening?* and uses tools of thick description—case studies, questionnaires, appreciative inquiry, participant observation, etc.—to answer it.

The interpretative task asks *Why is it happening?* and places the descriptive findings in conversation with frameworks that seek to explain the phenomenon experienced and examined. Typically drawn from the human sciences, these frameworks are often drawn from cultural, sociological, psychological, or anthropological fields.

These two core tasks bind practical theology unequivocally to concrete and lived contexts. Whether it starts with a crisis, established practice, or lived belief, practical theology begins, first and foremost, on the ground. This is a unanimous commitment across the field. Yet it is also what makes the field perplexing to outsiders (and sometimes to insiders). The need for rigorous attention to the descriptive and interpretative DNA of practical theology can makes it appear, to some, as "social science lite." It can be seen as a kind of sociology in the theological faculty, leading some to wonder about the difference between a sociology of religion and practical theology.

Nevertheless, for practical theology to continue to be concrete and lived it must not expunge these tasks from its operation. At the same time, it must also think of how such moves (in themselves) point to the

---

Theology and the One Body of Christ, ix–x.

13. Osmer provides a summary of these tasks. "*The descriptive-empirical task.* Gathering information that helps us discern patterns and dynamics in particular episodes, situations, or contexts. *The interpretive task.* Drawing on theories of the arts and sciences to better understand and explain why these patterns and dynamics are occurring. *The normative task.* Using theological concepts to interpret particular episodes, situations, or contexts, constructing ethical norms to guide our responses, and learning from 'good practice.' *The pragmatic task.* Determining strategies of action that will influence situations in ways that are desirable and entering into a reflective conversation with the 'talk back' emerging when they are enacted." Osmer, *Practical Theology*, 9.

theological nature of practical theology. After all, it appears *en vogue* and ruled as good scholarship to nearly take off the theological hat when doing descriptive and interpretative work, before (maybe) putting it on again later.

When this happens, the descriptive/interpretative tasks becomes locked in epistemology (what humans *know* as constructed and able to be observed) and escapes ontological articulations that touch on concrete and lived ways people lean into the mystery of reality itself, a reality bigger and more than socially constructed constructs. The divine cannot be captured in strict social constructionism without severe reduction. While seeking to avoid reduction but still wed to a hard social constructionism, practical theology runs the risk of avoiding the *theological* and succumbing to the human agent's social construction of God. Or more often, it simply stops talking of God and instead turns to religious phenomena— staying only at the level of the congregation for instance, and its interaction with political ideologies. Moving into the next two tasks is where we begin to push Osmer's perspective.

Two Other Core Tasks

Osmer explains that there are two other core tasks to practical theology, two tasks he calls the normative and pragmatic. The questions that mobilize these two tasks ask respectively *What ought to be happening?* (the normative) and *What then should we do?* (the pragmatic). Osmer explains clearly that though the normative is the heart of the specifically theological move in practical theology, it is not to say that theology has not been present prior to the operation of this task. As a matter of fact, in the appendix to his *Teaching Ministry of Congregations*,[14] Osmer explains that the outworking of these four core tasks, which are shared by all practical theologians are nevertheless mobilized in different ways, depending on one's view of praxis, theological anthropology, or cosmology.

Of these two tasks, the pragmatic, performative moment has been the one to which practical theologians most ardently cling. While practical theology has given its most direct attention to description and interpretation, it has not been shy about claiming its pragmatic mandate, distinguishing itself from pure sociology or anthropology by asserting that it is not only interested in describing and interpreting the world,

14. Osmer, *The Teaching Ministry of Congregations*, 303–17.

but in changing it.[15] For this change to happen, renewed, reimaged, or newly created forms of action are needed. So practical theology attends to honing the reflection on, and performance of, classic practices of the Christian tradition like liturgy or counseling; or it attends to the pragmatic actions of Christian life that are social, public, and even political. Yet the insistence on changing the world, and not just describing it, leads some to assert that practical theology is simply a normative sociology or political anthropology.

Whether such comments are made disparagingly or appreciatively, they reveal that this attention to pragmatic action takes place within normative commitments. To seek to change things is to make some normative assertion about the deficiency of the present and the new direction change needs to take. Osmer's question *What ought to be happening?* has most often been taken in this kind of ethical framework, leading practical theology to be seen by some (particularly Don Browning) as a kind of pragmatically engaged ethics.

While honoring the concrete and lived commitments of practical theology, this perspective on the pragmatic moment of practical theology nevertheless tends to flatten out divine action. Normativity becomes a dialogical engagement with Christian tradition that sets ethical (normative) directions for engagement, but divine action, as an independent and free reality, runs the risk of being lost.

Therefore, from our perspective, it may be better to see Osmer's normative question *What ought to be happening?* not solely in an ethical frame, but in a revelatory one. In other words, the normative questions asks, *What ought to be happening (what ways should we perceive of reality, ourselves, the church, our practice and conceptions of God) now that God has encountered us? What ought to happen now that we have experienced the event of God's encounter?* We might shift this question to, "Now what?"—after we've had an experience with living Christ in our very concrete and lived experience, the practical theologian must ask: "Now what?" now that we've called these experiences *real?*[16]

---

15. "In [practical theology's] focus on concrete instances of religious life. Its objective is both to understand and to influence religious wisdom or faith in action in congregations and public life more generally." Miller-McLemore, *The Wiley-Blackwell Companion*, 14.

16. This is to shift the normative question closer to what Andy (following others) has called *Christopraxis.*

The heart of the normative question is to articulate the "ought," not as defined by a kind of moralistic categorical imperative (Kantian), but as an event of encounter, as an ontological reality, as the unveiling of God's being next to our own. What ought to happen now that the Spirit has come upon us (Acts 2)? *Now what that the Spirit of the living Christ has fallen on us as a very ontological reality?* From the experience of this encounter in Acts, Peter and the disciples are pushed to performative action: to preach, in such a way that it is not only a "best practice" (three thousand are added to their number, as all hear them in their own languages) but as the very participation in the continued action of God (the Spirit moves to build Christ's church by overcoming the curse of Babel in the communion of Word heard and responded to).[17]

Though there are no unanimous ways on how practical theologians use the descriptive, interpretive, normative, and pragmatic tasks, it seems clear that practical theology needs them to secure its identity as a theological discipline with some value within the faculty and church. Osmer's consensus model of the four core tasks offers helpful traction as we grapple with both how practical theology misses the depth of divine action and why it must return to it. Without sufficient attention to normativity, which in Osmer's understanding is shot through the entire process of practical theological reflection, the field of practical theology risks absorption by social sciences, and the practice of ministry risks becoming another helping profession. Reclaiming normativity, on the other hand, restores to practical theology both its "practical" and its "theological" DNA—and paves the way for real, unique, and substantive contributions to theology for our time.

---

17. "While we have suggested that the starting point for Practical Theology is human experience, in fact this is not strictly the case. God and the revelation God has given to human beings in Christ is the true starting point for all Practical Theology." Swinton and Harriet, *Practical Theology and Qualitative Research*, 11.

Bibliography

Forrester, Duncan. "Can Theology be Practical." In *Practical Theology: International Perspectives*, edited by Friedrich Schweitzer and Johannes van der Ven, 15–25. Frankfurt: Peter Lang, 1999.

Hastings, Thomas John. *Practical Theology and the One Body of Christ*. Grand Rapids: Eerdmans, 2007.

Loder, James. "Normativity and Context in Practical Theology." In *Practical Theology—International Perspective*, edited by Friedrich Schweitzer and Johannes A. van der Ven, 359–73. Berlin: Peter Lang, 1999.

Miller-McLemore, Bonnie. *Misunderstanding About Practical Theology: Presidential Address to The International Academy of Practical Theology*. At the International Academy of Practical Theology, Amsterdam, July 2011.

———. *The Wiley-Blackwell Companion to Practical Theology*. West Sussex: Wiley-Blackwell, 2010.

Osmer, Richard. *Practical Theology: An Introduction*. Grand Rapids: Eerdmans, 2008.

———. *The Teaching Ministry of Congregations*. Louisville, KY: Westminster John Knox, 2005.

Root, Andrew. *Christopraxis: A Practical Theology of the Cross*. Minneapolis: Fortress, 2014.

Schweitzer, Friedrich, and van der Ven, Johannes A. *Practical Theology—International Perspectives*. Berlin: Peter Lang, 1999.

Swinton, John, and Harriet Mowat. *Practical Theology and Qualitative Research*. London: SCM, 2006).

Taylor, Charles *A Secular Age*. Cambridge, MA: Harvard University Press, 2007.

Consensus and Conflict in Practical Theology: Reflections

RICHARD R. OSMER

I AM DEEPLY APPRECIATIVE of the work that has gone into this book. Friends, colleagues, and former students have truly honored me with wonderful, evocative, and thoughtful chapters on topics that have been close to my heart over the years. I give special thanks to the editors of the project, who are located in different parts of the world. Thank you, Andy, Kenda, Mandy, and Blair for pulling this all together. And thank you, Friedrich, my longest European friend, for writing the foreword. In these dark days, it is especially important to remain in solidarity with our friends and colleagues around the world. For this reason, I also am very pleased that my former student and, now, colleague and friend, Shin-Geun Jang from South Korea, has been involved in this project. If the gospel is about God's reconciliation of the world in Jesus Christ and we are called to be Christ's ambassadors of reconciliation, then today we must keep our international relationships strong to resist the forces of evil that would divide us.

As I read the chapters of this book, I was reminded of the many gifts I received while teaching at Princeton Theological Seminary. Three in particular stand out. I have been very fortunate to teach at a seminary with such a long and strong tradition of practical theology. Excellent scholarship in the service of the church stood at the heart of this tradition. My wife, Sally, and I co-pastored congregations while students at Harvard and Yale, and after graduating from seminary, we co-pastored congregations in western North Carolina. While I pursued doctoral studies at Emory University, we served as pastors in large congregations in Atlanta. It always felt natural to me to think of my teaching, research, and relationships with students as a form of ministry. This was welcomed at Princeton. Many Princeton practical theologians had approached their work in this way before me. And the broader ethos of Princeton Seminary as a Reformed institution was shaped by John Calvin's belief that professors of divinity are doctors of the church who should be ordained. Scholarship and teaching not only serve the ministries of the church, but are a form of ministry in their own right. My sense of vocation and the institution where I worked fit together as calling and confirmation. For this, I am deeply grateful.

Teaching at Princeton Seminary brought a second wonderful gift: my closest colleagues. These included James Loder, David Wall, and Freda Gardner, and, later, Kenda Creasy Dean, Gordon Mikoski, and Bo Karen Lee. Kenda, Gordon, Bo, and I forged a remarkably collaborative relationship over the years. I was reminded of this especially as I read the chapters of this book by former doctoral students. While I advised the dissertations of a number of these students at PTS, I see the influence of Kenda, Gordon, and Bo in their chapters and, even more, in their vocations. None of these students were *my* students; they always were *our* students. This sort of close collaboration was a part of all our work in education and formation and was a special gift in my time at Princeton Seminary.

Reading this book also has made me aware of how fortunate I was to teach in a setting with such wonderful students in all degree programs. This was a third gift of my time in Princeton. I learned from students every bit as much as they learned from me. They challenged and extended my thinking. They forced me to become clearer about what I was trying to say and to take account of the wide range of cultural and ecclesial contexts they represented. Over the years, I came to think of teaching as dialogue. Looking back, I would have to say that learning through teaching supported my scholarship as much as my own empirical research and reading. Almost all of the books I have written were preceded by courses in which I invited students to engage the subject matter along with me.

It felt very natural for me, thus, to engage the chapters of this book as a kind of dialogue. I have no interest in clarifying or defending my own position on this matter or that. Rather, I want to share some of thoughts and questions evoked by the insights of authors I respect. Here are a few things that emerged in the inner dialogue prompted by my reading.

Discovering Practical Theology

The jointly-authored *Introduction* notes that that my journey as a professor at Princeton Seminary has included the incorporation of new subject areas over the years. I came as a professor of Christian education shaped by my work as a pastor and by my doctoral work at Emory under the tutelage of James Fowler, Charles Gerkin, and Rod Hunter. While at PTS, I later entered the Kairos School of Spiritual Formation and began to include courses that incorporated spiritual companioning: "Spiritual Guidance through the Lifecycle," "Spiritual Awakening Movements," and "Introduction to Spirituality and Missional Formation." Later, at my initiative, I formally gave up my chair in Christian education to become the Ralph B. and Helen S. Ashenfelter Professor of Mission and Evangelism. That journey provides the structure of this book.

The authors are quite insightful to set my engagement of these different ministries against the backdrop of changes taking place in mainline Protestantism. The precipitous decline of mainline congregations during the second half of the twentieth century has, indeed, made the engagement of spirituality and evangelism more important than ever. The *Introduction*'s authors also note that a constant drumbeat throughout my writing and teaching has been my engagement of practical theology. Why has the practical theology discussion been so important over the course of my career?

As I thought about this question, I was taken back to my own theological education. I studied for two years at Harvard Divinity School, mainly at the Center for the Study of World Religions, although I took four very important courses from Rosemary Radford Reuther and Juan Luis Segundo, who were visiting scholars. My wife, Sally, also was a student at Harvard. After two years, we transferred to Yale Divinity School to complete our Masters of Divinity degrees. While at Yale, I took a number of courses in which Karl Barth was prominent. My future colleague George Hunsinger was the TA in several of these courses, and he was a brilliant interpreter of Barth even as a PhD student. However, I took only *one* course at Yale that attempted to integrate theology and practice: "Pastor, Prophet, and Priest," which brought case material from our student placements into dialogue with theology. At Yale, preaching was taught by a person without a background in theology, and pastoral care and counseling were approached from the perspective of the psychology of religion. The professor of Christian Education was known for such poor pedagogy that nobody took his courses—including me. Other courses in "area four" (the so-called application area) were taught by adjunct professors: visiting pastors and expert practitioners in areas like family therapy.

Looking back, what was missing from my education at both Harvard and Yale was any real attention to practical theology as a field of study. There was little attention to practice as a constructive source of theological knowledge, and little effort made to integrate a student's experience across the theological disciplines. My budding interest in Barth was cordoned off from what I was learning about ministry as a student pastor. This led to a real deficit in my ability to draw on theology to guide, understand, and critique my congregations and leadership when I became a full-time pastor following graduation.

It was only upon entering the "Theology and Personality" doctoral program at Emory that I first encountered practical theology as a field of study. Chuck Gerkin, Rod Hunter, and Jim Fowler were major players in the practical theology discussion emerging during the 1980s when I was a doctoral student. In one of Hunter's courses, I was introduced to models of pastoral care, examining the ways theology and practice might be brought into conversation along different lines. Hunter also offered a course on the wisdom literature of the Bible, exploring a tradition of knowledge crafted to evoke wise judgments in particular circumstances. Rod believed that we might find clues here about the kind of theological knowledge constructed in practical theology.

Gerkin taught the doctoral seminar on practical theology and a course on Eric Fromm. I resonated strongly with his extensive use of case study material. This approach was prominent in the Clinical Pastoral Education movement in which Gerkin was a leader before beginning his teaching career at Emory. I had learned the case study method during a CPE intern year at Norwich State Hospital, a psychiatric facility for long-term and acute patients. While Gerkin was writing his classic book *The Living Human Document*, I worked as his research assistant. His approach to practical theology had a lasting impact on my understanding of this field, especially his dialogue with Jürgen Moltmann.

My relationship with Jim Fowler was more complex. Jim's research in *Stages of Faith* catapulted him onto the international stage of education, moral philosophy, and developmental psychology. Throughout the apex of his fame, Jim was a warm and caring mentor to me. He offered personal support and guidance, demanded academic rigor, and opened many, many doors. For example, when our second child arrived and my wife decided to step down as a pastor in a large church in north Atlanta, Jim made it possible for me to support our family financially by serving as the assistant director of research in the Center for Faith Development.

The Formation of a Practical Theologian: Emerging Trajectories, Enduring Questions

I have no doubt that my education as a doctoral student at Emory shaped my life-long interest in practical theology. It opened up trajectories that I continue to explore, and posed questions I still ponder. Looking back, I can identify its impact along four lines. First, my graduate education introduced me to practical theology as a field with a history and research focus. Rod Hunter in particular constantly pressed the question of the constructive contribution of the field. If practical theology does more than apply the research of the other theological disciplines to congregations, what is its constructive contribution to the larger theological enterprise and to public life? Gerkin and Hunter gave epistemic weight to practice in answering this question. Certain knowledge emerges from reflective practice that cannot be gained in any other way. Fowler focused on the empirical dimension of practical theology, not only teaching me how to carry out qualitative research, but also introducing me to the robust European discussion of empirical research in practical theology exemplified in the work of Johannes van der Ven and others. This went a long way toward helping me identify the unique contribution of practical theology as a field. My formation by Gerkin and Hunter, who taught pastoral care, and Fowler, who taught Christian education, also provided me with the important insight that practical theology can be a meeting place for the sub-disciplines of Christian education, pastoral care, preaching, leadership, and evangelism.

Second, my time as a doctoral student introduced me to the importance of engaging fundamental theological issues that are inherent to the work of practical theology. Although I didn't realize it at the time, I was being taught to value practical theology's dialogue with dogmatics and Christian ethics as much as its dialogue with the social sciences. I was encouraged to read theologians like Paul Tillich, Karl Barth, David Tracy, Gustavo Gutiérrez, and Reinhold Niebuhr, as well as theological ethicists like H. Richard Niebuhr and Paul Lehmann. Jürgen Moltmann was a visiting scholar while I was a doctoral student at Emory, and I had the good fortune of attending some of his classes. Moltmann would prove to become the most important dogmatic theologian I would engage for most of my career. His influence on my work is under-represented in this book, only appearing in the chapter by Shin-Geun Jang. It is Moltmann who represents best, I believe, what transversal rationality looks like in the interdisciplinary work of theology, repeatedly altering his dialogue partners as he takes up different doctrines. Moltmann provided me with theological frameworks for *Practical Theology: An Introduction* (for example, his inclusion of Jesus as sage in his creative reworking of the threefold office of Christ) and *The Teaching Ministry of Congregations* (especially his understanding of God's dealings with the world as a comprehensive narrative with various divine and human actors, which I recast as theo-drama).

Third, as a doctoral student, I was encouraged to think of practical theology as inherently inter- and multi-disciplinary. At Emory, I took courses on John Dewey from John Gowanlock in the philosophy department, and studied human development with Margaret Beale Spencer and Laurie Adamson in the psychology department. I also had the very good fortune of taking a doctoral seminar on Marx, Weber, and Durkheim from sociologist Steven Tipton, one of the primary authors of the then-newly released *Habits of the Heart*. I took comprehensive exams in psychology and social science and was constantly encouraged by Fowler, Gerkin, and Hunter to reflect explicitly on interdisciplinary method in theology in dialogue with Tillich and Tracy, as well as practical theologians like Don Browning, Rebecca Chopp, Sallie McFague, and Matthew Lamb. This fascination with interdisciplinarity would become a career-long interest that was deepened substantially at Princeton Seminary through regular opportunities to team-teach a doctoral seminar with my colleague Wentzel van Huyssteen, the James McCord Professor of Theology and Science.

Fourth, my relationships with Fowler, Hunter, and Gerkin opened up relationships to colleagues in the practical theology discussion. Through Hunter, for example, I met Seward Hiltner, and through Gerkin, John Patton. Fowler encouraged me to participate in the Association of Practical Theology, where I met Don Browning, who became a generous mentor, inviting me to participate in several multi-authored books. In the Association of Practical Theology, I first met young practical theologians from the University of Chicago, Garrett-Evangelical Seminary, Princeton Theological Seminary, and Claremont School of Theology who would later become leaders in the field: Pam Couture, Bonnie McLemore-Miller,

James Poling, Mary Elizabeth and Allen Moore, Daniel Schipani, and others. While at Princeton, my relationship to Fowler opened the door to collaboration with Hans van der Ven, Don Browning, Camil Ménard, Dietriech Roessler, Riet Bons-Storm, Friedrich Schweitzer, and Karl Ernst Nipkow in order to establish the International Academy of Practical Theology. In particular, this collaboration led to a long-term friendship and partnership with Friedrich Schweitzer that led to three books and parallel studies on confirmation in Europe and the United States.

In short, I learned as a doctoral student that practical theology is a fully academic, research-oriented field with dialogue partners in philosophy, the human sciences, and the other theological disciplines. I wrote a (very) long dissertation in which I approached Christian education as a form of practical theology. It is little wonder that I continued to think in terms of practical theology as I began to focus on Christian spirituality and evangelism later in my career.

How My Thinking on Practical Theology Has Changed

In recent years, my continuing interest in practical theology has focused on evangelism, church planting, and mission. I have been surprised that very few scholars draw on the practical theology discussion to think about evangelism and even fewer approach this field with a serious engagement of dogmatic theology. I count myself very fortunate to have had a colleague and friend at Princeton Seminary who engaged both fields: Darrell Guder. Before coming to PTS, Darrell taught evangelism in two seminaries and authored some of the very best books on this practice of ministry. He situates evangelism within a broader discussion of the *missio Dei*, the mission of God, and changes taking place in Christianity across North America. He argues—rightly, I believe—that one of the best theologians to have explored evangelism is Karl Barth. With George and Deborah Hunsinger as two of my closest colleagues on the Princeton Seminary faculty, I had additional Barthian dialogue partners close at hand. At the time I began seriously exploring evangelism through the lens of practical theology, two doctoral students I was advising, Nate Stucky and Blair Bertrand (both of whom have chapters in this book) were drawing extensively on Barth in their dissertations. The three of us, along with Tom Hastings (also a contributor to this volume), began to share our writings and discuss Barth on an ongoing basis.

This recent encounter with Barth has led me to rethink some of the ways I have written about practical theology in the past. When I wrote *Practical Theology*, I was trying to offer *"An Introduction,"* as the subtitle indicates. I focused on some of the key tasks that contemporary practical theologians pursue in their work. While all writing is situated, I tried not to advocate my own theological perspective at that point (Jürgen Moltmann) or my favorite dialogue partners in the human sciences (sociology and psychology). I hoped to introduce readers to a variety of perspectives and potential resources.

The book remains a helpful *introduction*. As I have focused more of my thinking on evangelism in dialogue with Barth, the way I think about practical theology has changed. I share here a brief summary of my current thinking.

1. I believe it is important for practical theologians to foreground their substantive theological convictions in their research and writing. This is particularly the case in reflecting on evangelism, which draws such highly charged positive and negative responses. Today, I find especially helpful Barth's understanding of election and reconciliation, which shapes his missional ecclesiology. Evangelism within this framework is *one* form of the church's witness, which encompasses the saying, doing, and being of the gospel in the service of God's reconciliation of the world in Jesus Christ.[1] Indeed, all forms of ministry participate in God's mission of reconciliation. The ministry of practical theology is to study, critique, and guide the missional witness of congregations in particular times and places.

2. An important assumption of my approach to practical theology today is the priority of ontology over epistemology. The being God determines our knowing of God. This is grounded in what many scholars call Barth's "actualism," a set of interlocking claims: God has God's being in God's acts; there is no hidden God behind the God revealed in the incarnation, life, death, resurrection, and ascension of Jesus Christ; our knowledge of God should take its bearings from God's self-giving in Christ. The modern and postmodern habit of starting with what we can or cannot know is reversed. We can know God only as God gives Godself to us, and this has taken place in a unique and unsurpassable way in Jesus Christ.

1. Saying, doing, and being the gospel is Darrell Guder's way of putting this point. See, Guder, *Be My Witnesses*, 91.

3. Without spelling it out in detail, I believe Barth's christocentric trinitarianism has important implications for the way we carry out theology. It bids us to give special attention to Scripture, for here God's reconciliation of the world in Jesus Christ is narrated and reflected on in the context of the story of Israel. Moreover, the inclusion of four, not one, Gospels in the canon, as well as Luke's story of the early Christian mission and a range of letters to congregations in diverse contexts (including Revelation's letters to the seven churches and vision of a new heaven and earth) orients us to the source and task of theology. The diverse material of Scripture is the source of our most important knowledge of God, telling us who God is, how God has acted in the past, and what God's people are called to do and be. Over the centuries, Scripture has been handed down and rehearsed in worship, studied in teaching, and used to comfort and criticize God's people prophetically. This is the task of theology in all its forms: to bring to mind the God attested in Scripture so that God's people might worship and serve the Lord in their own time and place. This is not merely a matter of repeating what theologians of the past have said. Nor is it simply a matter of finding the one, true "biblical" position on this matter or that. Rather, it is a matter of listening to Scripture as God's living Word that addresses God's people again and again in new times and places.

4. The centrality of Scripture's witness to God—the center of which is God-with-us in Jesus Christ—leads me to underscore practical theology's dialogue with various forms of theology that have emerged across the centuries to guide and criticize the church in its worship and service of God. Today, I give priority to practical theology's dialogue with Christian biblical studies, dogmatic theology, church history, and Christian ethics over its dialogue with philosophy and science. The latter remain indispensable dialogue partners in understanding our context and world. But we should not expect them to be as important to our constructive work in practical theology as the study of Scripture, the doctrines and history of the church, and Christian ethics. Moving beyond correlational models of practical theology and discovering how to engage the other theological disciplines is one of the most important challenges facing practical theology today.

5. My work on evangelism has led me to ask basic questions anew. What is the gospel? What does it mean for the church to bear witness to the gospel? How is the church's mission related to God's mission? The more basic these kinds of questions have become, the more I have found it necessary to learn from the other theological disciplines. Much of my most recent thinking about evangelism centers on gaining a better understanding of God's reconciliation of the world in Jesus Christ. At its most basic, evangelism in the New Testament is the announcement of good news. Jesus announces the good news of the dawning of God's kingdom in his words and works. Paul announce the good news of Christ's death and resurrection to all people because he believes it alters the situation of all people.

6. Following Barth, I emphasize Scripture's portrait of God's reconciliation of the world in Jesus Christ as an accomplished reality that is universal in scope. Christ dies that *all* might be pardoned. Christ lives in perfect faithfulness to God that *all* might be raised to new life in him. The objectivity of God's reconciliation is followed by its subjective appropriation by persons and communities at different times and places. But the soteriological moment is *not* when persons make a "decision for Christ." Scripture is clear that reconciliation is God's doing, and it has taken place in the events of Christ's life, death, and resurrection. That is the soteriological moment. Our subjective appropriation of this accomplished reality, moreover, does not follow one experiential pattern in all times and places. Paul's dramatic conversion is one way this takes place. But Peter's (and the disciples') slow unfolding journey toward recognition of Jesus as Savior and Lord is another. Persons and communities, like the Galatian church, may be persuaded to follow a different gospel and need to be re-evangelized. Evangelism is sharing the good news of the gospel. How people respond should not be forced into a cookie-cutter pattern, which ultimately is not Scriptural and overemphasizes human agency as the instrument of salvation.

7. I have come to believe that Lesslie Newbigin is right when he writes that the congregation represents the first hermeneutic of the gospel.[2] It is in the shared life of a concrete community of disciples that people first see and hear what is at stake in the gospel. My way

2. Newbigin, *The Gospel in a Pluralist Society*, 227.

of putting this is to say that *the congregation is the first evangelist.* If the gospel is the good news of God's reconciliation of the world in Jesus Christ, then congregations must become a reconciled and reconciling people in order to bear witness to the gospel. Congregations must embody a spirituality of reconciliation in their life together, and they must engage the world as a people committed to reconciliation. Barth aptly describes congregations' engagement of the world as a "revolt against the disorder" of the lordless powers.[3] In championing the Prince of Peace, congregations disturb the false peace that normalizes enmity, war, oppression, ethno-nationalism, racism, economic injustice, and violence. As reconciling communities, they stand in solidarity with the world, even as they stand against the world, for the world is loved by God, has been reconciled to God in Christ, and is moving toward the day when this reality will be revealed to all.

8. Evangelism is sharing the gospel of reconciliation with others. It takes place in many different ways: in conversations in families, in relationships at work or with friends, in small groups that welcome seekers, lapsed Christians, or people in crisis, and in one-with-one relationships. The approaches and models of evangelism will change. They are context-dependent. They are not as important as the substance of the gospel that is shared and the ways the gospel is embodied in the life and mission of congregations as reconciled and reconciling communities. Research indicates that mainline Protestant congregations do not engage in much evangelism. This is deeply troubling. The gospel is good news—the very best news possible. Did the mainline lose touch with the gospel somewhere along the way? Do its members prefer niceness and low commitment to the life-giving but demanding transformation inherent to learning a way of life that requires forgiveness, confrontation, deep learning, mutual sacrifice, and identification with the pain of the world? Is the evangelism deficit in the mainline really a gospel deficit? If so, then what might practical theologians have to say to this situation?

---

3. Barth, *The Christian Life*, par. 78.

Consensus and Conflict: An Appreciative Dialogue

This brief outline of some of the ways my thinking about evangelism have shaped my current understanding of practical theology provides a backdrop to my response to the chapters that come after the Introduction of this book. I view this as a dialogue in which I have much to learn, just as I gained so much from the students I taught at PTS. What I have to share in response is shaped by my thinking in the present more than what I have written in the past.

The Educator: Forming the Faithful

The first section, *The Educator: Forming the Faithful,* includes three chapters that exemplify the importance of biblical and theological reflection on the ministries of faith formation in the church. These chapters also invite us to recognize that the renewal and transformation of the church is likely to emerge from unlikely sources: children, young people, and newcomers.

Amanda Drury's beautifully written chapter explores the use of fantasy literature in imagining alternate worlds, especially the strange new world of the kingdom of God. As she puts it: "Children's fantasy literature tills the soil for the kingdom of God—it allows the kingdom of God to germinate through 1) calming the watchful dragons of myopic realism, 2) opening our ears to the testimony of children and 3) awakening within us a moral imagination to envision a new world." Drawing on Scripture, she reminds us that more than once Jesus pointed to children to teach adults what it means to enter the kingdom of God. So too, we must consider, not only the ways fantasy literature might form the imagination of children, but also, the importance of the imagination in the discipleship formation of youth and adults.

For most of my life, Christian education has over-emphasized cognitive/moral/faith development and critical reflection. We are challenged here to reconsider. Imagination is not something we leave behind as we grow and develop. It remains important to all forms of creativity. Mandy invites us to consider more deeply how we might engage the imaginations of children, youth, and adults in order to help them see their lives and world differently, from the perspective of God's kingdom. Jesus' most characteristic form of teaching used parables to this end. How might we engage the imagination in analogous ways today?

I have experienced Kenda Dean's magic before and have seen her use it on others. One part emerging insight; two parts Kenda's thinking and creativity; *voilà*, something wonderful and interesting suddenly appears. This is what I experienced when reading her chapter on my contribution to the theological turn in youth ministry. This turn is something Kenda and Andy Root are especially well-known for, but I suspect all of the Timothy Scholars[4] are contributors to this movement in different ways. The chapter explores why it is not adequate to focus exclusively on young people's "needs" and to think of Christian ministry primarily as meeting these needs—a common pattern when psychology or cultural interpretation dominate practical theology. The more important task is discerning God's mission and forming young people to participate in this mission as part of a community of disciples.

Among the many issues raised by this chapter, one is especially important to practical theology: How do we bring theology into conversation with other fields that are helpful in understanding the psychological, biological, and cultural contexts of teens and young adults? Focusing exclusively on their needs is not adequate. But ignoring their context and stage of life is not adequate either. Kenda's Wesleyan tradition offers a rich resource to reflect on these kinds of interdisciplinary issues, the so-called Wesleyan quadrilateral, which portrays Scripture, tradition, experience, and reason as sources of knowledge of God.[5] The relative weight granted to each of these sources is subject to debate. I am hopeful that the movement Kenda and others are championing will continue to take up the full range of theological issues involved in practical theology—from methodology to empirical research to good practice. As the chapter points out so nicely, every issue of importance to theology is at stake in the church's work with young people.

Jessicah Krey Duckworth's chapter on catechesis invites us to consider the relationship between formation and Christian education. Formation takes place through learning and participating in the practices of the Christian community, which embody a way of life. Christian education affords opportunities to learn the meaning of these practices,

---

4. The Timothy Scholars were a cohort of PhD students studying at PTS in the area of Christian education with a special emphasis on ministries with youth and young adults. They were supported by an outside donor seeking to strengthen the church's ministries with young people by strengthening this subject area in contemporary theological education.

5. Albert Outler coined this term; see Gunter et al., *Wesley and the Quadrilateral*.

to pose questions about them, and to change them when they are no longer responsive to people's lived experience and lose the capacity to bring them into a relationship with the living God. As Jessicah points out, formation and education were both present in the catechesis of the early Christian community, which provides us a kind of norm of good practice: "A dynamic catechesis seeks to interpret the heart of the gospel in light of concrete situations and experiences within the contemporary community of faith in order to facilitate encounter with Jesus Christ." She develops this further in dialogue with the theologian Mary Solberg's interpretation of Luther's theology of the cross.

Luther's portrait of the Christian life emphasized the "ever new" reception of God's grace. It is not the "more and more" of growth in faith; it is the "ever again" of faith that returns to and depends on God's grace afresh every morning because it is God's free gift that is received in its totality day by day—like manna in the wilderness. Jessicah is subtly relocating the entire practices discussion in this theological framework. She does so by sharing examples of catechesis involving children and newcomers in the faith community. Both represent those who "don't know," who are situated at the moment of receiving from others. But their receiving is a giving, for their questions and wondering invite adults and long-term members to begin again at the start and see things afresh. This is how the church is renewed, as grace is mediated through those who stand at the beginning and edges of the Christian way of life and remind long-time members that they must become like little children and new members if they are to receive anew the gift of God's love upon which they always depend.

The Spiritual Director: Testing the Spirit

I have the advantage of reading the chapters of this book after they were written. This allows me to see the three chapters of the second section, *The Spiritual Director: Testing the Spirit*, as fitting together. Angela Reed focuses on spiritual companioning; Nathan Stucky, on the theological presuppositions of the modern missionary movement during the colonial period as they continue to impact theological education. Too often, spirituality is viewed as inward-looking, focusing exclusively in the spiritual life of the individual, and mission as outward-looking, focusing on social change. As Bo Karen Lee shares in the last chapter of this section, our teaching in the Spirituality and Mission track in Education and Formation at Princeton Seminary has led us to view spirituality and mission as interrelated. You can't think about companioning ministries without also thinking about mission. You can't think about mission without also thinking about the spirituality of the church shaping the Christian imagination. It is helpful, thus, to read the three chapters together.

Angela Reed defines spiritual companioning as "a way of accompanying others in intentional relationships of prayerful reflection and conversation that help them notice God's presence and calling in their personal lives, local communities, and the world." By definition, thus, spiritual companioning pays attention to *calling*, the particular task or vocation persons are given by God. The context of this calling is their personal life, the community in which they live, and the broader needs of the world. Spirituality, thus, is not primarily a matter of personal benefit and psychological growth—though these may follow. It involves paying attention to the living God with the help of another person to discern the vocation God is calling a person to do and be.

Angela is somewhat unique in approaching the field of spirituality in terms of practical theology. Focusing on the case of Jason, she explores how this perspective might help us understand the kind of companioning Jason's spiritual direction group offered him as he worked through the loss of his father. She raises questions about the normative dimensions of spiritual companioning: the adequacy of Jason's image of God and the congruence of his beliefs, experience, and feelings. She also indicates that the congregation is the proper context of spiritual companioning, for it is only one practice among many that form persons in the Christian way of life, a life that includes "witness and service." She also raises one of the most important insights of contemporary practical theology: practice has epistemic weight. Learning through practice and studying practice is a source of knowledge that practical theology offers to the larger theological enterprise. How to conceptualize this source of knowledge in relation to Scripture, tradition, and the knowledge of the human sciences remains an important challenge for cotemporary practical theology.

Nate Stucky's chapter embodies beautifully what Barth calls the church's revolt against the disorder of the lordless powers.[6] Drawing on Willie Jennings's *The Christian Imagination*, Nate presses us to engage in a "deep exploration of the genesis of colonialism and the advent of racial

---

6. See Barth, *The Christian Life*, par. 78.

logic." He notes that Jennings argues that "the colonial moment—the moment when racial logic and destruction spread like cancer throughout the world—that moment depended on and grew out of a division between human identity and land in the mind of the colonizer." Jennings traces the way theological ideas like supercessionism, papal infallibility, and apostolic succession "bloat the church's sense of itself" and create a Christian imagination that sets the stage for the modern missionary movement in which "the colonizer becomes the (white) norm of Christ-likeness; and all lands and peoples are subject to the dominion and judgment of the colonizer." Nate raises a simple but fundamental counter-question: How did Christ enter the world?

> Some would say the world longed for a conquering emperor—a display of force that would set the world aright. Instead, the all-powerful Creator of the universe comes as an infant child to an unwed teen mother with livestock and lowly shepherds keeping watch. The Lord of the universe comes to a particular land, a particular time, and a particular place, and before engaging any public ministry spends decades learning. Jesus learns the language, the culture and customs, the land and geography, the food and the festivals, and only after these decades of simply being native to his place does he begin a public ministry.[7]

The chapter ends by returning to issues raised at the beginning. How do the presuppositions of colonialism continue to shape the Christian imagination informing theological education, and what contribution might new ventures, like the Farminary, make to breaking its logic?

Bo Karen Lee's chapter shares some of the thinking that went into the creation of the Spirituality and Mission track in Education and Formation at Princeton Seminary. She gives me far too much credit. At every step, her gifts as a historian and theologian of spirituality complemented my background in practical theology and Christian education. When I described the wonderful gift of a collaborative relationship with my closest colleagues at PTS, I certainly had Bo in mind. We were determined to bring spirituality and mission together. As Bo notes, I have sometimes drawn on David Bosch's concept of the church as a two-pointed ellipse in which the upbuilding and sending of congregations are both important. Practical theology informed by this ecclesiology necessarily holds

---

7. Stucky, *Consensus and Conflict*, 84.

spirituality and mission together and seeks to discover and nurture the deep connections between these constitutive elements of the church.

Bo helps us see why it is important to read Angela's chapter and Nate's together. Spiritual companioning cannot be done well without attending to the particularities of person, story, place, and events—as we see in the case of Jason. Yet, these particularities are always interpreted against the backdrop of the church's understanding of its mission: its calling to worship and serve God in the world. As Nate's chapter makes so clear, we still inhabit an imagination shaped by colonialism, which is perfectly comfortable with a spirituality focusing on individuals who are not challenged to confront the logic of racism, power, and privilege embedded in the imagination of the church. Discovering deep connections between new, post-colonial understandings of mission and life-shaping spiritual formation is one of the most important contributions practical theology can make in the coming decades.

The Evangelist: Sharing God's Good News

The third section, *The Evangelist: Sharing God's Good News*, is composed of three chapters that place evangelism in comprehensive theological frameworks. This is absolutely crucial to reimagining evangelism today. We cannot take it for granted that we know what evangelism is, for much of the thinking and practice of this ministry took shape during the colonial period and is limited by the kinds of distortions Nate Stucky pointed to in the previous section. We must think anew about sharing the gospel in dialogue with contemporary biblical scholars, dogmatic theologians, and good practice—as we see in this section.

No one has influenced my understanding of evangelism more than Darrell Guder, and I thank him for his generous colleagueship during the years I taught evangelism at PTS. If I left seminary many years ago ill-equipped to relate Karl Barth's theology to my ministry, Darrell has provided great help in overcoming this lacuna in the latter years of my teaching. His chapter represents an amazingly fine overview of missional theology shaped by Barth's perspective. Since I agree with so much of what he says here, I simply want to highlight some of the ways this chapter contributes to the current discussion of practical theology.

First and most importantly, Darrell makes it clear that, in the end, how we define the nature, purpose, and methods of practical theology must be shaped our substantive theological commitments. Of course, it is possible to define practical theology as a field and write general introductions, but the real work of practical theology takes place in the context of committed and articulated theological convictions about God, the church, salvation, and so forth. We need to acknowledge this and claim it. We are *doing* theology, not simply talking about theology. The missional theology articulated in the chapter represents the kind of theological work we should be doing.

Second, Darrell, like Barth, points to the damaging effects of the silo mentality in modern theology. His chapter embodies what it looks like to bring dogmatic theology, biblical studies, church history, and practical theology into conversation. Third, he implies, but does not fully develop, a key challenge in this dialogue: How and why do we choose certain dialogue partners in theology and not others? Biblical studies, today, for example is highly pluralistic. Darrell gives examples near the end of his chapter of the ways Paul's letters were written to form his congregations for mission. In other writings, he draws on the work of biblical scholars to spell out more fully what it means to approach Scripture with a missional hermeneutic. This has been a topic of discussion in a working group at the American Academy of Religion for several years. Practical theologians need to participate in discussions like this in order to make informed choices about contemporary biblical criticism. How should they negotiate historical, literary, rhetorical, feminist, theological, social science, and other approaches to Scripture?

Finally, Darrell mentions at several points the misleading ways the dichotomy between theory and practice is used to characterize the tasks of theology. This is particularly pernicious when practical theology is assigned the role of application, as if it did not contribute research and theory in its own right. But an important question remains, and it must be pressed to those of us influenced by Barth: what does practice actually contribute to the constructive work of theology? When we practice and study evangelism in particular contexts, for example, how does this shape our understanding of mission or witness or Barth's twelve forms of ministry/service? Do we learn from practice? If so, how do we describe its contribution? More work is needed on this issue.

My long-time friend and colleague Tom Hastings also offers an extended example of the way practical theology engages biblical studies, church history, and confessional tradition in reimagining the central practices of the faith community. Tom first engages Walter Brueggemann, who portrays the writings of the Old Testament in terms of three distinct kinds of literature that represent different ways of knowing and following God: (1) the intergenerational transmission of the Torah by the priests, (2) the disruptive announcement of judgment and hope by the prophets, who call for justice in the community, and (3) the education of individuals for wise judgment in everyday life by the sages, who also help the community to face up to the mystery of God's ways. Tom argues that this threefold pattern is appropriated and transformed by the early church in ministries of worship, witness, and wonder. He moves on to explore how these ministries were continued in the catechetical instruction of the Reformation period and their continuing viability today. He concludes by making a constructive proposal in which worshipping, witnessing, and wondering are central. Evangelism finds its proper context within this broader framework. This is a splendid example of constructive work in practical theology in dialogue with a range of theological disciplines.

As a former professor of evangelism at Wesley Theological Seminary and prominent pastoral leader in the United Methodist Church, Drew Dyson helps us see how the study of practice and theological construction go hand in hand. Drew made a highly persuasive case in his dissertation that John Wesley was the first missional theologian of the post-Reformation period. In this chapter, he turns his attention to three congregations' ministries of evangelism with emerging adults, concluding that a missional ecclesiology "awakens" emerging adults to faith and offers meaningful participation in faith communities. He draws out three threads of theological commitment discovered in these settings: "a clear understanding of individual and corporate Christian vocation, or purposeful work; a strong sense of identity and belonging within the community of faith; and a posture of radical openness and hospitality to the community beyond the church." These threads do not add up to a model or program that can imitated elsewhere. Rather, they are strands of missional ecclesiology that take on the hues of very particular faith communities located in different contexts.

Drew's chapter complements nicely the two other chapters in this section and goes a long way toward answering the question of the contribution of practice to the constructive work of practical theology. The study of practice provides us with cases of good practice that help us imagine how ministry in other contexts might be reformed. Moreover, it yields knowledge that poses questions to our colleagues in other fields of theology. Are their ecclesiologies sufficiently attentive to vocation, belonging, and radical hospitality? If not, then perhaps they should think again, for Drew has found these to be especially salient to ministry with emerging adults today, a group at risk of departing the church altogether.

The Practical Theologian: Legacy and Promise

The final section, *The Practical Theologian: Legacy and Promise*, draws attention to my ongoing interest in practical theology—from my work as a pastor while at Harvard and Yale to my doctoral studies at Emory to my most recent thinking about evangelism. These chapters take up issues of methodology in practical theology. Focusing on methodology exclusively and *ad nauseum* is problematic. But it is helpful while actually doing constructive work and even necessary in our age of intellectual pluralism. I have been especially blessed by thoughtful colleagues like Gordon Mikoski and excellent students, who later became colleagues, like Blair Bertrand, Andy Root, and Shin-Geun Jang, who took to methodological issues from the very beginning of their time at Princeton Seminary. I am pleased to dialogue with their thinking again.

Blair's chapter rightly locates me in the Reformed tradition and sets forth beautifully many of the ways this tradition has shaped my thinking. I am very much a Presbyterian pastor and theologian. I was raised in a southern Presbyterian church offering me excellent catechesis up to and beyond confirmation. Blair traces this influence on my work, not to pigeonhole me, but to raise the broader issue of the way traditions shape scholarship. He asks if this should be taken into account more fully in my depictions of "metatheoretical" issues in practical theology. Blair raises a number of important questions, and I can only take up one here: the relationship between theological tradition and what I have called theological rationale.

In light of what Blair writes, I am inclined to agree that tradition is a very good way of characterizing the entire cluster of decisions people make about metatheoretical issues and the way they "hang together" in a person's actual work. Concepts like "paradigms" and "research programs" have been used in similar ways. Tradition, however, is less restrictive and serves this purpose better. When used to reflect on practical theology, it would allow us to point, not only to higher-order metatheoretical decisions informing our constructive work as scholars, but also to other dimensions of our formation, like our emotions and habits of practice and thinking, that continue to shape our current work. As many have pointed out, it makes little sense to separate rationality from our bodies, dispositions, and history. Tradition is a helpful way for practical theologians to give an account of themselves as embodied beings.

I am not persuaded, however, that we need to abandon the concept of rationale to make this move. In passing, I should note that my brief comments on metatheoretical decisions in practical theology have always been highly tentative. While I point to four kinds of issues, I have never claimed that only these four are important. Rather, they are offered as examples of the kinds of decisions practical theologians make—often implicitly—as they engage in more focused work. If Blair develops a way of thinking about tradition that clarifies why certain metatheoretical issues need special attention, it may be beneficial to think in terms of overlapping and interacting traditions. Practical theology today is highly pluralistic, and one of its strengths since Vatican II is its ecumenicity— Catholics and Protestants in dialogue. From Wentzel van Huyssteen, I learned to view dialogue in pluralistic fields through the lens of "reflective equilibrium": looking across a field at a certain point in time and articulating what we have in common, as well as our differences. The reality of different traditions in conversation persuades me that something like the category of rationale might continue to be helpful.

Personally, I believe substantive *theological* commitments should be brought forward to ground one's understanding of practical theology. I am aware that not everyone works this way; many provide a rationale for their work in terms of the substantive concepts of philosophical, hermeneutical, or feminist traditions and, thus, work differently than I do. Moreover, many draw on theological traditions that are different than my own Reformed tradition. I do not want to argue that "all others must do as I do." Both dispositionally and intellectually, I am not Barthian in this regard, if this means yelling a loud "No!" towards those with whom I disagree. Mutual respect, conversation across differences, and working together for the common good is badly needed in our world, and practical theology should be one of the places this is practiced. Obviously, the themes of tradition, rationale, and reflective equilibrium deserve further attention, as do many others in the fine chapter that Blair has written.

I have great respect for the highly creative and genuinely constructive work Andy Root is doing in practical theology. He has the gift of addressing both a wide reading public and scholars who are interested in highly technical methodological and theological issues. I am particularly taken with his attempt to bring practical theology into conversation with critical realism and major theological figures like Eberhard Jüngel, Søren Kierkegaard, Dietrich Bonhoeffer, and Karl Barth. He is moving in directions very close to my own. This is why it is easy for me to imagine Andy and I beginning a conversation about issues we are both exploring. In that conversation, I would raise several questions.

First, what is meant by critical realism? There are a wide variety of critical realisms present in philosophy, science, and theology. As Blair would say, it is important to locate ourselves in a particular tradition. Second, what is the relationship between critical realism and *theological* critical realism? At times, Andy focuses on the latter, as in his discussion of God as act and being, as event, and as ministering presence. At other points, he uses the category of critical realism more generally—which seems to make it a *tertium quid*, the meeting ground for theology and other fields of study. Does this run the risk of importing an "immanent" or, perhaps better, an "alien" frame and allowing it to set the terms for theology? Taking advantage of critical realism's depiction of a stratified model of reality and refusing to turn theology into one more "level" within this account (e.g., at the foundation: Alister McGrath; at the top: Nancey Murphy and George Ellis) is one of the more challenging issues confronting theologians in dialogue with critical realism. Personally, I think addressing this issue from a theological perspective requires a forthright discussion of revelation, which I would welcome.

Third, while I agree with Andy's attempt to locate the empirical in practical theology within a framework shaped by substantive theological convictions, I wonder if the interdisciplinary task might be more complex than he suggests. Paul Ricoeur is reported to have said of Martin Heidegger: "I agree with where he ends up but believe he gets there too quickly; a detour is necessary."[8] A kind of detour might be helpful in thinking about the location of the empirical in practical theology. It is basic to critical realism's affirmation of a stratified model of reality that different levels of reality must be respected in order to avoid reductionism from the bottom up (explaining the discontents of civilization in terms of the individual psyche, as in Freud) or from the top down (explaining depression and suicide rates exclusively in terms of social integration, as in Durkheim). I believe this makes it impossible to think of empirical

8. I first heard this at a conference while I was a graduate student. For discussion of this point, see Ricoeur, *Hermeneutics and the Human Sciences*.

research *exclusively* in terms of concrete lived experience, as portrayed from the perspective of a particular view of divine and human action. Various kinds of empirical research are appropriate to the investigation of different levels of reality. Some of these are far removed from concrete, lived experience. For example, survey research appropriate to the sociological investigation of a large population can provide very helpful insight into general trends, as we see in the National Study of Youth and Religion. A complex interdisciplinary conversation is involved in practical theology's dialogue with this sort of research, which includes assessing the reliability of the research on social scientific grounds, interpreting the implications of the data for Christian practice in diverse contexts, and appropriating the findings in terms of a framework of divine and human action—to name but a few. Andy's chapter gives the greatest attention to the last of these, but a "detour" to other levels may be necessary in order to adequately describe practical theology's dialogue with empirical research. (I am sure Andy has much to say in response—may the conversation continue!)

I was delighted to read Shin-Geun Jang's chapter on Christian teaching as "Trinitarian Kenotic Praxis." He builds on and goes beyond my own constructive work in *The Teaching Ministry of Congregations*, where I draw on the theology of Jürgen Moltmann more directly than in my other books. I am particularly appreciative of Shin-Geun's ability to draw on this framework to critique and guide teaching in a South Korean church context. He embodies the very best of practical theology that is contextually sensitive and deeply theological.

I have found Moltmann's view of trinitarian praxis helpful along three lines: (1) it takes seriously the church as a contrast community that is called to embody the kenotic love of the triune God in its shared life; (2) it portrays teaching as a form of participation in God's praxis and, thus, as dynamic, communal, and participatory; and (3) it portrays the church as following God into the world in mission, a mission of self-giving love that cares for the human and natural world at every level of life. The emphasis is on our present participation in the life of the triune God. In terms of my current theological thinking, I cannot help but wonder if this sort of depiction of divine and human praxis adequately addresses what God and God alone has done on our behalf and in our stead. Where does the gracious work of God in the atonement fit into to this depiction of the Christian life? Where does it acknowledge the uniqueness of Christ's life of covenant faithfulness to God, upon which our own faithfulness depends? I raise these questions in reflecting on my own appropriation of Moltmann, and they may resonate with Shin-Geun as well.

Gordon Mikoski's chapter on my contribution to practical theology at Princeton Theological Seminary and beyond is very generous and builds on our common work in writing a book on the history of practical theology at PTS. He has been my primary dialogue partner on methodological issues at Princeton, and I look forward to his future contributions to the field, which I believe will be considerable. Since Gordon is my colleague and friend, he may a bit too complimentary, so I will add several critical comments about my work, especially *Practical Theology: An Introduction*.

I think this book gives the mistaken impression that theology enters in primarily at the normative moment of practical theological reflection. While it is true that I frame each of the four "moments" theologically (e.g., descriptive empirical work is a form of priestly listening), I do not address adequately the ways theology enters in every step of the way. The descriptive empirical and the interpretive moments, in particular, are portrayed in ways that are too close to social science and as leading up to the real work of theology, which is normative. At the very least, I should have been much clearer that empirical work is informed by theological commitments (Why study this issue? Why ask these particular questions?) and that the interpretation of data is theological as well as social scientific.

I also did not give sufficient attention to the dialogue between practical theology and the other theological disciplines in this book. I have addressed why I believe this is important earlier in this chapter and will say no more here. Finally, I think it is legitimate to ask if the book overemphasizes the tradition of critical reflection that has been so important in twentieth century practical theology. As shared above, I was shaped by Clinical Pastoral Education, the Lab School movement, and other forms of education that placed great emphasis on reflective practice. While I gesture toward other traditions like Christian spirituality, I wonder if practical theology in an increasingly secular West will have to give more attention to practices like prayer, worship, Scripture study, and communal discernment that root reflection in the Christian way of life. Critical reflection is an important second or even third step that must be grounded in formation. It plays a role in discernment, moral action, and the engagement of others in and beyond the church. It may well be that practical theology's close ties to critical reflection and reflective practice reveal ties to modern Western theology so deep that we will have to jettison this way of thinking about theology altogether as we encounter new patterns emerging in global Christianity.

By way of conclusion, I hope that my deep appreciation for this book has been evident throughout. Each chapter is special to me and has evoked an inner dialogue. The privilege of teaching and learning from so many students, colleagues, and friends has always stood at the heart of my vocation as a teacher. On the occasion of my retirement, I give thanks to those in this book and beyond who joined me on that part of my journey.

Bibliography

Barth, Karl. *The Christian Life, Church Dogmatics, Vol. IV, 4, Lecture Fragments.* Translated by Geoffrey Bromiley. Grand Rapids: Eerdmans, 1981.

Guder, Darrell. *Be My Witnesses: The Church's Mission, Message, and Messengers.* Grand Rapids: Eerdmans, 1985.

Gunter, Stephen, et al. *Wesley and the Quadrilateral: Renewing the Conversation.* Nashville: Abingdon, 1997.

Newbigin, Lesslie. *The Gospel in a Pluralist Society.* Grand Rapids: Eerdmans, 1989.

Ricoeur, Paul. *Hermeneutics and the Human Sciences.* Edited and translated by John Thompson. New York: Cambridge University Press, 1981.

Subject Index

Scripture Index

Made in the USA
Middletown, DE
24 October 2020